NEW ZEALAND

NEW ZEALAND

Elisabeth B. Booz

PASSPORT BOOKS

Trade Imprint of National Textbook Company
Lincolnwood, Illinois U.S.A.

Published by Passport Books in conjunction with
The Guidebook Company Ltd.

This edition published in 1991 by Passport Books,
Trade Imprint of National Textbook Company,
4255 West Touhy Avenue, Lincolnwood (Chicago),
Illinois 60646-1975 U.S.A.

Library of Congress Catalog Card Number: 90-63333

Grateful acknowledgement is made to the following authors and
publishers for permissions granted:

Rogers, Coleridge & White for
Spinster © Sylvia Ashton-Warner 1960

John McIndoe for
Maorie is My Name © John Caselberg 1975

Square One Books for
"The Crime of Being a Maori" © James K Baxter 1972

The extract from Whanau by Witi Ihimaera is reprinted by kind
permission of the Octopus Publishing Group (NZ) Ltd and the author.

Editors: Peter Fredenburg, Robyn Flemming and Sallie Coolidge
Picture Editor: Carolyn Watts
Maps Design: Bai Yiliang

Photography: Andris Apse (106, 126 middle right, 138-9, 151, 159,
166, 170-1, 188; Magnus Bartlett (65); Communicate New Zealand
(175, 181); Brian Enting (4-5, 9, 26-7, 31, 34, 39, 43, 52, 56, 60, 68-9,
76, 98-9, 102, 122, 126 all but middle right, 135, 177, 184-5, 196,
200-1, 208, 212-213, 217); Geoff Mason (18-19, 84, 89, 114, 162)

Printed in Hong Kong

Contents

Special Topics

Maps

Excerpts

Introduction

New Zealand has finally burst on to the world travel scene as a country to visit in its own right—one to spend a glorious time exploring. It is high time. For far too long this remarkable country was known only as the pleasant little place you visited if you had a few days left over from a trip to Australia. Somehow, the grandeur of its scenery, the opportunities for every kind of outdoor holiday, the excitement, the warmth of its people and the excellent tourist facilities all failed to grab travellers' attention. This undeserved neglect was abetted by certain misconceptions, some of which persist.

Many people are not exactly sure where New Zealand is. Some think the country is more or less attached to Tasmania, but a little further south—just a part of Australia, in a manner of speaking. Others believe that New Zealand is incredibly remote, somewhere near the South Pole—just a part of Antarctica, or almost. In fact, New Zealand lies exactly halfway between the South Pole and the Equator. If you placed it at the equivalent latitude in the northern hemisphere, 40 degrees north instead of south, it would lie level with Italy, which happens to be about the same shape (upside down and in mirror image) and only slightly larger.

New Zealand is much further from Australia than most people realize; it is more than 2,000 kilometres (1,300 miles) southwest of Sydney across the Tasman Sea. These two English-speaking nations are linked primarily by trade agreements and their common language. Each has its own independent government, its own history and customs, its own landscape and its own view of the world. New Zealanders do not like to be mistaken for Australians.

Antarctica is even further away, about 3,000 kilometres (1,900 miles) south of New Zealand. Part of Antarctica—Scott Base and the 730,000-square-kilometre (282,000-square-mile) Ross Dependency—is under New Zealand jurisdiction. The United States services its adjacent Antarctic station at McMurdo from a base in Christchurch, by a cooperative arrangement with New Zealand.

Many people think that New Zealand is just like England, and there is little point in travelling so far to see a place so familiar. In fact, no place could be much less like England than this land of golden, subtropical beaches, volcanoes, snowcapped mountain ranges and fern-filled rain forests. No industrial revolution ever blackened New Zealand's countryside, and no smog settles over its towns and cities. New Zealanders combine two cultures, one coming from the South Pacific with the Maori, the original settlers, and the other from Europe with the colonists who came later, mostly from England and Scotland. The resulting blend has evolved into an egalitarian, frank, attractive society that is neither English nor Polynesian—but pure New Zealand.

To be sure, there is an element in the New Zealand way of life that evokes nostalgic memories of a long-vanished England, an England of friendly policemen patrolling their beat on foot, of parks safe for walking in at night, of people who are polite to each other as a matter of course, who do not push and who go out of their way to help a stranger. Traffic was movement, not a jam, in that half-forgotten place, and the trees were filled with birdsong. This is how you will find New Zealand today—a far cry from what most other modern, industrialized countries have become.

Many people think they will not see anything in New Zealand that they cannot see in Australia. In fact, the continent of Australia and the string of islands forming New Zealand are as neat a contrast as you could ask for. Where Australia is a great, dry, desert-centred land with extremes of climate and bright colours under a blazing sun, New Zealand is a mild, green-and-golden land spread between snowy mountain peaks and a winding, accessible coastline of island-studded bays and harbours. Majestic desert sunsets and spectacular coral reefs attract visitors to Australia. Waterfalls cascading through mossy gorges, bubbling hot springs and cool fiords bring them to New Zealand. Distances are vast in Australia. Along New Zealand's slender length everything is relatively close, and visitors travel over an ever-changing scene as one compact region merges with the next. Australia can boast of its marsupials—some of the strangest animals in the world. New Zealand, with virtually no native mammals, is blessed instead with marvellous, unique birds. History, climate and the land have shaped people of contrasting character, too. A trip to Australia tells you little about New Zealand, and vice versa.

Many people think that, though New Zealand has beautiful scenery, the people are all boring and uncreative sheep farmers. In fact, New Zealanders are anything but boring. The idea that New Zealand is a cultural and intellectual backwater probably dates from before the Second World War, when great distances and relatively slow communications made it difficult for New Zealand artists to exhibit or travel abroad. Back then, New Zealand writers Katherine Mansfield and Ngaio Marsh went to England to find a wide audience for their books describing life in New Zealand. This is no longer necessary. Books written in New Zealand by Sylvia Ashton-Warner, Janet Frame, Witi Ihimaera and Keri Hulme are much discussed in England and America. Exhibitions of New Zealand art, such as Te Maori, travel the world, and a network of public galleries from Auckland to Dunedin mount an endless stream of major shows, while dozens of smaller galleries in the cities and provincial towns exhibit the works of local painters, print-makers and sculptors. The performing arts are bright and lively. Handicrafts, particularly those using ceramics and wool, are widely practised, appreciated and used throughout the country. Maori arts and crafts flourish in both their traditional and modern forms. The output is amazing, considering that New Zealand has

A Cultural Misunderstanding

We had seen Captain Cook and his sailors. They were a cheerful and merry tribe—good-natured, very affectionate (especially to our women), and gave us a quantity of useful things without asking for payment... We liked this tribe very much. But this new tribe, the missionary, puzzled and vexed us. The majority of them were very solemn, and had a gloominess about them as if all their relations had been eaten and they were powerless to get their revenge...

A great many meetings took place in different parts of our country, and it was generally settled that the missionary tribe should be allowed—though tolerated would be a better word—to try and persuade those who were willing to listen to their incantations or prayers. Our country was a free country, and everyone did as they liked, so long as nothing was done injurious to the welfare, prestige or mana of the tribe. Mark that... Listen! Some of our chiefs, bold, brave men... would on no account stand undue familiarity. They had a high-spirited, though very affectionate, race to lead—not control, mind—or guide, and to have to put up with insult without avenging it according to its nature would have been fatal to a chief occupying a leading position; and... injurious to the tribe, as it would render it contemptible to its neighbours. Taking this into consideration, will any reasonable person be astonished at the following action taken by my great-grandfather Kahu...

One day, as he was returning from a whapuku fishing excursion, he was met by a missionary on the beautiful surf-beaten beach of Tatahi, and as the men of the tribe dragged the large red canoe, fish and all, ashore, this person thus addressed my great-grandfather: "You are a wicked, bad man. You have not listened to my teachings; you have broken the Sabbath commandment by going over to fish. My God is angry. You and your people will all go to hell, and be burnt with fire for ever and ever, just like your wicked forefathers..." All eyes were turned from this man's face, and became fixed on my great-grandfather, who had been threatened by this missionary that he would be burnt with the fire that was now burning up his ancestors, male and female; that he was to be cooked with fire, and never to be done. Not a doubt existed—could have existed—in the hearts of the tribe as to what the result would be. No harm had been done to this stranger of a stranger tribe. He had asked for, and obtained, a piece of land in our tribal district to build upon; houses had been built for him and his gods; yams, kumaras, fish, crayfish, shellfish, eels, pigeons, kakas, and rats, each in its season, had been largely heaped up for him, as he said it was good to give to him and his god; and then, without any provocation at all, he had cursed my great-grandfather!

"Lay hold of him," cried my great-grandfather; "take him out of his kotiroa (long coat) and other clothes." This was done more quickly than a boiled kumara is taken out of its skin...and in less time than it takes to remove the feathers from a fat pigeon the man of incantation was in an oven, and prevented from creating further mischief. He had done quite enough as it was... Every day for a whole moon after this tauas came upon us, robbing us first and then condoling with my great-grandfather, and showing their respect for him to such a degree that when the tauas left off coming we had not a kumara left, nor had my great-grandfather a flax or kiwi mat in his house... The rest of the missionaries met when things had cooled down a bit, and told us through some of our slaves, who had been baptised and made catechists of, that a letter was being written to King George, who would send war parties in big ships and batter us. We believed this, as it was natural and right that the English king chief would want payment for the death of one of his wizards... though why he should have sent that style of men to our shores to curse us we could not tell.

John Caselberg, Maori Is My Name, *1975*

a population of only 3.2 million. The literacy rate here is one of the highest in the world, and New Zealanders are, per capita, the world's biggest book-buyers. Good bookshops with offerings from around the world can be found in every sizeable town.

As for the familiar image of New Zealanders as sheep farmers, times have changed. Sheep still outnumber humans 20 to 1, but only a small percentage of people actually farm full-time—and the ones who do are among the most interesting people you could meet. Although New Zealand's economy rests solidly on agriculture, its population has become mainly urban and suburban. The interests, habits and occupations of New Zealanders are very similar to those of people in other developed nations around the world.

Many people think that New Zealand is so small they can see the whole place in three or four days. In fact, New Zealand is roughly the size of Great Britain, Japan or the American state of Colorado. It is too full of variety to be sampled even casually in a few days. Its slim length, 1,600 kilometres (1,000 miles) from end to end, passes through a span of latitudes that ranges from flower-filled, frost-free Northland to misty, sub-arctic Stewart Island. Both of the main islands have breathtaking scenery, enchanting places to visit and exciting things to do, but to visit only one of them is to know only half of New Zealand, as they differ dramatically from each other. The warmer, emerald-green North Island was shaped aeons ago by the fire of volcanoes. The larger, more spectacular South Island has rocky mountains, sapphire-blue lakes and deep fiords that were slowly carved by glacial ice.

Tourism is an important factor in New Zealand's new, diversified economy, which has finally been yanked free from Great Britain's apron strings by the mother country's joining of the European Common Market. The New Zealand Tourist and Publicity Department (NZTP) has done an excellent job of developing facilities, keeping the natural beauty of the country unspoiled and making events of cultural interest accessible. New Zealand Visitor Information Centres are centrally located in over 100 cities, towns and villages to help visitors find accommodation, buy tickets and decide what to do, which sights to see and where to go next. New Zealand is still new enough to the tourism game for visitors to be treated as individuals. Only in rare cases, and only in the most intensely developed sites, such as Rotorua and Mount Cook, do they suffer the commercial hype of a tourist trap.

The Department of Conservation was established as a Cabinet-level ministry in 1987, combining under one authority many government functions relating to the environment, such as the administration and protection of wildlife refuges, forests, wilderness areas, marine reserves and national parks, making it New Zealand's watch-dog against the kind of damage to nature that is occurring in many other parts of the world. The Department of Conservation runs well-managed information centres at the headquarters of national parks and forest reserves and in all regional centres. For visitors interested in nature, the rangers in charge can be valuable sources of information and help.

There is so much to see and do in New Zealand, and such a selection of guidebooks covering the whole bewildering scene, that your problem as a visitor becomes trying to decide which sights and activities to concentrate on. The aim of this guide is to focus your attention on the country's five specialities worth travelling halfway around the world to sample. Any one, or any combination, will lead you through both islands, taking you off the beaten track and into easy, friendly contact with New Zealanders with similar interests and tastes.

Bird-watchers will encounter a rich diversity of bird life, including many unique species, to make this the bird trip of a lifetime (see page 17).

Anyone with a love of nature and a pair of good shoes will find New Zealand unique in the world for its network of wonderful walkways, well frequented by a population that walks for pleasure and health (see page 21).

Fishermen the world over have long known about New Zealand's trout-filled lakes and streams, but only now has access improved to the point that the best spots, while still pleasingly remote, are within reach and well supplied with good facilities (see page 23).

Golfers will find a true paradise in New Zealand, where the descendants of Scotsmen have created more splendid golf courses per capita than anywhere else in the world. Visitors are welcome everywhere (see page 25).

Sophisticated wine-tasters are becoming increasingly intrigued with New Zealand's fast-growing wine industry, and its cool-climate wines are making impressive showings on the international scene (see page 29).

This guide is organized in two parts: the North Island and the South Island. Each of these parts is divided in turn into five chapters corresponding to the regions of each island. Each chapter begins with a brief overview of places, sights and local history, followed by a more comprehensive description and travel tips. At the end of each chapter are 'Focus' sections marked by the symbols given above. These provide detailed information on the five specialities, gathering together the options in the region that you can take to pursue your own particular interests.

Bird-watching Areas

Bay of Islands
northern blue penguin, giant petrel, cape pigeon, white-faced storm petrel, fairy prion, shag, heron

**Ha
Hauraki Gulf**
little blue penguin, shearwater, gannet, arctic skua, giant petrel, white-faced storm petrel, cape pigeon, fairy prion

Little Barrier Island
wildlife sanctuary (permit required) stitchbird, saddleback, kokako kakapo, black petrel, Cook's petrel

Muriwai Beach
small gannet colony

Firth of Thames
godwif, knot, South Island pied oystercatcher, wrybill, sandpiper, turnstone, red-necked stint, gull, tern, shag, heron. banded dotterel, pied stilt

Manukau Harbour
spotted dove, pheasant, finch, whimbrel, other waders

Waikato Wetlands
bittern, heron, egre shag, spotless crake, kingfisher, pukeko, shining cuckoo, brown teal

Rotoehu State Forest
North Island kokako, kaka, wattlebird, forest species

Otorohanga
Kiwi House and Native Bird Park

Urewera National Park
shag, swan, blue duck, scaup, shoveler, robin, tui, morepork, falcon, pied tit, bellbird, long-tailed cuckoo, shining cuckoo, kaka, rifleman

Farewell Spit
godwit, knot, turnstone, whimbrel, black swan, pipit, goldfinch, California quail

Marlborough Sounds
sea and shore species, king shag breeding ground

Cape Kidnappers
gannet sanctuary with three large colonies

Paparoa National Park
Westland black petrel (winter breeder), yellow-breasted tit, tui, pigeon, bellbird, silvereye, grey warbler, kaka brown creeper, rifleman, yellow-crowned parakeet, blue duck

Mount Bruce
National Wildlife Centre

Nelson
waders and shore species in estuaries

Kapiti Island
sanctuary (permit required) whitehead, North Island robin, pied tit, grey warbler, tui, bellbird, little spotted kiwi, brown teal, blue penguin

Okarita
white heron sanctuary (permit required)

Rakaia River
banded dotterel, black-fronted dotterel, wrybill, plover

Avon-Heathcote Estuary
spotted shag, godwit, white-faced heron

Haast Pass
bush species

Milford Sound
Fiordland crested penguin, kakapo

Lake Pukaki & Godley River
waterfowl, wrybill, pied stilt, white-faced heron, spur-winged plover, banded dotterel, black stilt, chukor, falcon, kea, morepork, little owl

Lake Ellesmere
pukeko, black swan, duck, golden plover, pectoral sandpiper, curlew sandpiper, sharp-tailed sandpiper, greenshank, red-necked stint, wrybill, other waders

Tairaoa Head
royal albatross, yellow-eyed penguin, black swan breeding ground; spotted and Stewart Island Shag nesting area

Te Anau Wildlife Bird Reserve
takahe, falcon

Eglinton Valley
yellowhead, kaka, robin, yellow-breasted tit, rifleman, brown creeper, yellow-crowned parakeet, long-tailed cuckoo, kea, rockwren, grey warbler, bush species

Stewart Island
little spotted and Stewart Island brown kiwi (diurnal), kaka, red-crowned parakeet, New Zealand pigeon, sheerwater, little blue penguin, southern pelagic species

Bird-watching

The bird life of New Zealand can hardly be matched in the world, because of
the land's strange, solitary history. Eighty million years ago, the primal land
mass near the South Pole slowly broke apart to form the seven continents,
with a lone sliver of land adrift on the rim of a tectonic plate later becoming
the islands of New Zealand. These islands carried only birds, one mammal
(the bat), a few lizard-like reptiles and three kinds of frog.

New Zealand was a paradise for birds. Without fear of predators, many
bush birds lost the power of flight. Some developed strange feeding habits,
like the giant moa which grazed on the grasslands. Evolution continued in
isolation, producing about 250 species of birds, many of them unknown
outside of New Zealand. From time to time, strong westerly winds from
Australia blew in seeds, insects and birds to add new variety to New
Zealand's ancient forests. The first mammal predator to endanger this
birdland was man.

Polynesians, later called Maori, came to New Zealand about 1,200 years
ago, bringing with them dogs, rats and fire. Flightless birds made easy prey,
and the many species of moa were soon hunted into extinction. A thousand
years after the Maori, Europeans colonized New Zealand, and in the space of
one century inflicted more damage on the local bird life than the Maori had in
a millennium. They felled and burned forests and drained swamps to create
farmland. Homesick English and Scottish settlers systematically introduced
all kinds of flora and fauna from 'home' throughout the 19th century. About
30 European birds became established in the wild, but these generally did not
invade the habitats of native birds, choosing instead man-made environments
such as farmland and gardens, to which no endemic species had adapted.
Other imported animals, including predators of birds, produced ecological
havoc. By 1900, controls were imposed; since then, awareness of the need for
conservation has reached national proportions. These developments arrived
too late, however, for the roughly half of New Zealand's native bird species
that are now extinct. Others are endangered, such as the kakapo, a unique
flightless parrot, and the black stilt, the rarest wader in the world. Today, the
Department of Conservation carefully oversees the environment.

The considerable latitudinal (north-to-south) depth of New Zealand allows
a climate that ranges from subtropical in Northland to cool-temperate,
verging on sub-arctic, in Southland. The diversity of terrain—alpine regions
rising above the treeline, highland and lowland forests, native 'bush', open
grassland and a long, variegated coastline—creates habitats for an astonishing range of bird species, given the relatively small geographical area, and
makes the islands a delight to anyone with a pair of binoculars. New Zealand
celebrates its wealth of birds every morning at 6 o'clock by opening its
national radio programme with bird calls!

Walking Areas

Waitangi
mangrove
forest walk

Cape Reinga
& Ninety-Mile
Beach
beach walk

Mangawhai Head
cliff walk

Cooks Cove &
Tolaga Bay
rocky coastal
walk

Mount Manganui
coastal walks

Auckland
harbour walks

Rotorua
forest and
volcanic
walks

Waitomo
cave walks

Lake Taupo
forest and
volcanic walks

Taranaki-Egmont
National Park
mountain and bush
walks

Lake
Waikaremoana
lake walks

Cape Kidnappers
beach walk

Abel Tasman National
Park & Golden Bay
coastal, beach and forest
walks

Wanganui
city walks

Tongariro
National Park
mountain walks

Buller River
bush walks

Wellington
city walks

Punakaiti
dramatic coastal
walk

Kaikoura
Peninsula
coastal walk

Franz Josef &
Fox Glaciers
glacier walks

Christchurch
city walk

Hanmer Springs
hot springs and
forest walks

Mount Cook
mountain walks

Banks Peninsula
extinct crater rim walk

Milford Sound
Milford Track

Rakaia River
Gorge
river walks

Peele Forest
Park
forest walks

Queenstown
lake and mountain
walks

Te Anau
lake and
mountain
walks

Dunedin
city walk

Owaka & Catlin
River Valley
river, forest and
coastal walks

Stewart Island
native bush walks

© The Guidebook Company Ltd

Walking

For any lover of the outdoors, New Zealand's walking trails are among its greatest treats. The spectacular national parks (four in the North Island, nine in the South Island), numerous forests and countless scenic reserves all provide well-marked paths ranging from short nature walks with plants and trees labelled for identification to long, hard hikes (called 'tramps' in New Zealand) lasting for several days. A system of national walkways legislated into being with the Walkways Act of 1975 will eventually create an ambitious and imaginative network of walking trails across public and private land all the way from the North Cape to Stewart Island.

Walking is a national pastime in New Zealand. During school holidays whole families set out together with backpacks, food and sleeping bags to tramp one of the famous tracks. However, now that the population is 80 percent urban or suburban, shorter day walks within easy driving distance of towns have soared in number and popularity.

The main difference between walks and tramps is the amount of time and equipment needed. Another variable is the type of trail. Walkways in New Zealand have three classifications: a walk is a well-formed path suitable for the 'average family', perhaps simply an accessible section of a longer *track*, which is a well-defined trail, usually longer than a 'walk', suitable for people of 'good average physical fitness' (New Zealand's standard of 'average' being higher than in most countries); a *route* is a lightly marked trail, usually through wilderness, to be used only by well-equipped and experienced trampers.

This guide concentrates on some of the many wonderful walks throughout New Zealand that require no special equipment other than a pair of stout shoes and a light day-pack. They may vary in length from one or two hours to a full day's excursion, but in all cases the walker can get back to a hot shower, a good meal and a bed by the end of the day. The walks described here collectively offer a wide variety of scenery: mountains, rivers, forests, seasides, lakes, cityscapes, beaches, volcanoes, caves, and—best of all—the 'bush', which is the misleadingly dull name for New Zealand's ancient, magnificently towering and fern-filled indigenous forest. There are other fine walks beyond the scope of this guide; information on them is easy to find.

Boots that cover the ankles are best, not only for ankle support but also for protection against sandflies. New Zealand's weather is very changeable, so be sure to include a warm pullover, a windbreaker and a light, waterproof covering in your day-pack. Insect repellent (available in New Zealand) is another absolute necessity during most of the year.

Fly-fishing Spots

Rotorua Lakes ●
Waitahanui ● Lake
River ● Waikareiti ● Ruakituiri
Lake Taupo ● ● ● River
● Lake ● Wairoa River
Tongariro River ● Waikaremoana

Lake Rotorangi ●
● Patea River

● Wairau River
Buller River ●
● Nelson Lakes

● Grey River
● Lake Brunner
Hokitika River ●
Whataroa & Lake Wahapo ● ● Harihari
● Lakes Pearson & Grasmere

Lakes Moeraki
& Paringa ● ● Rakaia River

Lake Wanaka ● ● Lake Hawea
Eglinton River ●
● Lake Wakatipu
Lake
Manapouri ● Mataura River
● Oreti River ● Taieri River
Waiau River ● ● Clutha River
Aparima ● Pomahaka River
River

© The Guidebook Company Ltd

Fly-fishing

New Zealand is a fisherman's Mecca, its lakes and rivers teeming with trout and salmon, its beaches ideal for surf-casting. The North Island's east coast is known worldwide for big-game fishing. This guide focuses mainly on trout fishing with artificial dry or wet flies in lakes and streams. Trout fishing in New Zealand is entirely for sport. The country has no commercial hatcheries, so you never see trout on a menu. You must catch your own, but then any restaurant will happily cook it for your dinner.

Trout were introduced to New Zealand by immigrants from Britain when they found only native eel in the rivers. Brown trout eggs were brought from Tasmania in 1867, obtained from fish that had been sent there from England. Rainbow trout eggs reached Auckland from the Russian River hatchery in California in 1883. The eggs were rushed to Lake Taupo, where abundant food allowed the fish to grow to sporting size within three years. Lake Taupo and its tributaries have remained the favourite fishing spot ever since.

Brown trout were soon scorned as trash fish that took food from the more highly esteemed rainbows. After World War I, efforts to eliminate the browns included shooting them, but, mercifully, the fish survived. Today the brown trout is recognized as a top sport fish and an excellent meal.

There are two ways to get a fishing licence. The easiest way is to buy a special tourist 30-day licence. It costs about NZ$60, is valid anywhere in the country and can be bought at any office of the New Zealand Tourist and Publicity Department (NZTP). Or you can buy a licence for the day, week, month or whole season at any sports shop in any of the 22 fishing districts where you may want to fish. These licences are not valid for Taupo and Rotorua, however; in those two areas you must get a separate licence from a sports shop or hotel.

The fishing season runs from October to the end of June in most of the North Island, and from October to the end of April in the South Island. The southern lakes stay open until the end of May. Lake Taupo and the lower reaches of the streams entering its east side stay open all year round.

If you take a guide, he will probably provide such gear as waders, rods, reels, line, tackle and rain gear. Rental equipment tends to be expensive and may have had a hard life, so it is best to bring your own rod and tackle. A medium-weight two-piece rod, 2.5 to three metres (eight to ten feet), is recommended. Do *not* bring any flies made with chicken feathers, as the import of these is strictly forbidden to protect against the introduction of poultry disease. Spare lines or a fly-tying vice make much-appreciated gifts.

All rivers are open to anglers. However, if you must cross private property to reach a river, ask the farmer's permission to fish off his land.

Top Golf Courses

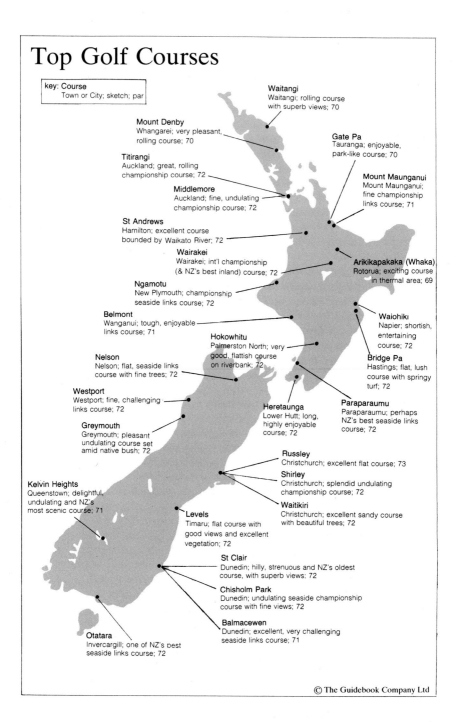

key: **Course**
Town or City; sketch; par

Waitangi
Waitangi; rolling course
with superb views; 70

Mount Denby
Whangarei; very pleasant,
rolling course; 70

Gate Pa
Tauranga; enjoyable,
park-like course; 70

Titirangi
Auckland; great, rolling
championship course; 72

Mount Maunganui
Mount Maunganui;
fine championship
links course; 71

Middlemore
Auckland; fine, undulating
championship course; 72

St Andrews
Hamilton; excellent course
bounded by Waikato River; 72

Wairakei
Wairakei; int'l championship
(& NZ's best inland) course; 72

Arikikapakaka (Whaka)
Rotorua; exciting course
in thermal area; 69

Ngamotu
New Plymouth; championship
seaside links course; 72

Belmont
Wanganui; tough, enjoyable
links course; 71

Waiohiki
Napier; shortish,
entertaining
course; 72

Hokowhitu
Palmerston North; very
good, flattish course
on riverbank; 72

Nelson
Nelson; flat, seaside links
course with fine trees; 72

Bridge Pa
Hastings; flat, lush
course with springy
turf; 72

Westport
Westport; fine, challenging
links course; 72

Heretaunga
Lower Hutt; long,
highly enjoyable
course; 72

Paraparaumu
Paraparaumu; perhaps
NZ's best seaside links
course; 72

Greymouth
Greymouth; pleasant
undulating course set
amid native bush; 72

Russley
Christchurch; excellent flat course; 73

Shirley
Christchurch; splendid undulating
championship course; 72

Kelvin Heights
Queenstown; delightful,
undulating and NZ's
most scenic course; 71

Waitikiri
Christchurch; excellent sandy course
with beautiful trees; 72

Levels
Timaru; flat course with
good views and excellent
vegetation; 72

St Clair
Dunedin; hilly, strenuous and NZ's oldest
course, with superb views: 72

Chisholm Park
Dunedin; undulating seaside championship
course with fine views; 72

Balmacewen
Dunedin; excellent, very challenging
seaside links course; 71

Otatara
Invercargill; one of NZ's best
seaside links course; 72

Golfing

An abundance of emerald-green, uncrowded golf courses set in stunningly beautiful scenery make New Zealand a golfer's paradise. The country boasts some 400 courses, both public and private (one for every 7,000 people), which is certainly the highest number of golf courses per capita in the world. Villages usually have a nine-hole course nearby—with wire strung around the greens to keep out sheep. Towns of over 12,000 have their own 18-hole courses, and all major cities have at least three of these. There are interesting courses throughout New Zealand, some of them real gems, some renowned worldwide. (The map opposite cites only some of the more exceptional and famous.) You can stop almost anywhere and be assured of a good, friendly game. There is no waiting, making three and a half hours the average time for playing 18 holes. Many people take advantage of the South Island's long summer twilights to enjoy a full round after dinner.

New Zealanders draw a distinction between a golf *course* and golf *links*. A links-type course is always situated beside the sea, on sandy soil, taking as its model St Andrews in Scotland, the paradigm of all golf links. Whatever their type, the courses in New Zealand are well designed, well turfed and well endowed with trees.

Golf clubs welcome visitors. Members of overseas clubs are usually accorded guest privileges at private clubs (300 of which are registered in New Zealand), so bring a letter of introduction from your home club secretary. Be warned that a green-fee player may occasionally have difficulty slipping in on a Saturday morning or run into ladies' day on a Tuesday or Wednesday morning. Once you are in, the style is friendly and casual. If you need partners, simply go to the pro shop and introduce yourself as a visitor. The pro will gladly set up a game for you. If you stop for a game and find the club house locked, just sign the visitors book, take a golf card, and put your money through the slit in the box provided. The green fee will be posted. At private clubs the fee is much cheaper than in the US; at public courses it is about the same. Golf carts are not used, as New Zealanders play for exercise. As one pro said, 'We want our visitors to be happy, but the Americans do long for carts, and the Japanese do long for caddies!' All golf courses supply two-wheeled, hand-pulled trundlers for hire at very cheap rates. Some trundlers even have fold-down seats so you can rest from time to time.

Nearly all pro shops can rent you eight golf clubs in a carrying frame and will let you keep them for a couple of weeks if you leave a deposit. However, many visitors prefer to bring their own clubs (which can easily be sold at the end of your trip, especially Pings) and feel it is easier to use a light golf bag than either a frame or trundler. Be sure to bring an ample supply of balls, as good-quality ones are outrageously expensive here. Bring a few extras as gifts!

Wine-producing Regions

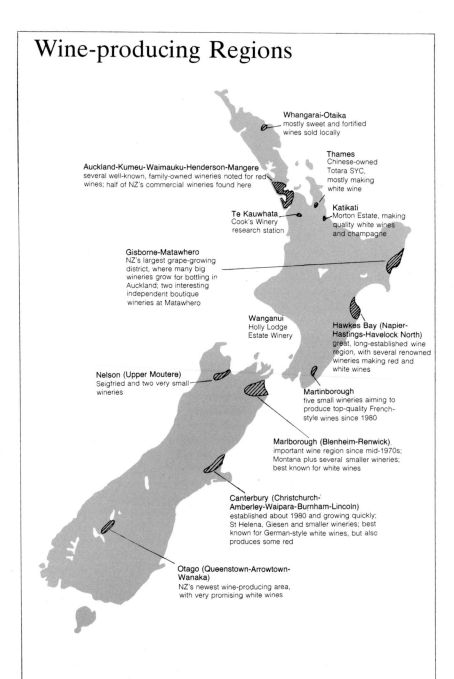

Whangarai-Otaika
mostly sweet and fortified
wines sold locally

Thames
Chinese-owned
Totara SYC,
mostly making
white wine

Auckland-Kumeu-Waimauku-Henderson-Mangere
several well-known, family-owned wineries noted for red
wines; half of NZ's commercial wineries found here

Katikati
Morton Estate, making
quality white wines
and champagne

Te Kauwhata
Cook's Winery
research station

Gisborne-Matawhero
NZ's largest grape-growing
district, where many big
wineries grow for bottling in
Auckland; two interesting
independent boutique
wineries at Matawhero

Wanganui
Holly Lodge
Estate Winery

**Hawkes Bay (Napier-
Hastings-Havelock North)**
great, long-established wine
region, with several renowned
wineries making red and
white wines

Nelson (Upper Moutere)
Seigfried and two very small
wineries

Martinborough
five small wineries aiming to
produce top-quality French-
style wines since 1980

Marlborough (Blenheim-Renwick)
important wine region since mid-1970s;
Montana plus several smaller wineries;
best known for white wines

**Canterbury (Christchurch-
Amberley-Waipara-Burnham-Lincoln)**
established about 1980 and growing quickly;
St Helena, Giesen and smaller wineries; best
known for German-style white wines, but also
produces some red

**Otago (Queenstown-Arrowtown-
Wanaka)**
NZ's newest wine-producing area,
with very promising white wines

Wine-tasting

The size and quality of New Zealand's fast-growing wine industry comes as a surprise to many people. Over 60 commercial wineries (mostly family businesses but also a few big international companies) produce 94 percent of the wine consumed here and export to more than 30 countries. New Zealanders are the most thoughtful wine drinkers in the southern hemisphere, with wine clubs functioning in every city and sizeable town. Though still small in the world market, New Zealand wines are attracting very serious interest from wine writers and from the trade in general.

New Zealand's vineyards actually lie nearer to the equator than those of Bordeaux, France, and the varieties of climate here closely resemble those of the major wine-producing areas of Europe. New Zealand is ideal for slow-ripening grapes, and its wines complement, rather than compete with, wines made from the fast-ripening grapes grown in Australia and California. Meanwhile, the depth of latitude means that the North Island can produce wines similar to those of France, while the South Island produces types more typical of Germany and Alsace. Unhampered by tradition, New Zealand vineyards have experimented with many types of vine in the past 25 years, selecting those most suitable to the various soils.

James Busby, a Scot, produced New Zealand's first recorded wine around 1835 in Northland. Wine-making spread with the farmer-colonists, but was almost halted towards the end of the last century by the vigorous assaults of temperance groups. Luckily, immigrants from Yugoslavia turned to wine-making in the Henderson Valley, near Auckland, around 1912, when earnings from the kauri gumfields (see page 59) dried up. Several wineries in Hawkes Bay, on the east coast, also began to flourish. Up until the 1960s, New Zealand wines were mostly sweet or fortified and thus suited only local tastes, but postwar affluence, overseas travel and a new sophistication brought a demand for drier and better wines. In the 1970s, Australian investment in some family companies hastened the changeover from American hybrid vines to European varieties. Much experimentation followed, with encouraging recognition at wine competitions. New wine areas in the South Island opened up, and an important new industry was launched.

New Zealand's elegant white wines, especially Sauvignon Blanc, have been strong international contenders. British wine columnist Harry Eyres finds even an ordinary New Zealand Sauvignon 'startlingly fresh and aromatic', far superior to Australian or Californian Sauvignons. Prize-winning red wines now come from the Kumeu region, near Auckland, and from Hawkes Bay. Late entry into competitive wine production has allowed New Zealand's vintners to combine advanced technology with traditional art, as winemakers trained the world over start to make their mark here. Informed wine-tasters are warmly welcomed at the cellars of most wineries.

Facts for the Traveller

Getting to New Zealand

By Air Flying is the only practical way of getting to New Zealand unless you have a great deal of time and money. More than 20 international airlines fly to New Zealand from all parts of the world. Air New Zealand is the national carrier, with flights from Los Angeles, Australia and many points in the Pacific Ocean.

The major international airport is at Auckland, near the country's northern tip, but an increasing number of carriers are also extending their service to Christchurch, in the South Island. At present, direct flights to Wellington, the capital, are possible only from Australia. Air New Zealand and Mount Cook Airlines have regular connecting flights from Auckland and Christchurch to all major towns. Half a dozen smaller domestic airlines fill in the gaps, reaching almost every corner of the country.

International arrivals in New Zealand are not permitted to disembark immediately, but must wait in their seats while the cabin is fumigated against any microbes that could threaten the country's vital agriculture. The process is soon over and is not unpleasant for the passengers.

By Sea Winter cruises to New Zealand (where it is summer) depart from England, North America and Hawaii. They are run by the Royal Viking Line, Royal Cruise Lines, the P & O Line and its offshoot, Princess Cruises. West Germany's Columbus Line takes up to eight first-class passengers on its freighters from US ports to Australia and New Zealand.

When to Go

Spring and autumn are the best times to visit New Zealand. (Remember that the seasons are reversed in the southern hemisphere, with spring occurring in New Zealand from October to early December and autumn from February to early May.) The worst time to visit is from mid-December until the end of January. This is the high holiday season, when it seems that every family in New Zealand takes a trip. Roads and trains are jammed, hotels and motels are booked up, and all tourist facilities are crowded. Other times to avoid, if possible, are the two-week school holidays in the middle of May and at the end of August.

Visas

All visitors must have a passport valid for six months beyond the expected time of departure from New Zealand, unless they are Australian citizens or nationals of Commonwealth countries who live permanently in Australia. Visitors from the US, Canada, the European Common Market countries,

Scandinavia and Japan, among others, do not need a visa for a visit of three months or less, but upon entering New Zealand they must show a return ticket, as proof that they will depart within three months, and evidence of 'sufficient funds', which means the equivalent of at least NZ$1,000 per month.

Customs

There are no restrictions on taking currency into or out of New Zealand. No customs duty is charged on personal effects and reasonable amounts of photographic equipment. Each adult can bring in six bottles of wine, one quart of liquor (spirits) and either 200 cigarettes, 250 grams of tobacco or 50 cigars. Golf clubs and fishing rods are permitted, but the import of fishing lures or flies containing chicken feathers is strictly prohibited to protect the poultry industry from imported diseases. (Well-made local flies and lures are available in the excellent sports shops operated in all the fishing areas.) Also forbidden is any kind of food except candy, cookies, tea and coffee.

Health

New Zealand is a very healthy country. You do not need a vaccination certificate or any shots, and tap water is safe to drink everywhere. Hospitals and doctors are of a high standard and reasonably priced. Dial 111 for an ambulance in cities. Emergency phone numbers are listed in all public phone booths and in the front pages of telephone directories.

Money

New Zealand uses dollars and cents, with banknotes in denominations of 1, 2, 5, 10, 20, 50 and 100 dollars and coins worth 1, 2, 5, 10, 20 and 50 cents. Travellers' cheques in US dollars and other major currencies can be changed at banks everywhere in New Zealand from Monday to Friday, 10 am – 4 pm. Hotels, restaurants and big shops also change travellers' cheques, but at a slightly lower rate. International airports have facilities for changing currency either coming or going. Credit cards are accepted almost everywhere; Visa and American Express are the most common.

Exchange rates vary according to international monetary conditions. In early 1989 NZ$1 was around US$0.64 or £0.36.

There is no tipping in hotels, restaurants or taxis.

Climate and Clothing

The weather in New Zealand is never extreme, though it may be wet. The North Island is the warmer of the two main islands. Auckland's average daily maximum temperature is 23°C (73°F) in midsummer (January) and 14°C

(57°F) in midwinter (July). Wellington is about 3°C (5°F) cooler. Snow caps the two highest volcanoes year round.

The South Island has a variety of climates. The north is sunnier, less windy and a little warmer than Wellington. East of the Southern Alps, on the relatively dry, warm side, Christchurch has an average daily maximum temperature of 22°C (72°F) in midsummer and 12°C (54°F) in midwinter. The mountainous West Coast is at least 3°C (5°F) cooler, with much rain or snow interspersed with sunny spells. The Southern Alps are permanently snowcapped. Queenstown, in the high country, has warm summers, with average highs of 22°C (72°F), and cold winters, with average highs of 8°C (46°F). Dunedin and Invercargill, in the far south, have an average high of around 19°C (68°F) in summer and 9°C (48°F) in winter, with occasional snow. Stewart Island is surprisingly mild—and unsurprisingly rainy.

While travelling around the country you encounter all kinds of weather. The best precaution is to wear light- or medium-weight layers that can be taken off or added as required—shirt, sweater, jacket or cardigan, windbreaker. Bring a bathing suit, good walking shoes, a rainproof outer covering and sunglasses. Shorts are acceptable for both men and women. Men need a jacket and tie occasionally, and women need a dress for fancy restaurants, the theatre and city life, but 90 percent of the time the New Zealand style is casual and comfortable, day or night. Clothes are expensive to buy in New Zealand, but bargains can be found in wool sweaters and sheepskin coats.

Electricity

New Zealand current is AC 230 volts, 50 cycles. Most hotels and motels provide AC 110-volt, 20-watt sockets for electric razors only. For other appliances, such as a hair dryer or travelling iron, you should bring a transformer. Most power sockets accept only three-pin, flat plugs, so for any appliances made outside New Zealand you will need an adaptor plug.

Getting Around

Air Air New Zealand, Mount Cook Airlines, Newmans Air and several regional airlines have scheduled services to the major cities, provincial towns and resorts. Most airports have charter planes as well.

Train New Zealand Railways offers passenger service on comfortable trains connecting several major cities on both islands. Sadly, there are very few smaller branch lines still operating.

Ferry A scheduled rail-car-passenger ferry service links the North and South islands, and a regular launch service links Stewart Island to the South Island.

Bus Long-distance motorcoach companies have highly developed networks. The government-owned New Zealand Railways Road Services

Mount Egmont (above);
Geyser at Rotorua (below)

runs efficient, comfortable 'Intercity' buses throughout both islands, often departing from railway stations. The biggest private coach companies are Newmans Coachlines and Mount Cook Line. Newmans is the larger, with routes over most of the North Island and part of the South Island. Mount Cook is newer, with 'jumbo-liners' featuring panoramic windows and on-board toilets. These run from Auckland to Wellington, but the company's main base is in the South Island. Smaller outfits, such as H & H Travel Line, provide scheduled regional services. Bus drivers, who like to play tour guide, historian and comedian rolled into one, usually keep up a running commentary on the passing scene that can be entertaining and instructive.

Cheap Passes Visitors who arrive via Air New Zealand are eligible for a 14- or 21-day air pass that allows unlimited, unrestricted stopovers on all Air New Zealand domestic routes at very reduced prices. The pass usually has to be purchased outside New Zealand. Check with your travel agent. New Zealand Railways offers its 8-, 15- or 22-day Travelpass (extendable by as much as six days), which allows unlimited travel by train, Intercity (NZRR) Services, and inter-island ferry. A Kiwi Coach Pass allows unlimited coach travel on Intercity (NZRR) Services, Newmans Coachlines or Mount Cook Line.

Car or Camper Rental As attractive as public transport may be, a rental car or camper is still the best way to see New Zealand. Hertz, Avis and Budget have offices in all major towns and tourist spots. They are more expensive than in North America but convenient if you are touring through several regions and want to drop off your car at a distant destination. Rental cars cannot be transported between the islands, but you can arrange for a new one to be waiting for you at the ferry landing. Local car rentals are often cheaper if you are staying in one area. Look under 'rental cars' in the yellow pages and phone to compare prices. Petrol is expensive — about NZ$1 per litre (or about NZ$4 per US gallon). Current driver's licences from the US, Canada, Britain and Australia are valid, as is the common international driver's licence.

Rental campers or motor vans are offered by eight companies in various sizes and models accommodating up to six people, with sleeping and limited cooking facilities but no toilet or shower. They can be rented in Auckland, Wellington and Christchurch. The New Zealand Visitor Information Centre, the New Zealand Tourist and Publicity Department (NZTP) Travel Office and the Automobile Association (AA) in these cities have full information and can help with rental arrangements. Prices vary with the season. A vast network of campgrounds and motor camps throughout the country have laundry facilities, central toilets and showers, and communal kitchen and dining room. Some even have swimming pools and TV.

Traffic keeps to the left, and all cars have right-hand drive. Roads are well surfaced and signposted, with distances given in kilometres (1 kilometre =

0.6214 miles). Four-lane highways are found only near big cities.

The AA has offices in every large town. Membership in an affiliated AA overseas entitles the visitor to free maps, comprehensive accommodation guides and tourist information.

Maps

The AA's detailed road maps of New Zealand (free to members) are very good in themselves, but they do not join up precisely, leaving unmapped gaps. Also, they are titled by district (such as Waitakere, Waikato, Wairarapa or Whangarei) and are confusing to a non-New Zealander. The AA comprehensive map book (for sale) is better. Shell road maps of New Zealand, available at Shell petrol stations, show distances and driving times. They are coherent and very useful for planning ahead.

Information

Tourist information is abundant and easy to find. The government-run New Zealand Tourist and Publicity Department (NZTP) has information offices in major cities in the US, Britain, Australia, Canada, Japan, Germany and Singapore. Within New Zealand, it operates New Zealand Visitor Information Centres (marked with the international 'i' sign) in over a hundred cities, towns and tourist areas—almost anywhere you are likely to visit. The NZTP supplies advice, brochures, maps, timetables and just about any information you would want about the locality. NZTP Travel Offices do the same thing and, in addition, provide a complete travel service, planning itineraries and finding and booking accommodation and transportation. The Automobile Association, with offices in all main towns, is another good source of information, maps and advice.

National Parks and state forest areas have helpful, educational visitor information centres run by the New Zealand Department of Conservation.

Accommodation

New Zealand is so well supplied with hotels, motels, lodges, bed-and-breakfast guesthouses, motor camps, hostels and campsites, ranging from high luxury to unadorned simplicity, that it is beyond the scope of this guide to make particular recommendations. There are two excellent guides that will steer you to the type of accommodation you want and can afford.

New Zealand Accommodation Guide, put out by the NZTP, is free and available at all NZTP Travel Offices and overseas information offices. Towns are listed alphabetically, and accommodations in each town are classified as hotels, motels, motor inns, guesthouses, bed-and-breakfasts, tourist flats, cabins and so on. Symbols are used to indicate what each one provides, and current prices are given. Street maps of main cities are included. This listing is updated annually.

AA Accommodation Directory is more complete, and all premises have been inspected by the Automobile Association. It comes in two volumes, one covering the North Island and the other the South Island. Towns are listed alphabetically, accommodations are classified by type (each listing supplemented with a lot of detailed information), and hostelries in different categories are given AA ratings with stars. The advertisement pages have photographs as well. You have to buy these volumes, but they are worth it, even if the annual updating is a bit slow. As the AA and NZTP guides are by no means identical, it is good to get both.

Also available are three guides published by Jason Publishing Company in Auckland: *Jason's Hotels, Resorts, Lodges: A New Zealand Accommodation Guide, Jason's Motels and Motor Lodges, New Zealand* and *Jason's Budget Accommodation, New Zealand-wide.* These can be useful, but the entries are not rated; some are given in bold type with extensive detail, while others, equally good in our experience, are listed simply by address and phone number in small type.

It is wise to book arrival accommodation in Auckland or Christchurch from abroad, but from then on independent travellers can do their own planning on the spot. All accommodations can be arranged ahead by phone, and two or three days' notice is sufficient during most of the year. However, during the peak holiday season from mid-December to the end of January, you need to book well in advance, especially for favourite fishing lodges, golf hotels and tourist spots like Mount Cook, Tongariro National Park, Fox Glacier, Franz Josef Glacier and Queenstown.

Hotels The government-operated Tourist Hotel Corporation (THC) provides the top luxury-resort accommodation on both islands, especially in areas of special interest and beauty, like Mount Cook and Chateau Tongariro, where the hotel is the centre of activity. Dominion Breweries (DB) has hotels throughout the country. International hotel chains such as Hyatt Kingsgate, Regency, Regent, Sheraton, TraveLodge and Vacation Hotels operate in large centres and tourist resorts. Independent hotels are usually clean and comfortable and appealingly smaller and more old-fashioned than the chains.

Hotels are either 'licensed' (permitted to sell liquor to the public), 'tourist licensed' (permitted to sell liquor only to hotel guests) or 'unlicensed' (not permitted to sell liquor).

Lodges Privately run lodges cater to sportsmen, often in scenic or wilderness settings. Fishing lodges offer a spectrum of accommodation from luxury to simple, as well as experienced guides (at extra cost) and special facilities for smoking or canning.

Motels New Zealand motels are very different from their counterparts in other countries. 'Motel flats' are complete little apartments with a fully equipped kitchen, usually two bedrooms, a bathroom with a shower, a living room and TV, with laundry facilities nearby. They offer exceptional value for small groups travelling together. Best Western and Flag Inns operate throughout the country. 'Serviced motels' are like regular motels, without kitchens but usually offering breakfast.

B & Bs Bed-and-breakfast guesthouses are usually very comfortable, reasonable in price and a fine way to meet New Zealanders. The breakfasts can be sumptuous! *The New Zealand Bed & Breakfast Book*, compiled by J and J Thomas (Wellington: Moonshine Press, 1987), is an excellent guide (though a great many B & Bs are not included), describing each house, its owner and its facilities, so you can choose intelligently and call ahead. New Zealand Visitor Information Centres can often tell you about local B & Bs that are not listed outside the region and make arrangements for you.

B & Bs are small and friendly, giving excellent value for money. Some have rooms with private bathrooms, but most have showers and toilets down the hall. All have a sitting room with TV, and many provide dinner on request. Over 30 of them have formed a nationwide federation that puts out a brochure, *New Zealand Bed & Breakfast Hotels*, which is available in New Zealand Visitor Information Centres and many hotels.

Motor Camps These offer all kinds of budget accommodation and campsites, from furnished trailers (caravans) to cabins and well-equipped flats. Sheets and bedding can be rented if they are not provided.

Hostels You do not have to be youthful to stay at youth hostels. By joining the Youth Hostels Association (YHA) for a nominal fee, you can get clean, comfortable, very cheap accommodation throughout New Zealand. The YHA handbook, *New Zealand: Come Hostelling*, gives basic information on hostelling and descriptions of every hostel, with photographs. **YMCA**s and **YWCA**s in larger towns and cities offer similar accommodation, but with more privacy, in single or double rooms.

Farm Holidays Many farm families take guests, either in their home or in separate quarters. Standards of comfort and cleanliness are high. Visitors are treated like members of the family and given the opportunity to observe a working farm, take part if they want to, or just rest in the country. A stay can range from one night with breakfast to weeks with full board. A number of organizations arrange these visits. Visitors can choose the type of farm and location they want. Details are available at any NZTP Travel Office in New Zealand or overseas at NZ Tourist Information Offices.

Food and Drink

New Zealand meals are typically hearty and filling. Refined continental cooking and other cuisines are found in the top restaurants in big cities. Prices are comparable to those in North America and Western Europe, but as there is no tipping in New Zealand the total cost is less.

New Zealand lamb is famous worldwide and the most commonly found meat in homes and restaurants, usually roasted with herbs. It often appears on menus as 'hogget', meaning one-year-old lamb, which is as tender as baby lamb but more flavourful. Beef is excellent and not too expensive, but you should probably ask to have it served rare, as New Zealanders prefer it well done. Domestic venison—often served as stew—is a speciality worth trying. It is more tender and less gamy than the wild variety. Chicken and duck are found everywhere. If you are brave, try muttonbird, a Maori delicacy that appears ready-cooked in fish shops in winter. It tastes like seagull and is best when smoked.

Seafood is superb and plentiful year-round. Rock lobsters (also called crayfish) abound in spring and summer, and all kinds of shellfish are fresh and delicious. The top specialities are succulent bluff oysters in autumn and winter, and green mussels (the colour describes the shell, not the meat). Among the best ocean fish are blue cod, snapper, John Dory, grouper, orange roughy (a type of perch) and tarakihi. Whitebait is a much-prized, tiny, transparent fish that is usually served fried in an omelette-like 'whitebait fritter'. Salmon appears on menus in New Zealand, but never trout. However, if you have caught your own trout, then most restaurants will be very willing to cook it for you.

Vegetables are abundant throughout the year. Meat courses are usually served with at least three or four vegetables. Fruit grows in several parts of both islands and is best bought fresh at roadside stands. There are many familiar fruits, such as apples, pears, peaches, nectarines, apricots and grapes, but try kiwi fruit, feijoa and tamarillo, which are as delicious as they are different. Fresh fruit is not usually served in restaurants. The national dessert is 'pavlova', a sinful concoction of meringue, sliced fruit and whipped cream. All dairy products are of superior quality, and the ice-cream is about the best in the world. Try 'hokey pokey' (butterscotch) ice-cream. New Zealand has a good variety of domestic cheeses, which follow English, French and Swiss types.

Tea shops are a fixture in every town. New Zealanders habitually stop whatever they are doing for a morning and afternoon tea-and-snack break — or coffee, if they prefer. Long-distance motorcoaches observe these breaks punctually, but the quality of fare in most rural tea shops is terrible. 'Pie' means meat pie; if a sign says it is 'home made' it might be good, with tender meat and flaky crusts, but the factory-made variety is dismal. Sandwiches are thin and anaemic, the absolute bottom being cold spaghetti on white bread with a dab of tomato sauce. On the other hand, some tea shops are gems, serving hot scones with strawberry jam and cream.

If at all possible, try a *hangi*. This is a Maori-style feast steam-cooked in an underground oven. It includes *kumara*, or Polynesian sweet potatoes, the Maori staple, and many other delicious dishes, both familiar and not, served as a buffet. Rotorua is the place to find them.

Beer is the national drink, and New Zealand has several good breweries. Hard liquor is also available. Pubs and bars are open from 11 am to 10 pm (11 pm on Saturday), except on Sundays, Christmas Day and Good Friday. Guests registered in a licenced hotel can be served drinks at any time. Among friends it is customary to 'shout' (buy) a round of drinks ('I'll shout you a drink'). Licenced restaurants serve drinks and wine with meals. Unlicenced restaurants almost always invite you to bring your own wine or beer and often display a BYO (bring your own) sign. New Zealand wines are excellent, both whites and reds, and special space is devoted to them throughout this guide.

Food and Drink Terms

Most of the terms below originated in Britain, but the list of 'translations' may be useful to American readers.

after   dessert
aubergine   eggplant
bangers   sausages
bickies or biscuits   crackers or cookies
capsicum   green pepper
chips   french fries
chook   chicken
cuppa   a cup of hot tea (or coffee)
dairy   neighbourhood store selling dairy products, canned goods, fruit, ice-cream cones and newspapers; open every day, early and late
entrée   appetizer course, eaten before the main course
greengrocer   fruit and vegetable shop
junket   a thin dessert resembling yoghurt
Marmite and Vegemite   salty, fortified yeast extracts that can be spread on bread and butter at breakfast instead of jam; an acquired taste
milk bar   shop selling dairy products, hot snacks and candy, often combined with a neighbourhood dairy
mince pie   hamburger meat pie (the size of your fist) enclosed in pastry
peckish   hungry
pudding   dessert of any kind, eaten at the end of a meal
supper   a snack before going to bed, not the main evening meal
take-aways   food to go; fast-food counters are called 'take-away bars'
tea   this can mean a cup of hot tea (any time of day), the customary mid-morning or mid-afternoon 'coffee break' of tea and snacks, or a full-fledged evening meal; if you are invited for 'tea', find out what your host or hostess means before you go
tomato sauce   the closest thing to ketchup, which does not exist in New Zealand

Shopping—Best Buys

Outstanding New Zealand wool products are sold all over both islands. Wonderful hand-knitted sweaters, weavings, woollen jackets, sheepskin rugs, coats and cars-eat covers are not cheap, but are definitely less expensive than elsewhere (except, perhaps, Hong Kong). Prices are often better off the beaten track than in the main tourist centres. Suede clothing and leather goods are also of very high quality. Greenstone jewellery is a bargain, cheaper than most other kinds of jade and sometimes beautifully worked in Maori designs.

Maori woodwork, finely carved in traditional motifs, makes for an interesting souvenir. Good pottery is much used and appreciated in New Zealand. Fine ceramics are most easily found around Nelson, Wellington and Auckland. Bulky or heavy purchases can be mailed home, and most shops are glad to ship them for you.

National Holidays

1 January	New Year's Day
6 February	Waitangi (National) Day
Good Friday	
Easter Monday	
25 April	Anzac Day
First Monday in June	Queen's Birthday
Fourth Monday in October	Labour Day
25 December	Christmas Day
26 December	Boxing Day

Local Holidays

22 January	Wellington
29 January	Auckland and Northland
1 February	Nelson
8 March	Taranaki
23 March	Dunedin, Otago and Southland
17 October	Napier and Hawkes Bay
1 November	Marlborough
1 December	Westland
16 December	Christchurch and Canterbury

Annual Events

January

Auckland   Annual Yachting Regatta, New Zealand Open Tennis
                         Tournament, New Zealand International Grand Prix
Wellington   Trentham Thoroughbred Sales

February

Bay of Islands   Treaty of Waitangi Celebrations

March

Hamilton   Ngaruawahia River Regatta (with Maori canoes)
                         Masterton Golden Shears Sheep Shearing Contest
Bay of Islands   International Bill-fish Tournament

April

Auckland   New Zealand Easter Show, Auckland Festival
Hastings   Scottish Highland Games

May

Auckland   Great Northern Hurdles and Steeplechase Meeting

July

Wellington   Wellington Hurdles and Steeplechase Meeting
Mount Hutt,
South Island   International Ski Races

November

Christchurch   Canterbury Show
Rotorua   International Trout Fishing Contest (into December)

North Island

The North Island is shaped like a lopsided, elongated diamond. Northland, the long, subtropical northern point, is joined to the rest of the island by a narrow isthmus on which sits the city of Auckland. It is flanked to the east across the Hauraki Gulf by Coromandel, a slim peninsula pointing north. The western point of the diamond forms around a single snowcapped volcano, Mount Egmont/Taranaki. The island's richest farmland lies in the west, between Auckland and the volcano, with its centre at the city of Hamilton. The eastern point of the island, the East Cape, is a densely forested, sparsely populated region, but the east coast around Hawkes Bay produces abundant fruit and wine. The south point focuses on Wellington, the capital of New Zealand. A range of rugged green mountains runs from Wellington to the East Cape, following the same geological fault that creates the South Island's mountainous spine.

In the middle of the North Island, a volcanic plateau rises from the Bay of Plenty, between Coromandel and the East Cape, to the volcanic peaks of Tongariro National Park. Major earthquakes and volcanic eruptions have occurred in the North Island within living memory, so an early warning system is in operation. At the very centre of the island, surrounded on all sides by thermal activity, is Lake Taupo.

Almost three-quarters of New Zealand's three million people live in the North Island, a large proportion of them in and around Auckland, which is by far the largest city. Most of the Maori live in the North Island, too, mainly in the north and east, where their traditions remain strong.

The first Polynesian settlers came into New Zealand at the north tip and spread southward. So did the Europeans, many centuries later, after whalers and timber speculators had put their first town at Russell, on the far northern Bay of Islands. Before long, small colonies dotted the coast at Wellington, Wanganui and New Plymouth. The Maori were helpless in the face of such an influx. In 1840, Maori chiefs, who had no concept of land ownership, signed over New Zealand to the British government at Wanganui, near Russell. The subsequent Land Wars—long, vicious struggles between Maori tribes and colonists—tore the North Island for two decades. By century's end, Europeans occupied all the farmland and were ready to develop the North Island's prosperous agriculture.

Four national parks preserve areas of outstanding natural interest and beauty—the two volcanic regions of Tongariro and Taranaki, the eastern lakes and virgin forests of Urewera, and the historic Wanganui River. Tourists usually head straight down the middle of the island from Auckland to Wellington by way of Rotorua's thermal springs, the glow-worm caves of Waitomo, Lake Taupo and the Tongariro volcanoes. They short-change both the North Island and themselves by doing so, because nearby are dozens of

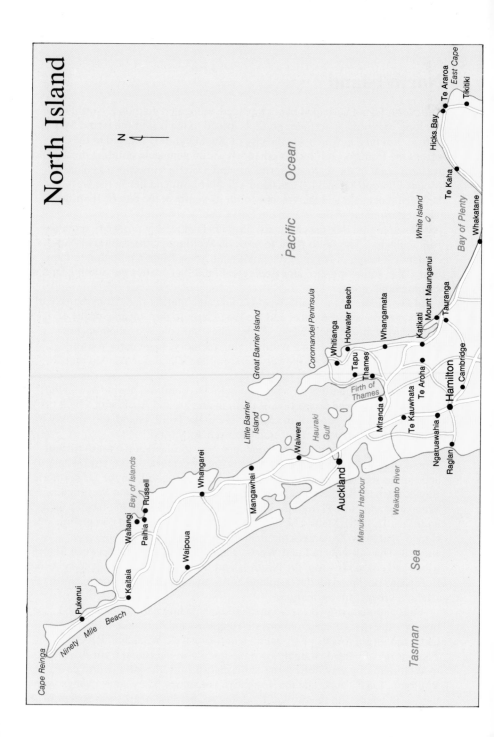

North Island

Cape Reinga

Ninety Mile Beach

Pukenui

Kaitaia

Waipoua

Bay of Islands

Waitangi
Paihia Russell

Whangarei

Mangawhai

Little Barrier Island

Great Barrier Island

Waiwera

Hauraki Gulf

Auckland

Manukau Harbour

Waikato River

Tasman Sea

Coromandel Peninsula

Whitianga

Hotwater Beach

Tapu
Thames

Firth of Thames

Miranda

Te Kauwhata

Ngaruawahia

Raglan

Whangamata

Katikati

Mount Maunganui

Tauranga

Te Aroha

Hamilton

Cambridge

White Island

Bay of Plenty

Te Kaha

Whakatane

Hicks Bay

Te Araroa

East Cape

Tikitiki

Pacific Ocean

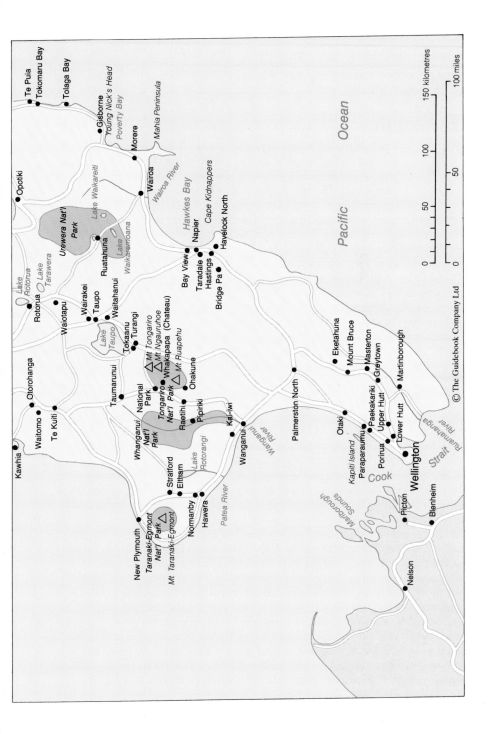

© The Guidebook Company Ltd

exciting, curious, welcoming spots that draw added charm simply from being off the beaten track.

The North

The subtropical northern part of the North Island enjoys the gentlest climate in New Zealand, with warm (but never unpleasantly hot) summers and frostless winters. Rain showers occur all year round. The two peninsulas of Northland and Coromandel received the earliest European visitors, who lived through wild times as fortunes were made and lost in whaling, timber and gold. Today, the climate and natural beauty of these peninsulas make them a magnet for New Zealand holiday-makers, though foreign visitors often bypass them in favour of the well-worn tourist track to the south. Northland's spectacular Bay of Islands, above all, should not be skipped over, its compelling scenery and fascinating history meriting far more international attention than they now receive. On the other hand, Auckland, New Zealand's biggest and most cosmopolitan city, is never missed. Conveniently situated in the north between two sparkling harbours, it is the point of arrival and departure for most international visitors. Some enjoy its wealth of sights, activities and excursions so much that they never get any further.

Auckland

New Zealand's principal metropolis spreads over at least seven extinct volcanoes on a neck of land only 1.5 kilometres (a mile) wide at its narrowest. On the west, Manukau Harbour spreads as broad tidal mud flats towards the Tasman Sea. On the east, Waitemata Harbour opens into the Hauraki Gulf, spanned by the long, eight-lane Harbour Bridge, which replaced ferry boats in 1959. The gulf is dotted with sailboats and islands. The symmetrical cone of Rangitoto Island, the closest, is a sleeping volcano that last erupted 200 years ago.

Early settlers did not come to Auckland as a well-organized, closely knit colony, as they did to Wellington, Christchurch and Dunedin. It was founded as the capital of New Zealand in 1840 on the site of a deserted Maori stronghold straddling the isthmus. One purpose of the siting was to protect the more thickly settled Bay of Islands up north from Maori attack. Officials, shopkeepers and labourers straggled south from Russell; the soil was fertile and Waitemata Harbour made a good port, so the population grew. Auckland's new inhabitants coveted the rich Maori lands to the south and were soon mired in the merciless Land Wars, which lasted 20 years and resulted in the ousting of the outnumbered Maori. The discovery of goldfields on the nearby Coromandel Peninsula stimulated commerce, and Auckland kept on growing. The city remained the capital for 25 years until 1865, when

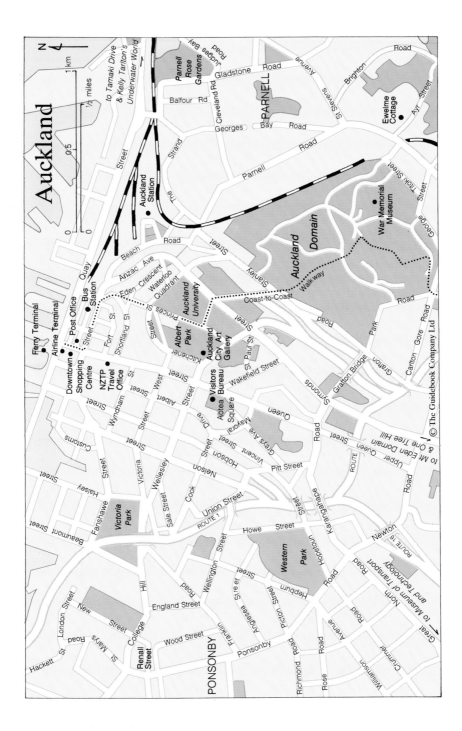

the government moved to the more central city of Wellington. Today, Auckland is home to 850,000 people, more than a quarter of New Zealand's entire population. Its promise of opportunity, education and advancement has drawn immigrants from islands all over the Pacific Ocean. With their numbers added to the indigenous Maori, Pacific peoples now comprise 17 percent of Auckland's population, making it the biggest Polynesian city in the world.

Getting There

Auckland is the hub of an excellent transportation network. A dozen airlines use the international terminal at the airport in suburban Mangere, 20 kilometres (12 miles) south of the city. Local airlines serve cities throughout New Zealand from the adjacent domestic terminal, which is linked to the international terminal by a shuttle bus. The 'Airporter' coach runs between the airport and city centre every half hour. Some visitors travelling on leisurely schedules and generous budgets arrive on the cruise ships that regularly dock at Prince's Wharf in Waitemata Harbour.

New Zealand Railways provides comfortable trains, one by day and one overnight, for the 11-hour trip between Auckland and Wellington, with stops at several points between.

Long-distance bus lines such as Mount Cook Line, Intercity (NZRR) Services, Newmans Coachlines and Main Line Coachlines have routes all over the North Island served from terminals in Auckland.

Information and Orientation

There are several places to go in Auckland for information and help with travel plans, tours, accommodation and bookings of all sorts. The **Travellers Information Centre** at Auckland Airport's international terminal is open daily 6.30 am–11 pm. Phone 275–7467 or 275–6467. The **NZTP Travel Office** downtown at 99 Queen Street is open weekdays 8.30 am–4.45 pm. Phone 798–180 or 275–9597. The **Auckland Visitors Bureau** up the road at Aotea Square (299 Queen Street) is open weekdays 8.30 am–5.30 pm and weekends 9 am–3 pm. Phone 31–899. **Touristop Tourist Services** in the Downtown Airline Terminal on Quay Street is open daily 8.30 am–5.30 pm. Phone 775–783.

Major national and international car rental companies have offices at the airport and downtown. The main city bus station occupies a full city block directly behind the post office, at the lower end of Queen Street. The **Bus Place**, 131 Hobson Street, has information, timetables, maps, special passes and tickets for sightseeing. A helpful telephone information service, known as **Buzzabus** (phone 797–119), may save footsteps by telling what bus to take to your destination and where to board and by answering other questions. Buzzabus operates from Monday to Saturday 6 am–11 pm and on Sunday 7.30 am–10.30 pm. Taxis are not easy to hail on the street. They wait in line (taxi ranks) at several corners in the centre of town or respond to phone calls. The biggest companies are Auckland Co-operative Taxi Society (phone 792–792) and Alert Taxis (phone 392–000). Bicycling on the city streets is not recommended, but bike-rental shops are found near most city parks.

Sights

Queen Street, Auckland's main boulevard, is near many of the main hotels. It runs north–south from the waterfront to suburban Newton along the floor of a now-built-up valley, with side roads climbing its steep sides. Small shops, big department stores, cafés, restaurants, arcades and two New Zealand Visitor Information Centres can be found on it. The Downtown Shopping Centre, opposite the main post office at its lower end, has over 70 shops.

Victoria Park Market, about three kilometres (two miles) from the centre of the city, is a lively, popular marketplace with plenty of bargains on almost anything from fresh fruit and vegetables to books, clothes, pottery and handicrafts. There are several food shops and an international food hall. The market can be reached most easily—and fairly cheaply—by taxi.

Two attractive, fashionable suburbs with beautifully restored Victorian buildings are Parnell to the east and Ponsonby to the west. Both have intriguing boutiques, gourmet restaurants and cafés. At **Parnell**, two special attractions are historic, kauri-wood Ewelme Cottage, at 14 Ayr Street, off Parnell Road, and gorgeous Parnell Rose Gardens, with some 4,000 roses in bloom between November and March. Parnell can be reached by a hike across Auckland Domain or by bus. **Ponsonby**'s special appeal lies in its narrow, steep streets (Renall Street, off Ponsonby Road, is perfectly preserved) and picturesque views. It can be reached by bus or by hiking alongside Victoria Park and over College Hill.

Several of Auckland's volcanic peaks served the Maori as fortresses and are now public parks with spectacular views over the city and harbours. **Mount Eden** is the highest point, with the grandest view. About four kilometres (2.5 miles) south of the central city, this park can be reached by bus from the downtown bus terminal. **One Tree Hill**, in large Cornwall Park, two kilometres (1.2 miles) further south, can be seen from a distance topped by a single pine tree and a tall obelisk. You can walk or drive to the top through groves of trees and fields of grazing sheep for a magnificent view. The Auckland Observatory is near the Manakau Road entrance. **Auckland Domain** (the grandiose word *domain* simply meaning 'park') is a large green area east of the city centre and west of Parnell, within walking distance of either. It contains nice gardens, a planetarium, a fine museum and plenty of activities, such as kite-flying.

The **War Memorial Museum**, at the top of Auckland Domain's hill, is

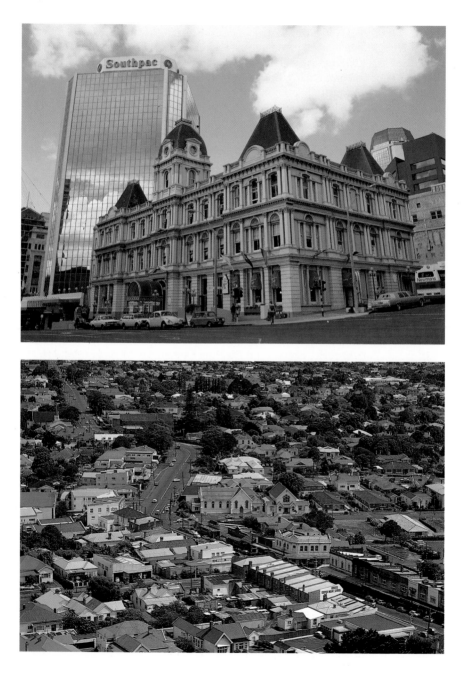

the best place in town to gain an introduction to the culture of the Maori and their remarkable art of decorative carving, which records their myths and history. The Maori Court contains a magnificent 25-metre (80-foot) -long war canoe, a carved gateway and a great carved house among its masterpieces, along with many artifacts and portraits of tribal chiefs. The museum also houses the South Pacific Island Collection and the Hall of New Zealand Birds, with the amazing assembled skeleton of an extinct giant moa. Open 10 am–5 pm.

The **Auckland City Art Gallery**, on the edge of Albert Park at Wellesley Street East and Kitchener Street, has a representative collection of contemporary New Zealand art and a good international display of drawings and prints. The classical old masters and historical paintings all help to make this one of New Zealand's outstanding art museums. Open 10 am–4 pm.

The **Museum of Transport and Technology**, on the Great North Road at the edge of the Western Springs Reserve, is an intriguing place to spend half a rainy day. It contains every imaginable kind of machine from trains and planes to player pianos, computers and whole fire stations, all in perfect working condition. When the sun comes out, visit the adjacent 12-hectare (30-acre) replica of a Second World War airfield, complete with authentic and working war equipment, or take an antique tram ride to the **zoo**. Open daily 9 am–5 pm.

Kelly Tarlton's Underwater World, at Orakei Wharf on Tamaki Drive, is one of the most imaginative seawater aquariums anywhere. It is built in what were once the city's huge storm tanks under the highway. A moving walkway carries visitors underwater along a clear plastic tunnel for an eight-minute trip through various marine habitats. Sharks and giant manta rays swoop overhead while curious fish peer at the humans. A sidewalk lets you step off the conveyor for longer, closer looks en route. Open daily from 9 am to 9 pm.

Hauraki Gulf and its islands can be explored by boat. Start with the helpful information centre of the Downtown Ferry Terminal at the end of Queen Street. Phone 33–329 or 790–092. Captain Cook Cruises leave from the wharf across from the Downtown Airline Terminal on Quay Street. Phone 394–901. Blue Boat Ferries make scheduled runs to several islands from West Prince's Wharf on Quay Street. Phone 34–479.

Northland

This long, ragged finger of land pointing north from Auckland for about 450 kilometres (280 miles) is mostly hilly, subtropical farmland with patches of forest enclosed within a spectacular shoreline. Until the 19th century it was largely covered with magnificent ancient forests. New Zealand's first European colonists settled on its east coast at the Bay of Islands. Their rough, tough town of Russell, also known as 'the hellhole of the Pacific', was the country's first capital, an honour it relinquished to Auckland in 1840. The great forests of kauri trees were levelled by timber speculators, and the ravaged land was further abused in the relentless search for buried kauri gum, a valuable export, until the early years of this century. Parts of the far north have never recovered and remain sparsely populated, semi-fertile grazing land. Yet, most of Northland has blossomed into rich farmland, while the coasts are a paradise for vacationers, boat-owners and deep-sea fishermen.

Northland's biggest town and main port is Whangarei, on the east coast. Further north, the Bay of Islands attracts year-round visitors to the towns of Paihia, Russell and Waitangi, which overlook the beautiful, island-studded bay. At the extreme north, a slim peninsula extends northward from Kaitaia, bounded on its west side by unbroken Ninety-Mile Beach (actually 64 miles, or 103 kilometres, long). At the tip of the peninsula are the North Cape and

The Troublesome Treaty of Waitangi

Waitangi is a word visitors keep hearing. Waitangi Day is New Zealand's national day, a holiday celebrated on 6 February with ceremonies and pageantry, or a day at the beach. Waitangi village, on Northland's Bay of Islands, is a must on tourists' itineraries. The village's Treaty House is its historical shrine, where the Treaty of Waitangi, signed by Queen Victoria's envoys and the Maori chiefs in 1840, sealed an agreement that Britain would take possession of Aotearoa, the Maori's beloved Land of the Long White Cloud, and add it to the far-flung British Empire.

For 150 years New Zealanders of British descent have prided themselves on the fact that their country was acquired by legal means, rather than by crude conquest—notwithstanding that the treaty was never ratified.

Great Britain's motives at the time were above reproach. The newly founded colony's coastal waters, its forests and its native people were being ruthlessly exploited by European whalers, sealers and lumberjacks, escaped Australian convicts and the other speculators, adventurers, mountebanks, missionaries and desperadoes who are drawn to wild frontiers. The Maori, their traditions crumbling under this abuse, were 'selling' land in exchange for alcohol and muskets. The Maori needed protection, the general lawlessness was getting out of hand and, to add urgency to the problem, the French were showing interest in colonizing the place. It clearly was time for the Crown to step in.

An ineffectual British resident named Busby was transferred from Australia to take the situation in hand, but without the troops, arms or authority needed to succeed. Finally, in 1840, Captain William Hobson was sent from London to replace him. His instructions were to annex the country with the 'free and intelligent consent of the natives'.

Cape Reinga, surrounded by turbulence caused by the meeting of the Tasman Sea and Pacific Ocean currents. Northland's less-developed west coast has the country's last big stand of kauri trees, which are preserved in the Waipoua Kauri Forest and Trounson Kauri Park. One giant is believed to be 2,000 years old! Dargaville, the largest west coast town, lies at a river mouth on isolated Kaipara Harbour. A hundred years ago, this sleepy settlement, now seemingly buried in dairyland, was a major port in the brisk trade of kauri gum and timber.

Getting There

Mount Cook Airlines flies from Auckland to Kerikeri, at the Bay of Islands, with a connecting coach service to Paihia. Intercity (NZRR) Services runs to Whangarei, Bay of Islands and Kaitaia. However, the best way to visit

---

From London, this seemed a humane, logical approach. Hobson, helped by Busby and the missionaries, drafted a treaty whereby the Maori would relinquish their sovereignty to the British Crown in exchange for a guarantee of Maori rights, which included the peaceful possession of their lands (which could, however, be sold to the government) and the privileges accorded other British subjects. The representatives of the Crown and a number of Maori chiefs signed or marked the treaty amid great pomp and circumstance on Busby's front lawn, and the way was opened for systematic colonial settlement to begin.

The treaty was carried around the country for other Maori leaders to sign. A handful refused, and one or two thought it was a receipt for gifts. None understood the notion of sovereignty or of outright ownership of land, which traditionally had been communally occupied by the Maori tribes, with sacred areas honoured by all.

The treaty's guarantees were soon forgotten as colonists flooded in, hungry for farmland. The Maori were dispossessed, overwhelmed by sheer numbers, despite their last-ditch efforts to save their land and identity in 20 years of bitter and bloody struggle known as the Land Wars.

Today the Maori, in a newly assertive mood, are challenging the Treaty of Waitangi. The government has set up the Waitangi Tribunal, including jurists of both Maori and Pakeha (European) descent, to consider thousands of Maori claims against Crown land, which though owned by the government is often leased out. Possession of much of the South Island and some parts of the North Island hang in the balance. Meanwhile, Canada's momentous decision in 1988 to return vast tracts of land to indigenous Indians and Eskimos has people all over New Zealand watching and wondering.

Northland is by car. Highway 1, the main road, links Auckland and Kaitaia, via Whangarei. Some 50 kilometres (30 miles) before Whangarei, Highway 12 loops around to the west coast, through Dargaville and the kauri forest, rejoining Highway 1 near the Bay of Islands. Highway 10 makes a northern loop by following the east coast from the Bay of Islands to Kaitaia. Thus it is possible to see most of Northland without ever backtracking.

Sights

After Auckland, Highway 1 passes through a prosperous farming area known as the Hibiscus Coast. Roadside stands sell fresh fruit and vegetables. **Waiwera**, 48 kilometres (30 miles) north of Auckland, is a small spa with thermal pools ranging in temperature from 33° to 40°C (91° to 104°F). The popular pool area is set among lawns, with entertainments like waterslides and movies. Open 9 am–9 pm.

   Whangarei, Northland's only real city, lies at the head of a protected deepwater harbour thronged with sailboats and commercial shipping. The New Zealand Visitor Information Centre, downtown on Rust Avenue, has free maps and literature. The **Clapham Clock Collection**, next to the rose gardens on Water Street, is worth a visit to see the hundreds of clocks and watches of every type and description, the oldest dating from 1636. Open weekdays 10 am–4 pm and weekends and holidays 10.15 am–3 pm. Photogenic **Whangarei Falls** plunges 25 metres (80 feet) over a forested cliff into a deep green pool about six kilometres (four miles) east of the city centre on Ngunguru Road. Several walkways offer spectacular views.

   The **Bay of Islands** received its name from Captain Cook when he first saw its 150 islands rising from the warm, azure sea inside a convoluted bay. **Paihia** is the main town. Its busy waterfront at the end of Williams Street has the New Zealand Visitor Information Centre and Maritime Building, where excursions, accommodation, tours and further travel can be arranged.

   Waitangi, across the river from Paihia, holds the historic Treaty House set in the Waitangi National Reserve. Here Maori chiefs signed a treaty with the British in 1840 surrendering their country and adding New Zealand to the British Empire. The colonial Treaty House is set in lovely grounds overlooking the bay. Open daily 9 am–5 pm. Nearby is the Waitangi **Whare Runanga**, a splendidly decorated Maori meeting house. The carvings are the work of several North Island tribes. The house itself was offered as a gift to the nation on the 100th anniversary of the treaty. Below the house an open pavilion shelters a great war canoe 35 metres (115 feet) long and carved from kauri trees, which is launched during celebrations every February with a Maori crew of 80. The Shipwreck Museum occupies the barque *Tui*, which is moored at Waitangi Bridge. Jewellery and gold coins feature among the relics of several famous shipwrecks. A fascinating film explains the salvage operations.

Russell, on the opposite side of the bay, is reached by a car ferry from Opua, just south of Paihia, and by passenger ferry from Paihia or Waitangi. A small road winding around the bay offers a longer, less-used route. Leave Highway 1 at Kawakawa for Taumarere and branch left after about five kilometres (three miles). Charming, old-world Russell retains little hint of its bawdy, brawling, lawless past, but the Captain Cook Memorial Museum gives some of that flavour. A good one-hour tour of the historic sites is run by Russell Mini Tours, leaving Russell Wharf daily at 11.15 am and 2.15 pm.

Kaitaia is the main town of the far north and the take-off point for Cape Reinga. The Far North Regional Museum has excellent displays on ancient Maori culture and the Dalmatian gum-diggers who displaced it. **Cape Reinga**, at New Zealand's northernmost tip, was the sacred spot from which, according to Maori legend, the spirits of the dead departed across the Pacific to Hawaiki, their mythological homeland. A 116-kilometre (72-mile) unpaved road runs the length of the narrow peninsula from Kaitaia, giving views of both the Tasman Sea and the Pacific Ocean. A tiny settlement at the cape includes a post office-cum-souvenir shop and a lighthouse. Marvellous views from the headland take in the coast and the clashing seas, where waves are said to reach ten metres (30 feet) in stormy weather. At low tide, the hard sand of **Ninety-Mile Beach** serves as an alternate road up the peninsula's west coast. Mount Cook Line and other companies offer day trips (including a picnic lunch) that go one way by the beach and the other by road, stopping en route at various scenic sights and the intriguing **Wagener Museum**, on Houhora Heads Road, east of the main road just south of Pukenui.

The Far North Information Centre is at 6–8 South Street, Kaitaia. Mount Cook Line's office is on Commerce Street. All hotels have brochures about different tour options. If you are travelling by car, it is best to leave it in Kaitaia and take a bus or four-wheel-drive vehicle to Cape Reinga because of tricky quicksand along the streambed leading inland from the beach.

Waipoua State Kauri Forest, the oldest and largest remnant of New Zealand's once-great kauri forests, lines unpaved but good Highway 12 for 16 kilometres (ten miles). Two of the primeval giants are awe-inspiring. Te Manhuta (Lord of the Forest) is 1,200 years old and the biggest-known kauri, standing over 51 metres (167 feet) high and 13 metres (43 feet) in girth. It is signposted along a short track close to the road. Te Matua Ngahere (Father of the Forest), also signposted, stands at the end of a beautiful forest glade, 15 minutes' walk from the road. This immense tree is believed to be about 2,000 years old. **Trounson Kauri Park** is a smaller but splendid kauri forest, with fine walking paths. A five-kilometre (three-mile) detour branches left from Highway 12 south of Waipoua Forest.

The Giant Kauri

The king of New Zealand's magnificent forests is the kauri, *Agathis australis* — but, sadly, few of these remain. In the same league as California's giant redwoods, the kauri's enormous size and staggering old age make it a rarity worth pondering. Early forms of the tree lived on a primal southern land mass before the seven continents took shape 190 million years ago. One giant still standing in the Waipoa Kauri Sanctuary is thought to be 2,000 years old.

The Kauri's silver-grey trunk soars towards a canopy of thick, leathery leaves, a perfectly straight shaft left clean as the kauri sheds its lower branches. This results in startling beauty, but also invited destruction, as kauris made excellent ship's masts. The straight-grained, unknotted hardwood also could be ripped into clear, wide planks for building the rest of the ship.

The first Europeans in New Zealand were sealers and whalers from Australia. They made a base in Northland's protected Bay of Islands, where they refitted their ships and took on provisions and Maori crewmen. Their numbers swelled until the fur seals were slaughtered to near-extinction, and by 1820 the town of Russell had taken shape. Timber traders moved in to fell the kauri forests almost as ruthlessly as the seamen plundered the coast,

The kauri forest, which stretched through Northland to beyond Auckland and across the Coromandel Peninsula, survived somewhat longer than the seals. The Royal Navy and shipbuilders of all kinds set up operations in Kaipara and Hokianga harbours, and sawmill settlements dotted Northland's west coast between them. In Coromandel, about 300 dams built of kauri timber backed up the water of streams which then floated the harvest of logs to the sea. The timber boom could not last because the kauris grew too slowly to replace themselves, needing 80 to 100 years to become commercially millable, or 800 years to reach full maturity. By 1860 the big forests were gone.

But there was still money to be made off the kauri. Dead trees left deposits of resinous sap as hardened gum in the soil. Beds of the petrified gum lay underground where prehistoric forests had once stood. The Maori chewed the fresh gum, burned it as fuel, especially for long-burning torches, and used its soot for tattooing. The gum commanded a high price abroad as a base for varnish and linoleum, and a 'poor man's gold rush' gathered steam. By 1880, some 2,000 gum-diggers had swarmed to the gum fields, most of them coming from Dalmatia, on the coast of present-day Yugoslavia, to escape conscription into the Austrian army. The gum trade peaked around 1990, and when the gum fields were exhausted the Dalmatians moved south to the area around Auckland to plant vineyards—inaugurating New Zealand's wine industry.

The devastation of the kauris produced useless land—kauri bark, shed over centuries, leached the soil, and gum-diggers reduced it to potholes. Fertilizers and much hard effort have finally created farmland. In 1952, public pressure saved the last of the kauris when Waipoua and Omahuta were proclaimed forest sanctuaries. The Otamatea Kauri and Pioneer Museum, at Matakohe, records the whole kauri saga in exhaustive, fascinating detail.

Karekare, North Island (above);
Knights Point (below)

Coromandel Peninsula

This 100-kilometre (60-mile) finger of land across Hauraki Gulf from Auckland separates that body of water from the Bay of Plenty. Its steep, wild mountains and lovely coasts, a couple of hours' drive from Auckland, are favourite haunts for nature-loving New Zealanders but are not well known to outsiders. Like Northland, Coromandel has had a chequered history. Its kauri forests were ruthlessly plundered for timber and gum, and a gold rush in 1867 brought short-lived prosperity, swelling its population for a decade before giving out. Today, its untamed scenery and calm isolation attract many craftspeople as residents.

Thames, at the base of Coromandel's west coast, is the peninsula's largest town, accessible by Intercity (NZRR) Services. Mercury Airlines flies in from Auckland. The New Zealand Visitor Information Centre on Queen Street has maps and details on the whole peninsula. The coast north of Thames to **Tapu** is a delight of rocky headlands and perfect sandy coves.

A paved road crosses Coromandel's mountain spine from Thames to the east coast. A scenic, steep gravel road crosses from Tapu, and a slow gravel road loops around the north end of the peninsula. **Whitianga**, the main town on the east coast, has a sheltered harbour famed for big-game fishing and a long beach. To the south, little **Hahei** is charmingly situated by a pink sand beach, and **Hot Water Beach** has a natural area where you can scoop out your own thermal pool in the sand to enjoy a hot soak. **Whangamata**, still further south, has a beach famous among surfers for its big, long waves.

Focus

Manukau Harbour, southwest of Auckland, has vast mud flats inhabited by shore birds. The oxidation ponds of the Manukau Sewage Purification Works, just north of the airport, are a major habitat for waders. The purification works are on Island Road, off Greenwood Road. The office gives permission to visit the ponds. Open 8 am–5 pm weekdays. Then continue out Island Road to Puketutu Island to see spotted doves in one of their rare breeding areas. Pheasants and various finches are also quite common here. On Manukau Harbour's south shore, towards Clarks Beach, the Karaka shell banks attract a good variety of waders, including whimbrel in summer. High tide at Manukau is three hours later than in Auckland.

The islands in **Hauraki Gulf**, east of Auckland, provide breeding grounds for little blue penguin and 13 species of petrel and shearwater. Take a ferry from Auckland's harbour out to Waiheke, the largest island, and keep an eye out for gannet, little blue penguin and arctic skua near the shore. Out in the gulf, look for giant and white-faced storm petrel, shearwater, cape pigeon and fairy prion. Timetables for the ferry are at the ticket office on Quay Street, between Queen's Wharf and Prince's Wharf.

Muriwai Beach, on the west coast about 40 kilometres (25 miles) north of Auckland, has a small colony of gannets that nest between August and February. Leave Route 16 just north of Waimauku and follow the signs to Woodhill Forest Headquarters for an entry permit. The gannets occupy a fenced reserve on the cliff top above Maori Bay. A track leads up from the old quarry parking area to a spot where the birds can be safely watched at close quarters.

Northland has New Zealand's foremost sanctuary for endangered species, **Little Barrier Island.** Free from predators and strictly protected, the island is a refuge for stitchbirds, saddlebacks, kokakos and a tiny kakapo community. The last black petrels and a small colony of Cook's petrels still survive there. Besides rare and endangered species, a rich variety of native and introduced birds inhabit the island. Permits to visit Little Barrier Island can be obtained from the Hauraki Gulf Maritime Park Board, Department of Conservation, Auckland. Open 9 am–3 pm. Phone 799–972. Boats can be chartered at Sandspit or Leigh, about 60 kilometres (37 miles) north of Auckland. Be sure to check in with the island's resident ranger on arrival.

Whangarei Harbour has mud flats on the south side where godwit, knot and other Arctic migrants stay in summer. The rocky north shore shelters little blue penguin, heron, oystercatcher, tern and other species. The New Zealand dotterel breeds at several points around the harbour.

The **Bay of Islands** offers a fine chance to see pelagic birds by boat. An excellent launch trip is the daily four-and-a-half-hour 'cream run' that leaves Russell at 9.20 am and Paihia at 9.45 am, heading far enough out among the islands to encounter a wide variety of Pacific sea birds.

The **Firth of Thames,** in south Hauraki Gulf between Auckland and Coromandel, has mud flats and shell banks perfect for migratory waders. The Miranda Naturalists' Trust protects the coastline just north of **Miranda,** which is about 70 kilometres (45 miles) southeast of Auckland. There is free access from the coast road, and vehicles can reach the beach at Access Bay. Thousands of godwits, knots, South Island pied oystercatchers and wrybills arrive in waves between September and February. Other migrants include sandpipers, turnstones and red-necked stints. Gulls, terns, shags, herons, banded dotterels and pied stilts are year-round residents. Miranda is a must.

In **Auckland,** a pleasant **waterfront walk** gives a view of the city's famous sailboats. Start at the post office (corner of Quay and Queen streets) and walk seven kilometres (4.3 miles) east via the Tamaki Drive causeway and Takaparawha Regional Park to Mission Bay. There are several bus stops along the way. Allow two hours.

The **Coast-to-Coast Walkway** crosses Auckland's isthmus from the Pacific Ocean side's Waitemata Harbour to the Tasman Sea side's Manukau. It is clearly marked and deservedly famous. There are magnificent views of the city and both harbours from gardens and parks that include two extinct volcanoes. An excellent pamphlet with a detailed map is available from the Auckland Visitors Bureau. Start at the Ferry Terminal, at the bottom of Queen Street. The route winds through the Domain, Auckland's largest park, over the city's highest point and through the green oasis of One Tree Hill before emerging at suburban Onehunga, on Manakau Harbour. Bus stops, public toilets and coffee shops are plentiful along the route. The whole walk is 13 kilometres (eight miles) long. Allow four and a half hours.

In **Northland**, there is a good cliff walk at **Mangawhai Heads**, about 20 kilometres (12 miles) northeast of Wellsford, which is 98 kilometres (61 miles) southeast of Whangarei. This coastal walk along a five-kilometre (three-mile) stretch of cliffs, beach, forest and farmland gives splendid views over the Hauraki Gulf. Leave Highway 1 at Kaiwaka and follow the signs to Mangawhai Heads. The walkway begins on the north side of Mangawhai Harbour, across the water from a wildlife sanctuary on a long sandspit. The walkway follows the beach for a kilometre (half a mile) before climbing the high cliffs amid large pohutukawa trees. It turns inland at a natural amphitheatre known as the Giant's Staircase, which offers pleasant vistas of the surrounding country, and ends where low cliffs approach the cape of Bream Tail. Here a colony of shags occupies a pohutukawa tree. At low tide, the return trip may be made along the shore, but this is rocky in places. The walkway is closed from August to October for lambing on the farmland. Allow two and a half hours for the round trip.

Within the **Waitangi Natural Reserve** on the **Bay of Islands**, a six-kilometre (four-mile) -long trail follows the Waitangi River to Haruru Falls at the edge of the park. The trail starts 500 metres (0.3 miles) from the carpark north of the visitors centre. It leads through a native rain forest and, by boardwalk, through a mangrove swamp full of wildlife. The falls are splendid after rain. Allow two and a half hours.

Cape Reinga, the sparsely populated tip of Northland, is where the spirits of deceased Maori traditionally depart New Zealand for the afterlife, and there is a good beach walk along this untamed coast. Get a map of the walking trails from the New Zealand Visitor Information Centre on South Road in Kaitaia or from the ranger at Waitiki Landing, about 95 kilometres (60 miles) further north. A big map is also located in the Cape Reinga carpark. Take drinking water, suntan lotion and insect repellent. The walk (part of a much longer track) starts at the carpark or on the path to the lighthouse. From the clifftop you have a fine view of the coast and the turbulence caused by the meeting of the waters of the Pacific Ocean and the Tasman Sea. A steep climb leads down to Te Werahi Beach, which the trail follows to its southern end at Te Werahi Stream. This takes about one hour. From the ridge above Te Werahi Stream, a loop walk to Cape Maria van Diemen is signposted. This detour takes about one and a half hours and brings you to a fine picnic place with spectacular views of the coast and the sea. You can return to the lighthouse by the beach or leave the beach and follow the well-marked track back to the road. The circle takes three hours without the detour.

 The far north is the only part of New Zealand without superb fly fishing. Instead, it offers world-famous big-game fishing and surf-casting.

The **Bay of Islands** draws big-game fishing enthusiasts from all corners of the earth. The biggest striped marlin in the world are caught here, along with many other species of game fish. The season for marlin is from December to May, and for yellowtail from June to September; shark season runs the year round. Several deep-sea boat charter companies in Paihia offer all kinds of amenities. The Bay of Islands Swordfish Club in Russell also charters boats. Light tackle fishing is another year-round sport and is relatively inexpensive. For 24-hour information phone Paihia 27–311.

Ninety-Mile Beach, on the west coast, is unsurpassed for surf-casting. One of the world's largest surf-casting contests is held here every January, drawing huge crowds of anglers who compete for big cash prizes.

Whitianga, on the east coast of the Coromandel Peninsula, is only a little less famous than the Bay of Islands in the world of big-game fishing. Boat charters to fish the waters of Mercury Bay can be arranged at the Whitianga Visitors Information Centre, but bookings should be made well in advance. The season runs from 26 December to the end of April, with February and March considered the best months.

Auckland has a dozen golf courses set between the sparkling waters of its two harbours. Two are world famous. **Titirangi Golf Club**, at New Lynn in the western suburbs, was designed 50 years ago by Alister McKenzie, the same Scot who helped Bobby Jones to design the famous course in Augusta, Georgia, that is the home of the Masters Tournament. The hilly, challenging, but shortish course is set in a magnificent area of native forest alive with birds. The greens and the view are outstanding. Par 70. Phone 875–749. **Middlemore Golf Club**, in the southern suburb of Middlemore, is equally prestigious and somewhat longer, its undulating terrain bordering the salt marshes of Curlew Bay. Par 72. Phone 276–6149.

Three other courses are well worth noting. **Muriwai Links Course** at Muriwai Beach, about 40 kilometres (25 miles) northeast of Auckland, is a fine challenge laid out on sand dunes overlooking the turbulent Tasman Sea. Some golfers count it as a 'must'. Par 72. Phone WM–411–8454. **Chamberlain Park Municipal Golf Course** is on Highway 16 near the centre of Auckland. The well-designed public course welcomes all and can be very crowded on weekends. Par 70. Phone 866–758. **Manukau Golf Club** is just

off Highway 1 in the southern suburb of Takanini. The well-wooded course beside Manukau Harbour resembles both links and inland courses. Its fourth hole, played across the sea, reminds Americans of the seventh hole at Pebble Beach. Par 72. Phone 266–6986.

In **Northland**, the best-known course by far is rolling, seaside **Waitangi Golf Course**, with its unsurpassed views over the Bay of Islands. Arnold Palmer praised it in 1978 as worth the trip. It is an easy walk from the THC Waitangi Hotel. Par 70. Phone Paihia 27–713. Many golfers also recommend the nearby **Kerikeri Golf Club**. Phone KC–78–837. At Whangarei, the **Mount Denby Golf Club** offers a very pleasant game across rolling terrain. Par 72. Phone 70–775.

Auckland is the centre of New Zealand's wine industry, though no longer the main grape-growing area. It has more wineries (well over 20) than any other part of the country. The giants of the industry— Montana, Corbans, Cooks, Villa Maria and others—mature and bottle their wine here with grapes drawn from many regions. The Wine Institute— founded in 1975 to represent all wineries, great and small, and to instil some order in the industry—is also in Auckland. The government's research station is nearby (see *Focus*, page 115).

Most of Auckland's wineries are small or medium-sized and are still run by the families who founded them. The descendants of Yugoslavs from Dalmatia predominate. Described below are some of the vineyards most praised by wine writers and judges. (Montana is not included here. Its vineyards near Blenheim in the South Island are set up for tours and tastings.) All the wineries welcome visitors, and Vineyard Tours operates organized tours to selected wineries near Auckland from Monday to Saturday, 10 am– 3 pm, including lunch, pickup and return to any city hotel. Phone 398–670.

West Auckland's Henderson Valley, the cradle of New Zealand's wine industry, has faced competition in recent years from newer wine-producing areas and loss of land from encroaching motorways and suburbs.

Babich Wines, on Babich Road, Henderson, is one of the best and largest of the family-owned wineries, the bulk of whose grapes now come from contract growers. The attractive home vineyard is run by two sons of the founder, a Dalmatian immigrant who turned from gum-digging to wine-making in 1919. Its strengths are very dry Sauvignon Blanc and fine Pinot Noir. Make two left turns off Swanson Road at Metcalfe Road. Phone 833–8909.

Collard Brothers, 303 Lincoln Road, Henderson, is a small family winery with a limited production of regional varietal wines. The three Collard brothers enjoy a high reputation for white wines, especially Chenin Blanc. The wines are hard to obtain due to a strong local following and mail order business. A visit to the winery is the answer. Phone 836–8341.

Corban Wines, 426–48 Great North Road, Henderson, produces premium wines from Gisborne, Hawkes Bay and Marlborough grapes. The old homestead and winery at Henderson were built by a wine-wise Lebanese immigrant whose first vintage was 1908. The Corban family is still very influential. The winery has an underground wine shop and is best known for whites, especially Rhine-Riesling and Fumé Blanc. Phone 836–6189.

Delegat's Vineyard, at the end of Hepburn Road at Glendene, just east of Henderson, is a family company headed by the son of its Yugoslav founder. It first won recognition for its Chardonnay. Top wines are now sold under the Proprietor's Reserve label. Try the Fumé Blanc. Phone 836–0129.

A dozen other wineries scattered around Henderson also produce good wines. They all welcome visitors and are fun to see.

High land prices around Henderson encouraged the planting of new vineyards in **northwest Auckland**, along Highway 16, at the villages of Kumeu, Huapai and Waimauku. The area is drier than Henderson, and its red wines are outstanding. Much fruit is brought in from elsewhere for bottling. The eight wineries are mostly Dalmation family businesses.

Matua Valley Wines, on Waikoukou Valley Road, Waimauku, is a top boutique winery, with an octagonal vineyard. It was founded in 1974 by Ross and Bill Spence, both experienced winemakers. The excellent Reserve Pinot Noir is available only at the vineyard. Phone 411–8301.

Coopers Creek Vineyard, between Huapai and Waimauku, was started in 1982 by New Zealander Andrew Hendry and Californian winemaker Randy Weaver. This small winery uses traditional techniques of maturation in French oak casks. It has a keen local following and growing exports. Phone 412–8560.

At **Nobilo Vintners**, Station Road, Huapai, three Nobilo brothers continue Yugoslav traditions, emphasizing red wines grown entirely at the Huapai vineyard. The top wines are Cabernet Sauvignon, Pinot Noir and Pinotage (a South African cross of Pinot Noir and Cinsault). Phone 412–9148.

San Marino Vineyards is on the main road at Kumeu. Winemaker Micheal Brajkovich, son of the founder, uses classic French techniques. The 'Kumeu River' premium label won high praise in 1988 international competitions. Chardonnay and Sauvignon are outstanding. Phone 412–8412.

Selaks Wines, just outside Kumeu, is another Yugoslav family enterprise, started in 1934. Its white wines are superior. The winery has an insulated tunnel that imitates the chalk cellars of Champagne for its bottle-fermented *méthode champenoise* sparkling wine. Phone 412–8609.

In **south Auckland**, at 5 Kirkbride Road, near Auckland Airport, **Villa Maria** is New Zealand's third-largest wine company, with classic Yugoslav origins. It is still family owned and recently acquired two independent wineries in Hawkes Bay. Although contract growers supply 98 percent of its grapes, the home vineyard still exists. It specializes in premium varietal

Maori carvings

wines, of which the Reserve Cabernet Sauvignon is exceptional. Phone 275–6119.

Driving **southeast of Auckland**, towards Tauranga on Highway 2, you pass three wineries worth noting. The small **de Redcliffe** vineyard is on Lyons Road near Mangatawhiri, the first village on Highway 2. Owner Chris Canning spent years in Italian and French vineyards and produces high-quality wine. **Totara SYC**, the only Chinese winery in New Zealand, is about five kilometres (three miles) off Highway 2 on the first turnoff to Thames. It is known for fortified wines, a blended white to accompany Chinese food and an agreeable Chenin Blanc. **Morton Estate**, on Highway 2 near Katikati, 30 kilometres (19 miles) from Tauranga, combines wine-making skill with high technology. It was founded in 1979. Its winemaker, John Hancock, has built a high reputation for Chardonnay, Sauvignon Blanc and very good sparkling *méthode champenoise*.

The Centre

 The centre of the North Island is a volcanic plateau where hot springs bubble, geysers erupt and steam seeps unexpectedly from cracks in the forested mountainsides. In the middle of the plateau lies Lake Taupo, teeming with rainbow trout, in the gigantic crater of an ancient volcano. South of the lake, Tongariro National Park has three volcanoes rising abruptly from the plateau, one smouldering, another sleeping and the third a snowcapped peak whose slopes draw skiers and climbers from all over the island. The city of Rotorua, New Zealand's foremost tourist resort, lies north of the lake, halfway to the Pacific Ocean and in the centre of spectacular volcanic scenery complete with thermal activity and a string of lakes.

An added attraction of Rotorua is that the city is a traditional home of the Maori. Modern Maori are now integrated into Western life, yet their culture remains very much alive, the survival of many traditional customs, arts and crafts everywhere in evidence. Many Maori perform music and dances for tourists, cashing in on the area's general prosperity.

North of Rotorua, the broad Bay of Plenty, as it was appreciatively named by Captain Cook, stretches from the Coromandel Peninsula to the East Cape. White Island, 50 kilometres (30 miles) offshore, belches steam and ash from its cone, marking the northern end of the volcanic zone. The Bay of Plenty is lined with golden beaches and backed by fertile fruit and dairy farms. It would seem far from all the geological excitement seething beneath the earth's surface were it not for the symmetrical silhouettes of extinct or sleeping volcanoes on the skyline and the relaxing hot pools dotting the area. Tauranga and Mount Maunganui are twin seaside resorts at the bay's western end, renowned for surf and deep-sea fishing, while Whakatane is the holiday centre for sun, sea and sport at its eastern end.

Bay of Plenty

The Bay of Plenty is indeed a delightful area of plenty. It is famous for kiwi fruit, which have become New Zealand's fourth-largest export, after timber, meat and dairy products. Highway 2 runs along much of the Bay of Plenty shore between Auckland and Gisborne. Air New Zealand serves Tauranga and Whakatane from Auckland, Wellington and other cities. Intercity (NZRR) Services links the area with all parts of the North Island.

Tauranga (not to be confused with Turangi, south of Lake Taupo) is the area's main city and port, through which passes much of the export timber cut from replanted forests around Rotorua. Tauranga's gentle climate makes it a favourite retirement area and centre for holidays and sports, especially big-game fishing. The New Zealand Visitor Information Centre is on the Strand. This pleasant city has a well-preserved historical area dating from the early 1800s. It is still called the 'Camp', after the original military settlement overlooking the bay. The first mission house, the Elms, built between 1838 and 1847 and containing some original furnishings, is one of the oldest homes in New Zealand. Open for guided tours Monday to Saturday at 2 pm. The fine garden, laid out in the same period, is open to the public 9 am–5 pm.

Mount Maunganui, across the harbour, stands 232 metres (761 feet) high. Once an island, the 'Mount' is now joined to the mainland by the slim isthmus on which the town of Mount Maunganui sits. Several tracks lead to the wooded peak of the Mount, which offers superb views on all sides. (Allow one and a half hours round trip.) Rare hot saltwater pools at the base of the Mount offer soothing relaxation. The surf and golden sand of magnificent Ocean Beach stretch for 15 kilometres (nine miles) along the bay and can be reached from Marine Parade, on the eastern side of the Mount.

Whakatane, the main town of the eastern end of the Bay of Plenty, is smaller and full of flowers in summer. It also offers splendid surf and sand at Ohope Beach, six kilometres (four miles) east of the town. Big-game fishing, jet-boating on the Rangitaiki River and 'flightseeing' over White Island's active volcano are easily arranged at the New Zealand Visitor Information Centre on Commerce Street.

Rotorua

Rotorua is at the centre of a thermal wonderland, halfway along a volcanic fault stretching from fuming White Island in the north to Mount Ruapehu, in Tongariro National Park, in the south. The city hugs the shore of Lake Rotorua, the largest of a dozen beautiful lakes strung through the northern volcanic plateau. To the east looms Mount Tarawera, a ravaged volcano that split asunder during a violent eruption in 1886. In Rotorua the sulphurous smell in the air and the unexpected sight of steam rising from cracks in the ground never let you forget that the earth has a molten core.

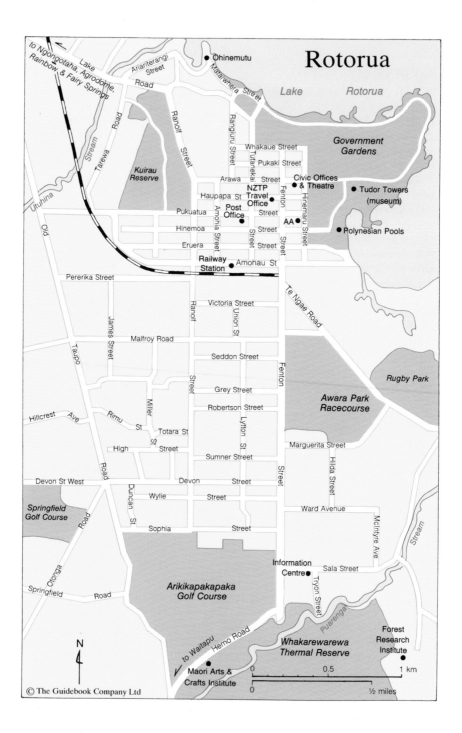

Rotorua

Lake

to Ngongotaha, Agrodome, Rainbow, & Fairy Springs

Lake Road

Ariariterangi Street

Ohinemutu

Matawhera Street

Lake Rotorua

Ranolf Street

Tarewa Road

Ufuhina Stream

Rangiuru Street

Kuirau Reserve

Government Gardens

Whakaue Street

Tutaneka Street

Pukaki Street

Arawa Street

Civic Offices & Theatre

Tudor Towers (museum)

Haupapa St

NZTP Travel Office

Fenton Street

Hinemaru Street

Pukuatua

Post Office

Street

AA

Polynesian Pools

Amohia Street

Hinemoa Street

Eruera Street

Old

Railway Station

Amohau St

Pererika Street

Victoria Street

Ranolf Street

Union St

Te Ngae Road

James Street

Malfroy Road

Seddon Street

Fenton Street

Rugby Park

Taupo

Rimu St

Miller St

Grey Street

Robertson Street

Lytton St

Awara Park Racecourse

Hillcrest Ave

Totara St

High Street

Marguerita Street

Sumner Street

Hilda Street

Devon St West

Devon Street

Duncan St

Wylie Street

Road

Ward Avenue

McIntyre Ave

Sophia Street

Springfield Golf Course

Otonga Road

Springfield Road

Arikikapakapaka Golf Course

Information Centre

Sala Street

Tryon Street

Puarenga Stream

N

to Waitapu

Hemo Road

Maori Arts & Crafts Institute

Whakarewarewa Thermal Reserve

Forest Research Institute

0   0.5   1 km

0   ½ miles

© The Guidebook Company Ltd

Maori tribes lived around Rotorua for hundreds of years before European settlers arrived, drawing benefit from the curative mineral springs and natural hot water. After the Land Wars of the 1860s and 1870s, the area drew visitors in ever-growing numbers to marvel at the famous Pink and White Terraces, natural crystalline silica steps that descended like stairs to the lake. These were destroyed by Mount Tarawera's violent explosion, which also buried three villages and claimed more than 150 lives. By the turn of the century, Rotorua was a fashionable spa in the European mould, with a bathhouse and sanatoriums. It has never lost its popularity and today offers modern tourists an appealing array of sights, activities and events.

Getting There

Air New Zealand, Mount Cook Airlines and Newmans Air serve Rotorua from most North Island cities. Intercity (NZRR) Services connects it with all major towns, and the New Zealand Railways Road Services Travel Centre on Amohau Street has information and timetables for both long-distance travel and local tours. Mount Cook Line runs to points south, including Taupo, Turangi and Wellington. Main Line Coachlines links Rotorua with Taupo and Auckland. Highway 5 joins the city with Hamilton, Taupo and Napier. Several car rental companies have offices here. The railway, alas, does not come through.

Sights

Almost everything in and around Rotorua is commercially packaged and costs money, but the unique character of the place makes much of it worthwhile. The NZTP Travel Office, at the corner of Fenton and Haupapa streets, and the Rotorua Tourist Information Centre, at the corner of Sala and Tryon streets, are very helpful, providing information, maps and bookings of all sorts. The most popular attractions focus on the thermal phenomena or Maori life and culture.

Whakarewarewa, commonly known as plain 'Whaka', combines both. The dramatic thermal reserve is close to the city, at the end of Fenton Street. The entrance is through a replica of Rotowhio Pa, a fortified Maori village. Free Maori guides are available to accompany visitors and are a real bonus for their knowledge and insight into Maori lore. The walkways through Whaka Thermal Reserve pass pools of bubbling mud, steaming silica terraces and (if you are lucky) geysers. The geysers lost some of their pizzazz when the area's thermal energy was diverted to industries and homes, but they are expected to be restored by an ordinance closing many of these in the near future. The tour ends at Rahui Maori Village, where the guide may show how food is cooked in thermal water and other Maori customs adapted to the volcanic environment. If you keep your ticket stub you can wander back the way you came instead of exiting here. Opposite the main entrance is the

Maori Carving

Of the various traditional Maori arts—carving, music, dance, rock-drawing and tattooing—wood carving, or *whakairo rakau*, was the most important and remains the most vigorous today. Objects made from jade-like greenstone and bone were also skilfully carved.

In pre-European times, master carvers were of noble rank, as carving was a sacred act of deepest significance to the tribe—recreating and perpetuating the ancestral myths. Carvers were always men, and women were not permitted even to watch the process, just as they were banned from viewing other tribal rites. Trained in the art from early childhood, a great carver enjoyed as much status and renown as any mighty warrior. Highly symbolic, curvilinear carved designs embellished almost every object the Maori used.

The blades of adzes and gouges were made of chipped rock. Chisels for making fine details were of greenstone, which could be honed to a surprisingly sharp, long-lasting edge. Tall native trees offered excellent, straight-grained wood for carving, and their size allowed carvers the freedom to work on a grand scale. Totara was the favoured wood, followed by kauri.

Carving reached its highest form in the elaborate decoration of buildings — especially food storage houses and the all-important meeting houses, which still serve as the focal point and spiritual centre of every Maori community. The meeting house is conceived as a living being. The head is represented by a central mask below a standing figure atop the gable. The arms are the ornamental boards covering the edge of the roof, often completed with fingers at the lower ends. The ridgepole is its spine, the rafters its rib cage, and the interior its belly. The carvings and paintings on different parts depict the ancestors, gods and mythological events most intimately connected with the life of the tribe. They constitute a visual history that, together with story-telling, transmits the soul and culture of a tribe.

A distorted human figure, male or female, is the most common subject in Maori carving. The head is magnified, as it is the container of *mauri ora*, the life spirit. Slanted eyes and three-fingered hands are thought to be superimposed bird features. Also common is the beaked *manaia*, a half-bird, half-human deity. The *marakihau*, half-fish, half-human, has a tube-like tongue capable of sucking up whole canoes. The *pakake* is a whale, and the *moko* a great lizard. *Tiki*, the term for any carved human figure, is applied now to the well-known greenstone charms (*hei-tiki*), whose original purpose and meaning have been lost.

The greatest examples of Maori carving are found in the major museums. The Maori themselves have never looked on a work of art as an object but rather as a living treasure with a soul. Such treasures belong to their tribe of origin forever and are only held in trust by museums. Meanwhile, young carvers are once again learning their traditional art from masters at Rotorua's Arts and Crafts Institute and other places, and a few contemporary Maori sculptors are exploring new ways of expressing ancient beliefs.

Maori Arts and Crafts Institute, a government-assisted training school aimed at keeping the standard of Maori arts and crafts at a high level. On weekdays, Maori boys work under master carvers, and women demonstrate flax weaving.

For a dip in the thermal waters visit the **Polynesian Pools**, a complex of hot mineral springs and public and private pools renovated in 1972 on the site of the 19th-century spa by the lake on Hinemoa Street. Bathing suits and towels can be hired. Open daily 9 am–10 pm. Up The **Government Gardens**, adjacent to the Polynesian Pools, is a lovely, uncommercialized park of flower gardens interspersed with thermal hot spots; white-clad residents play bowls or croquet on the manicured lawns. The park is overlooked by impressive **Tudor Towers**. Originally the Tudor Bath House, it now contains the Rotorua Museum, which is worth a visit, and a small art gallery with rotating shows. Open weekdays 10 am–4 pm and weekends 1–4.30 pm. Behind it, **Fleur International Orchid Garden** displays hundreds of varieties amid streams and waterfalls in two naturally heated plant houses.

Waimangu Thermal Valley, about 25 kilometres (15 miles) southeast of Rotorua, was created along with Lake Rotomahana by the devastating Mount Tarawera eruption of 1886. A three-kilometre (two-mile) walk offers stunning views of craters, cauldrons, steaming red cliffs and a boiling lake. Minibuses give free lifts back up the hill. Half-day and full-day tours are run by New Zealand Railway Road Services.

Waiotapu is a fascinating thermal reserve, noted for its many-coloured phenomena, about 30 kilometres (19 miles) south of Rotorua, signposted off Highway 5. Easy pathways lead past variegated craters and silica terraces to a waterfall that changes colour after rainstorms and to the fizzing Champagne Pool.

Maori concerts, with dances and traditional games, are given in costume at the Maori Cultural Theatre, Tudor Towers and Ohinemutu. Several big hotels offer concerts in the evening along with a *hangi*, or traditional Maori feast, steam-cooked underground. The hangi offers authentic Maori dishes along with familiar fare. Early reservations are essential.

Ohinemutu was the original Maori village by the lake around which Rotorua grew. Its modern Maori inhabitants now live in Western-style houses, making full use of the thermal activity for cooking, washing and heating, but hold to their Maori customs and lifestyle. The *marae*, or communal compound, has a splendidly ornate meeting house, some of the interior carvings 200 years old. It is used for meetings, community affairs and regular evening concerts at 8 o'clock. Phone 82–269 or 86–456 for reservations. St Faith's Anglican Church, opposite the meeting house, interprets the Christian faith through Maori art in a beautiful synthesis. An etched window depicts Christ in a chief's kiwi-feather cloak, apparently walking on the water of Lake Rotorua. The tombs of Maori leaders are all above ground, safe from steam.

Te Wairoa Buried Village, 14 kilometres (nine miles) from Rotorua, near Lake Tarawera, is the partly excavated ruins of a Maori village buried under two and a half metres (eight feet) of mud and ash by the 1886 eruption. This tranquil place, away from the active hot spots, is full of strange stories and interesting relics. The nearby Blue and Green lakes and Lake Tarawera make for a pleasant half day.

Mount Ngongotaha, 12 kilometres (7.5 miles) west of the city, offers a fine panoramic view over the whole area. You can drive to the top or ride up by gondola lift on Skyline Skyrides to a restaurant high on its slopes. Another option coming down is by luge on a kilometre (half-mile) -long slide. Nearby on Highway 5, the **Agrodome** offers an hour-long show featuring well-trained sheep, skilled sheepmen who can shear off a whole fleece in less than two minutes, and fabled New Zealand sheepdogs performing their tasks. Shows are at 10.30 am and 2.30 pm. At **Rainbow** and **Fairy Springs**, five kilometres (three miles) north of town on Highway 5, there are crystal clear waterfalls, pools and streams set among ferns and forest. Trout protected here from fishermen grow to an enormous size.

Many more sights and excursions can be enjoyed singly or in combination. 'Flightseeing' by floatplane from the lakefront jetty or by helicopter or plane from the airport is an exciting way to see Mount Tarawera's gaping crater, the lakes and the geothermal areas. Ask at one of the information centres about the various possibilities and costs.

Lake Taupo

The largest lake in New Zealand, Lake Taupo lies bright blue and clear in the crater left by a gigantic prehistoric eruption. White pumice beaches, colourful cliffs and hot springs around the shore all act as reminders that the lake forms part of a great volcanic fault.

Taupo, 84 kilometres (52 miles) south of Rotorua on Highway 5, is a pleasant, low-key resort town at the northeast end of the lake, with a wonderful view across the water to the volcanoes in Tongariro National Park. It attracts year-round visitors for the unsurpassed lake fishing; golf, hiking and water sports are also popular activities. Maps and information about local attractions are available from the Taupo Information Centre, near the lake end of Tongariro Street. Colourful Wairakei Thermal Valley and the mighty Wairakei Geothermal Power Station nearby, about 20 kilometres (12 miles) north of Taupo, make an exciting side trip. The Geothermal Bore Field Information Centre, on Wairakei Road, has a good audio-visual show. Conducted tours of the power station start from here.

Turangi, on the Tongariro River south of the lake, is a much smaller town, devoted mainly to trout fishing and the management of the Tongariro Power Development Project. The Tongariro Information Centre and

Museum, on Ohuanga Street, has abundant information about the town and the surrounding area. Open from Monday to Thursday 8 am–5 pm and from Friday to Sunday 8 am–4.30 pm.

Tongariro National Park

This vast tract of land south of Lake Taupo was New Zealand's first national park—and one of the first in the world. It forms the southern anchor of the volcanic plateau. The whole beautiful area, rich in Maori legends, was presented as a gift to the nation in 1887 by a wise Maori chief who foresaw the danger of partitioning by land-hungry settlers. Said Chief Horonuku Te Heuheu Tukino, 'It shall be a sacred place of the Crown and a gift forever from me and my people.'

Mount Ruapehu (2,797 metres, or 9,176 feet) is the highest mountain in the North Island and snowcapped the year round. In winter, its ski lifts and tows bring hordes of skiers to its upper slopes. The volcano is mildly active; its green, acidic, ice-rimmed Crater Lake simmers and steams. From time to time, most recently in 1975, the mountain erupts, letting loose *lahars* (mud flows).

Mount Ngauruhoe (2,291 metres, or 7,516 feet) looks the way a volcano should, with a perfectly symmetrical cone and a plume of steam rising from its crater. It smoulders constantly and, once in a while, most recently in 1954, puts on a display, belching out showers of ash and lava.

Mount Tongariro (1,968 metres, or 6,457 feet), which gives its name to the park, is the most northerly and lowest of the three volcanoes. Its truncated peaks contain several small craters, some of which give off steam or gas, but Tongariro has not erupted in recent times.

On the windy, rain-shadowed eastern side of the mountains, the Rangipo Desert presents a desolate, gravel-strewn landscape. By contrast, the hills and valleys on the western side are covered with forest, heather and rich vegetation. Tongariro National Park is bounded east and west by Highways 1 and 4 respectively, and north and south by highways 47 and 49. The railway runs through National Park township and Ohakune on the west side, and Intercity (NZRR) Services connects all the major towns. Highway 48, the only road to enter the park, leads to the elegant THC Chateau Tongariro and Whakapapa Village (also called Chateau), where the New Zealand Visitor Information Centre and park headquarters are located. The famed THC Chateau offers luxury accommodation with four-star restaurants, golf, swimming pool and other pleasures. The moderately priced Ruapehu Skotel has many types of rooms and a cafeteria. Whakapapa Village has a motor camp and store.

A number of short walks on good tracks start near Whakapapa Village. Other lovely walks with views and waterfalls branch off Okahune Mountain Road, on Mount Ruapehu's southwest flank. The information centre has maps and brochures. In clear weather, drive from Whakapapa Village up Bruce Road to the 'Top o' the Bruce' for panoramic views and incredible sunsets.

Focus

If **Rotorua**'s relentless tourist hype starts to get to you, take a walk along the lakefront between Government Gardens and the Polynesian Pools in one of the town's few uncommercialized spots. At the wildlife sanctuary you may see a number of birds, including black-billed and red-billed gulls, which seem to thrive in the harsh thermal environment. A nesting colony occupies a low island at Sulphur Point from September to January. The lovely redwood forest near the headquarters of **Whakarewarewa State Forest Park** (just beyond the famous Whaka thermal area) is renowned for its numerous finches. At Lake Rotoehu, northeast of Rotorua, the indigenous Rotoehu State Forest is home to a great variety of forest birds including kaka and North Island kokako. In dry weather the trails may be closed for fire protection, so inquire first at the Department of Conservation. Phone 479–179 between 8 am and 4.30 pm.

Lake Taupo is poor in birds (except gulls) on the northern and eastern shores due to the constant activity of fishermen, but on the shallow, reedy southern shore you will find spotless and marsh crake, fernbird, shag, bittern, dabchick and many varieties of duck.

In **Tongariro National Park** look for pipit, skylark and banded dotterel the open country on the dry eastern side. On the forested western side, the bird life is much richer. The two-hour forest walk around virgin Lake Rotopounamu is highly recommended for its prolific combination of water birds and bush birds, including New Zealand pigeon, bellbird, rifleman, grey warbler, North Island tomtit and fantail. Instructions for reaching the lake are given in the Walks Focus below.

Rotorua has, besides the downtown lakeshore walk recommended above for bird-watchers, a fine walking area nearby at Whakarewarewa Forest Park, just beyond the Whaka thermal area. The forest was planted after the devastating eruption of Mount Tarewera in 1886 and has flourished for over a century. Stop first at the Park Information Centre on Long Mile Road for information and free maps. There are eight well-marked walks through the forest ranging in time from 1.5 to eight hours. The shortest one, in a grove of California redwoods, is among the most beautiful.

At **Taupo**, the ten-kilometre (six-mile) -long Taupo Walkway includes two great spectacles—Huka Falls and Aratiatia Rapids. It can be walked by sections or along its whole length. The three-kilometre (two-mile) -long walk from Taupo to Huka Falls begins at Spa Thermal Park on County Avenue, off

Spa Road. It crosses a hot-water stream by boardwalk, then follows the bank of the Waikato River to the 11-metre (36-foot) -high waterfall. There are toilet facilities at the bridge above the falls. Allow two hours up and back. Or you can drive to the Huka Falls Bridge, signposted off Highway 1 two kilometres (1.2 miles) north of Taupo, and join the scenic walkway there. It continues near the river for seven kilometres (four miles) with views of waterfalls, rapids and the Wairakei Geothermal Power Station. The walk ends at Lake Aratiatia, near the power station's spillway. The amazing Aratiatia Rapids, downstream of the spillway, flow only when the gates of the power station are opened, releasing a mighty torrent of water, normally 10–11.30 am and 2.30–4 pm. The rapids are most spectacular when the water first surges through, so the times given above should be verified at the Taupo Information Centre. If you can arrange transport at the Aratiatia exit, the walk from Huka Falls takes two and a quarter hours. The whole walk from Taupo takes three hours one way.

Turangi has a very peaceful walk around **Lake Rotopounamu**, near the edge of Tongariro National Park, which is also recommended for birdwatchers. From Turangi turn right on Highway 41. After four kilometres (2.5 miles) turn left on to Saddle Road (Highway 47) at the sign for Chateau Tongariro. Drive about seven kilometres (four miles) over Te Ponanga saddle to the start of the track, which is signposted on the left. Parking is on the right. After an easy 20-minute climb through fern-filled native bush, the path branches down to the unspoiled forest-clad lake. The flat round-the-lake walk through native flora takes one and a half to two hours.

Tongariro National Park offers so many good short walks (ranging from 20 minutes to two and a half hours) on such a variety of terrain that it is best to get a set of free brochures, maps and advice from the park headquarters before making your choice. A superb, longer volcanic walk is an easy day's hike to **Ketehai Springs**, on the north side of Mount Ngauruhoe. It is one leg of the longer Tongariro Traverse Track, which many trampers consider the best walk in the North Island. It starts at the carpark one kilometre (half a mile) along a well-marked but unpaved road off Rangipo Road (Highway 47A), about 12 kilometres (seven miles) from Rangipo or four kilometres (2.5 miles) from Papakai. Kevin and Sylvia Mora's shuttlebus company in Turangi can provide transport. Phone (0746) 8392.

The clear track takes you through a delightful region of upland forest and streams to the timber line. The track continues, marked with poles, across tussock grass to Ketetahi Springs, where you will find boiling mud, hot springs, small geysers, blowholes and steam vents. Keep left at the track junction to reach the Ketetahi Hut. Do not stray from the marked track in this area, because the ground is treacherous. If the steam thickens and blocks your view, wait for it to clear before walking further. The warm stream below the thermal area has some good bathing spots. There are no facilities for changing, so wear a bathing suit under your clothes and bring a towel along with your picnic. Drinking water is available at the Ketetahi Hut up the mountain above the springs. Allow two and a half hours to the springs, slightly less returning.

Huge **Lake Taupo**, in the middle of the North Island, is the fishing mecca of New Zealand, with year-round trout fishing from boats or the shore of the lake itself and in the lower reaches of rivers flowing into it. Local guides claim a 97 percent success rate for their fishing expeditions. The trout consider Lake Taupo an inland sea and go up its adjacent rivers to spawn. Before the area was so well known, four- to five-kilogram (ten-pound) catches were fairly common. The average now is 1.5 to two kilograms (three to four pounds) for rainbow trout and two to 2.5 kilograms (four to five pounds) for brown trout. Bigger fish can often be had where streams enter the lake. The limit is eight per day, and you need a government fishing licence for the Taupo–Rotorua area (available in any sports shop, hotel or information centre) unless you have an all-purpose 'tourist licence'. Ask wherever licences are sold for the local fishing regulations.

The township of **Taupo** draws great numbers of fishing enthusiasts. It is set up for tourists, with many attractions and amenities for the fishing community, such as smoking and freezing facilities, and offers easy access to the east-shore river mouths. From the late afternoon to sunset it seems that the whole population of the town goes out to fish! The village of **Waitahanui**, about ten kilometres (six miles) south of Taupo on Highway 1, is a fishing centre at the mouth of the Waitahanui River, where three- to 3.5-kilogram (six- to eight-pound) catches are not unusual. Local wits claim that the anglers lined up at sunset across the river mouth form a 'picket fence'. In any case, you will need thigh or chest waders. The village has three motels that cater specially for fisherfolk. There is parking on both sides of the main bridge.

The **Rotorua Lakes**, to the north, also offer splendid year-round trout fishing, from either boats or the shore. **Lake Tarawera**, possibly the best, is well stocked with rainbow trout, which are harder to catch but bigger than most found in Lake Taupo, often weighing 3.5 to 5.5 kilograms (eight to 12 pounds). If you fish in Lake Rotorua, do it only for the sport—the lake is polluted, making the fish unsafe to eat.

The lower reaches of surrounding rivers seem to attract the largest rainbow and brown trout. **Turangi**, which proclaims itself the 'Trout Capital of the World', is situated on the famous **Tongariro River**, from which 800–900 tonnes of trout are taken by sports fishermen annually! Turangi is much smaller and quieter than Taupo, but its lodge and motels offer all facilities for cleaning, smoking, freezing and vacuum packing, and any restaurant will cook your trout for your dinner. There is good fishing within walking distance, and two shuttle bus companies make daily runs to the more remote fishing spots. Phone 8226 or 8392. It is interesting to see the Tongariro Trout Hatchery, three kilometres (two miles) south of Turangi on Highway 1, with its underwater viewing chamber and good information centre. Open daily 9 am–4 pm. Phone 8170.

The village of **Tokaanu** lies right at the mouth of the Tongariro River and is much favoured by fisherfolk. The historic settlement has the added attraction of being in a thermal area with public and private hot pools.

Knowledgeable guides abound in all of the fishing centres. They can be hired by the day or half-day (minimum three or four hours), and their fees include tackle, equipment—often food and drink, too. Unless you are a real pro, you have a better chance of success with a guide than on your own.

The **Bay of Plenty** has a trio of lovely courses. The **Tauranga Golf Club** at Gate Pa meets the high standards of the many keen golfers in the area. Flowering shrubs and trees lining the fairways make it especially beautiful. Par 70. Phone 88–465. In the general vicinity, **Mount Maunganui Golf Club**, on Fairway Avenue, is the home of the New Zealand PGA championship tournament. The excellent links course offers a fine test of skill. Par 71. Phone 53–889. **Whakatane Golf Club**, at the eastern end of the bay, is also a good links course, highly enjoyable to play. Par 72. Phone 7921.

Some golfers put the Taupo–Rotorua area at the very top of their list. In **Taupo**, first prize goes to the **Wairakei International Golf Course**, rated by some as New Zealand's top course. It is operated by the Tourist Hotel Corporation at the THC Wairakei Hotel, six kilometres (four miles) north of Taupo, and is open to visitors. The very long, well-designed course has three sets of tees for each hole, in effect creating three courses of varying difficulty within one 18-hole framework. The 14th hole, nicknamed the 'Rogue' after a past volcanic eruption, is especially memorable. This course is a must on any golfer's list. Par 72. Phone Taupo 48–152.

The **Rotorua Golf Club**'s 80-year-old Arikikapakapaka championship course offers a unique golfing experience amid astounding scenery. The short, exciting course, opposite the Whakarewarewa thermal area at the south end of Fenton Street, is sprinkled with extinct mud pools and occasional active steam vents. In some spots the ground is hot. A very explicit score card points out a strategy for each hole. Par 69. Phone 83–725. Nearby, the club's entertaining (and easier) nine-hole course (opposite the Thermal Motor Camp on Old Taupo Road) has natural hazards that include bubbling mud, boiling pools and steam vents. The third fine course at Rotorua is **Springfield Golf Course**, a pleasant, rolling, tree-lined course right in town at the western end of Devon Street. Par 72. Phone 82–748.

🍷 The central volcanic plateau is the only region of the North Island where no vineyards exist, but it is well supplied with good hotels and restaurants that let you sample the whole range of New Zealand wines.

The East

 When Captain Cook first touched the coast of New Zealand, it was on the east coast, near modern-day Gisborne. Unfriendly Maori tribes and his failure to get the supplies he needed led him to name his landing place Poverty Bay. The name stuck, but it has proved a complete misnomer, as the east is now one of the North Island's richest farming and fruit-growing regions.

The east begins up north with the East Cape, which juts out to separate the Bay of Plenty from the Pacific Ocean. Steep, forested mountains cut it off from the rest of the North Island, leaving its population, which is heavily Maori, thinly spread around the coast. At the base of the East Cape is Gisborne, which, lying close to the International Date Line, prides itself on being the first city in the world to see the rising sun each day. Indeed, the sun often shines on the fertile vegetable farms, orchards and vineyards around the city. The balmy climate, beaches perfect for swimming, surfing and fishing, and the easy-going pace of life bring New Zealand vacationers thronging to Gisborne, but it is frequently missed by overseas visitors.

South of Gisborne, Hawkes Bay scoops a large bite out of the east coast. The biggest city here is Napier, with its sizeable twin city of Hastings nearby. A devastating earthquake nearly destroyed them both in 1931, killing hundreds of people. It raised new land and changed the configuration of the coastline, but today the rebuilt cities make it hard to imagine the catastrophe. Havelock North completes the triangle of towns that anchor the southern end of Hawkes Bay.

The pleasant town of Wairoa straddles both banks of the Wairoa River at the north end of Hawkes Bay and gives access by road to Urewera National Park, the nation's third biggest. The huge protected area of virgin forest covers a remote mountain range between Wairoa and Rotorua, its headquarters on the Wairoa side of the range, on the banks of the bright blue, star-shaped Lake Waikaremoana.

Getting There

Air New Zealand flies to Gisborne and Napier from both Auckland and Wellington. New Zealand Railways has daily trains between Wellington and Gisborne stopping in Napier. Intercity (NZRR) Services and Mount Cook Line link the east coast cities with Auckland, Rotorua and Hamilton. New-

mans Coachlines has a Wellington–Napier route. If you are travelling by car,
Highway 35 winds picturesquely around the coast of the East Cape from
Opotiki on the Bay of Plenty to Gisborne, while Highway 2, the main road,
cuts across the base of the cape by a less interesting route. The roads meet
again at Poverty Bay, and Highway 2 continues south along the east coast to
Napier and Hastings. Two roads run inland across the largely unpopulated
mountains to the main tourist areas. Small Highway 38 leads from Wairoa
through Urewera National Park to Rotorua. The larger Highway 5 follows an
old Maori track from Napier to Taupo.

The East Cape

This peninsula can be circled by car or Intercity (NZRR) Services bus by a
rugged, magnificently scenic road around the coast and the main highway
across the base. Only a few roads penetrate into the mountains and gorges of
the wild interior, all of them narrow and difficult dead-ends. The drive
around the coast road takes six hours without stops, but there are plenty of
reasons to stop and make it a full-day trip. Groves of ancient pohutukawa
trees burst into flame-red flower in summer beside rocky coves and deserted
beaches, and many villages along the way are worth exploring.

    Opotiki, where the west end of Highway 35 branches off Highway 2, lies
60 kilometres (37 miles) east of Whakatane on the Bay of Plenty. The little

port town has one claim to fame: an attack on the church by Hauhau fanatics in 1865, during the Land Wars, led to the particularly grisly murder of its resident German missionary. The Church of St Stephen the Martyr, on Church Street, displays a glass case with blood-stained relics of the horrid incident.

Te Kaha, 69 kilometres (43 miles) to the northeast, is a picturesque old whaling settlement on a cove from which open-boat whaling continued into the 1930s. The intricately carved meeting house has some of the best Maori carving in the region.

Hicks Bay, 84 kilometres (52 miles) beyond Te Kaha on the north coast, also has an outstanding meeting house with century-old interior carvings. The rafter designs glorifying the death of warriors in battle are unique to the East Cape.

Te Araroa, beneath the tall cliffs of a narrow bay 24 kilometres (15 miles) further on, boasts the largest pohutukawa tree in New Zealand. A 42-kilometre (26-mile) detour leads to the **East Cape Light House**, perched on the high cliffs of the island's most easterly point. Visitors are welcome between 1 and 3 pm.

Tikitiki, 150 kilometres (93 miles) from Gisborne on the east coast, lies inland along the Waiapu River. The marvellously ornate St Mary's Church is a memorial to soldiers of the Ngati Porou tribe who died in World War I. The carved panels and rafters recount the history of this Maori tribe, the principal one on the East Cape.

Te Puia Springs, 103 kilometres (64 miles) from Gisborne, is the site of an important hospital and relaxing hot pools. A short walk to the source of the springs ends with a good view over the surrounding countryside.

Tokomaru Bay, 92 kilometres (57 miles) from Gisborne, is the first point at which the road touches the east coast shoreline. Once a busy commercial port for freezing works, which are now abandoned, the town has a well-carved, modern meeting house near the wharf.

Anaura Bay, 23 kilometres (14 miles) further south, is worth a detour for its unspoiled stretch of golden sand and its scenic walkway (see *Focus*, page 000).

Tolaga Bay, 54 kilometres (34 miles) from Gisborne, is a pretty inlet where the road again touches the shore. Captain Cook spent a week here, re-plenishing supplies.

Gisborne

Perched at the north end of Poverty Bay, at the junction of two rivers and in easy reach of beautiful beaches, is the attractive little city of Gisborne. Gladstone Road, the main street, is adorned by an impressive clock tower and two tall masts holding aloft models of Captain Cook's ship, the *Endeavour*. These are lit up at night. The New Zealand Visitor Information Centre is at

209 Grey Street, which crosses Gladstone Road at the clock tower. Next to the information centre a small park surrounds a fine totem pole, a gift from Canada in 1969 in commemoration of Captain Cook's landing 200 years earlier.

The southern point of Poverty Bay is a headland of white cliffs named **Young Nick's Head**. Sailing south from Tahiti, Captain Cook offered a reward of a gallon of rum and the honour of having a coastal feature named after him to the first crew member who sighted land. This turned out to be 12-year-old Nicholas Young, dubbed Young Nick. Other crew members, whose names are forgotten, no doubt helped the lad to dispose of the rum, but Young Nick's name lives on at this prominent landmark.

Kaiti Hill Lookout is the spot from which to get a spectacular view of Gisborne, its two rivers, the surrounding countryside, the harbour and all of Poverty Bay. Cross the Gladstone Bridge and look for signposts on the right.

Voyager Kupe and Captain Cook

Two great explorers came to the shores of New Zealand from opposite ends of the earth, eight centuries apart, and both are revered by their people for discovering a 'virgin' land they could make their own.

The first was Kupe, a forebear of the Maori, whose legend was passed down in story and song, for lack of a written language. He came by canoe from a Polynesian island, remembered only by the legendary name of Hawaiki, but probably located close to Tahiti. Without compass or sextant, he set his course across the vast Pacific, navigating by the stars, the direction of the wind, the temperature of the ocean currents and the shape of the clouds. He landed in the far north in about AD 950 and named the new country Aotearoa, meaning 'Land of the Long White Cloud'. Kupe circled both islands, which he found uninhabited, attaching names and tales to many landmarks. Then, remarkably, he made his way back to Hawaiki. Two centuries later, Chief Toi and his grandson Watonga repeated Kupe's voyage, returning home to verify and enlarge upon the knowledge that Kupe had brought them. Curiously, though, tradition says that this time they found people living in Aotearoa.

Around 1350, a great migration set out from Hawaiki. Seven or more laden canoes travelled in pairs and reached the coast of Aotearoa at different points. (Even today, the main Maori tribes are known by the name of their canoe.) If there were earlier settlers, they must have been eliminated or absorbed by the Maori, for no trace of them remains.

Captain James Cook was not the first European to find this land. In 1642 Abel Tasman, the Dutch explorer after whom Tasmania is named, had anchored briefly off the northwest tip of the South Island before Maori warriors

At the foot of Kaitai Hill, on Kaitai Beach Road by the river mouth (the beach is not for swimming), the **Captain James Cook Memorial** marks the place where the Englishman first landed. Across the road, a short track leads up Kaitai Hill to **Cook Memorial Park**, which is steeped in history. The observatory there has three telescopes for public use. At the foot of Kaitai Hill at Queens Drive and Ranfurly Street, the **Poho-o-Rawiri Meeting House** is one of the largest decorated Maori meeting halls in New Zealand. The carvings and woven reed-work were executed by the Arawa tribe in Rotorua. If the main door is closed, use the side door or ask the caretaker (who lives in the adjacent building) for permission to enter.

Gisborne Museum and Arts Centre, on Stout Street by the Peel Street Bridge, has on its grounds Wyllie Cottage, Gisborne's oldest house. The museum traces east-coast history with a collection of Maori and colonial artifacts, including a whaling boat used at Te Kaha on the East Cape.

drove him away. He thought he had sighted the Great Southern Continent, which geographers theorized must exist to counterbalance the land masses of the northern hemisphere. His find was given the name Nieuw Zeeland, after a province of Holland.

More than a century later, in 1769, James Cook landed at the North Island's East Cape and claimed New Zealand for Britain. This brilliant Yorkshireman, trained as a seaman on coal ships in the wild North Sea, served in the Royal Navy in time of war, his skills attracting the attention of his superiors. When he was chosen to head an expedition that included a search for Tasman's Great Southern Continent, Cook requested a coal ship, a humble vessel in the eyes of some, but stable under sail and provided with a huge hold for supplies. He carried on board the converted *Endeavour* a team of scientists who recorded every detail of the voyage, and by his experiment of feeding his crew sauerkraut, which is rich in vitamin C, he found a cure for scurvy, the killer disease of sailors.

Though Cook's first encounter with the Maori was as hostile as Tasman's, he persevered. He mapped the entire coast of New Zealand and befriended other Maori tribes before going on to circle Antarctica and prove that the great unknown continent did not exist—at least not as envisioned. Cook visited New Zealand on three separate globe-encircling voyages that established a new map of the world. His reports of the beautiful land, rich in fish and timber and peopled with skilled, intelligent tribesmen, soon brought European sealers, whalers and lumberjacks to gather up its wealth—and missionaries to gather up its souls. Miners, farmers and settlers followed in their wake.

Wairoa

This is the only sizeable town at the north end of Hawkes Bay. It lies slightly inland on both banks of the broad Wairoa River. A lighthouse dating from 1877 stands incongruously by the palm-lined riverbank near the bridge, having been saved when it was replaced on Portland Island in 1958. The incandescent light, once visible for 39 kilometres (24 miles), enlivens the river every evening. The Wairoa Bridge was washed away by the rampaging, debris-filled river in March 1988, when Cyclone Bola came howling through, dumping 915 millimetres (36 inches) of rain on the Gisborne area in 30 hours and causing immeasurable damage. The two isolated halves of the town are now joined by ferry and a bridge upstream, requiring a 13-kilometre (eight-mile) detour, while the main bridge on Highway 2 is being rebuilt. It is expected to reopen before the end of 1989.

Two roads connect Wairoa and Gisborne. Highway 2 follows the spectacular coastline of white sand, sparkling water and pohutukawa trees. This road cuts behind the sparsely populated Mahia Peninsula at the northern extremity of Hawkes Bay, passing through **Morere**, 40 kilometres (25 miles) from Wairoa, a delightful green oasis with hot springs. Highway 36 follows a lovely, less-travelled route inland through the hills, passing many small settlements. The genuine, untouristy Maori village of **Te Reinga**, beside Te Reinga Falls, stands at the junction of the Ruakituri and Wairoa rivers. Its simple, unpretentious *marae* (communal compound) offers a welcome to travellers. The damage caused by Cyclone Bola can be seen along the route in landslips all over the hills and mountains. Near Gisborne, fields covered with silt may take years to recover their former fertility.

Urewera National Park and **Lake Waikaremoana** are easily reached from Wairoa. Highway 38, connecting Wairoa and Rotorua, a distance of 222 kilometres (138 miles), traverses Urewera National Park and the Huiarau Mountains by a winding, beautiful route. The park headquarters are on the shores of the lake at Aniwaniwa, 62 kilometres (39 miles) from Wairoa. It is the most convenient spot from which to start fishing or exploring the park's virgin forest on foot (see *Focus*, page 000). The village of **Ruatahuna**, close to the park on the Rotorua side, is the traditional home of the Tuhoe people. From here, a small detour of four kilometres (2.5 miles) leads to **Mataatua**, where the truly magnificent Te Whai-a-te-Motu Meeting House was completed in 1888. Among the splendid interior carvings, those at the base of the centre poles show two of the Tuhoe ancestors wearing European neckties, a measure of the impact made by Western culture on sacred Maori traditions.

Hawkes Bay

There are two major towns in Hawkes Bay, New Zealand's fruit basket.
Napier is 'Art Deco City', a charming period piece of the 1930s. The

town's distinctive style was born of a tragic earthquake. Without warning, a devastating shock convulsed the province of Hawkes Bay in February 1931, killing 256 people, flattening much of the city and starting fires that swept through whatever remained. High cliffs crumbled, and the bed of Napier's inner harbour rose above sea level, creating 3,343 hectares (8,260 acres) of new land. Large swamps and a lagoon vanished at the spot where Napier Airport stands. Suburbs and industrial areas now cover the new land.

Marine Parade, the waterfront avenue, was built over the rubble of the collapsed city. The long, attractive esplanade is bordered by Norfolk pines and faced on the west by low buildings in 1930s style. The sea side of the Parade is dotted with attractions for visitors, including the New Zealand Visitor Information Centre, opposite Emerson Street, which has free maps, brochures and timetables.

Walking north from the information centre and the sound shell, you pass the Colonnade, where a market is held on weekends. Across the Parade, the **Lilliput Complex** is a tiny, animated village with its own railway. Times of operation are available from the information centre. The **Hawkes Bay Art Gallery and Museum**, just off the Parade at Herschell Street, has a fine collection of ancient Maori and Moa-hunter artifacts and a horrifying audio-visual presentation recreating the 1931 earthquake. Open weekdays 10.30 am–4.30 pm and weekends 2–4.30 pm. Beyond a fountain, a floral clock and a swimming pool (open only in summer, 10 am–5.30 pm), the well-designed

Nocturnal Wildlife Centre is one of the best in the country, having not only kiwis but also several other nocturnal animals and birds. Open daily 9 am–4.30 pm. The animals are fed at 2.30 pm. Finally, a climb or drive up to **Bluff Hill Lookout**, signposted from Lighthouse Road, gives an excellent cliff-top view over the city, harbour and coast. (Take a city map.)

South of the information centre, **Marineland** has regular shows at 10 am and 2 pm, in which dolphins, seals and sea lions perform acrobatic and swimming stunts. **Hawkes Bay Aquarium**, one of the biggest in the southern hemisphere, is excellently designed, with three floors of display tanks around a huge oceanarium.

Hastings, 21 kilometres (13 miles) south of Napier, is its twin city and rival. Napier's port exports Hastings' fruit, food and farm products, and each of these two municipalities feels itself to be the true centre of Hawkes Bay. The 1931 earthquake damaged Hastings severely, but today the rebuilt town is a pretty one of parks and gardens surrounded by vineyards and orchards.

Havelock North, five kilometres (three miles) southeast of Hastings' commercial centre, is a quiet, mostly residential, tree-filled town that has kept its countrified qualities. **Te Mata Peak**, rising south of the town, offers a magnificent view over all of Hawkes Bay from Cape Kidnappers to Mahia Peninsula. The orderly streets of Hastings nestle among lush orchards and market gardens, Napier sprawls back from the Bluff Hill headland, and the fertile plain stretches away to the rugged Kaimanawa Mountains. A six-kilometre (four-mile) -long road leads to the summit, signposted off Te Mata Road. The 2.2-kilometre (1.4-mile) Te Mata Peak Walkway over the last stretch offers an alternative 45-minute route for the energetic.

Focus

East Cape, north of Gisborne as far as Tokomaru Bay, is the best place in the North Island to see wekas, which are tough, inquisitive, flightless rails. Wekas virtually disappeared from the North Island in the 1920s and 1930s, probably due to disease. A few survivors continued breeding on the East Cape and formed the base of a remarkable and wide-spread comeback over the last 30 years. The **Gisborne Botanical Gardens**, on the banks of the Taruheru River, shelter a rare species of weka that is still found only here. The paradise shelduck is another East Cape denizen that has recently increased in great numbers. The birds are nearly always seen in pairs, the male and female very different in colouration.

Lake Waikaremoana and **Lake Waikareiti**, on the southeast edge of Urewera National Park, form a rich centre for birds. Shags, swans, various ducks, scaups, shovellers and dabchicks stay near the water. Blue ducks can be found on streams—the forest rangers keep track of their whereabouts. Abundant forest birds include robins, tuis, moreporks, falcons, pied tits, bellbirds, long-tailed and shining cuckoos, kakas and riflemen, among others.

Hawkes Bay's great attraction is the gannet sanctuary at Cape Kidnappers, about 30 kilometres (19 miles) from both Napier and Hastings, the only large mainland nesting site in the world. Three colonies, numbering about 3,000 pairs, offer an unforgettable sight (and smell, so stay upwind). The sanctuary is open from late October through June (the birds leave in March); it is closed for nesting and mating from July to October. Private cars are banned beyond Clifton, but you can walk along the beach below the cliffs when the tide is out (about five hours round trip; see *Focus* on walks, page 94), or ride the beach route on a tractor-pulled trailer (four hours round trip; time of day depending on the tides). Four-wheel-drive vehicles are somewhat more expensive, but they operate overland at any time of day (three hours round trip). Consult the New Zealand Visitor Information Centre at Napier or Hastings for all details on transport, or call Gannet Safari, phone 750–350 or 750–152.

Black-fronted dotterel, an Australian wader first recorded nesting near Napier in 1954, is a species to watch for. It is now firmly established around Hawkes Bay and starting to appear in South Island riverbeds.

East Cape boasts two spectacular coastal walks north of Gisborne at bays where Captain Cook landed in 1769.

Cooks Cove is about 53 kilometres (33 miles) north of Gisborne, just south of Tolaga Bay. Turn seaward off Highway 35 on to Wharf Road, about two kilometres (a mile) south of Tolaga Bay township, and go left at the end of the road to a carpark. The walkway, across from the carpark, climbs to a splendid cliff-top lookout over Tolaga Bay then follows a farm track to a fine lookout over Cooks Cove. An easy path to the shore passes the famous 'Hole in the Wall' that astonished Captain Cook's crew. The walkway crosses private property and is closed in August and September for lambing. Take your own drinking water. Toilets are at the wharf near the carpark. Allow two and a half hours for the five-kilometre (three-mile) round trip.

Anaura Bay, about 70 kilometres (43 miles) north of Gisborne, is a bit shorter. Turn seaward off Highway 35 on to Anaura Road at the road sign. The walkway starts at the north end of the beach, 500 metres (a third of a mile) beyond the Recreation Reserve campground, by a tin haybarn. The walk offers magnificent views of the coast, crosses part of Waipare Forest and follows Waipare Stream through the native bush of Anaura Bay Scenic Reserve. The track emerges on Anaura Road about a kilometre (half a mile) south of the starting point. The 3.5-kilometre (two-mile) walk takes about two hours.

Urewera National Park, New Zealand's third-largest national park, has dozens of good forest tracks, including five short walks to waterfalls. The

Final Harvest

U ntil last year, the Mahana clan would get together at a family
meeting, dub in some money and buy seed to plant in the family
paddocks. Then they would fix a time for the planting, calculating it
the old way by the shape of the moon and the position of the stars in
the night sky. Once that was done, they would all come together at
the planting.

It used to be a good time. A family occasion. A gathering of the
Mahana clan. Kids and all would come to follow the tractor and
plant the seeds in the furrows. And although it was hard work it
didn't seem to take long because everybody was too busy chucking off
at each other to think of how hard the work was.

—Hey! Cover that plant properly with the dirt, ay!

—Worry about your own plant! And while you're at it, don't you
know how to plant in the straight line?

—Who says I'm not planting straight! It's not me, it's the furrows
that are crooked.

—Don't blame the furrows, ay! You must have had too much to
drink last night!

— Me?

—Yes, you! And just look at the son of yours! Hey, Boy! You
only have to dig a small hole for the plants. You think you're going
to China?

—You watch your own son! He's not watering those plants at all!

—So? What with your boozing last night, you got enough water
in you for all the plants!

And so it would continue all that day. The laughter and the light-
hearted exchanges, and the constant bending into the planting. And
at smoko times, the clan would all rest beneath a willow tree and eat
some kai. Then back to the work again until night had fallen.

Sometimes, the planting would take a whole week, depending on
how many paddocks the clan had decided would be planted with seed.
One week among the very few weeks that all the Mahana families
became one family. A happy week of shared muscle and sweat. Of

laughter. Aroha. Until the planting was over.

Then would come the waiting time. The waiting for the maize and potatoes to grow. And each Mahana family would come out to the land to weed the growing plants and water them when it was their turn.

But once the crop was ready, the Mahana clan would come together again. They would gather at the harvest and there would be fulfilment of family reaping a shared labour.

This day, Rongo Mahana has come for this year's harvest. He has come with spade in hand to this paddock. He has come alone; he has come in sadness. There is no sense of fulfilment.

For last year, Rongo Mahana planted this one paddock by himself... And this day, he has come alone to the harvest.

— Times are changing.

Rongo throws the sacks on the ground. He sits on one of them and unlaces his shoes. He puts his boots on. Then he stands with spade gripped in his hands and pushes it into the earth to uncover the potatoes clinging to the roots of an upturned plant. He bends and pulls at the potatoes, his fingers searching the soil for any others which have not been exposed by the cleaving spade. And he piles them in the furrow between this row and the next before thrusting the spade again beneath the next plant in the row. Spade turning earth, body bending and fingers scrabbling in the dirt. Spade cleaving earth, body attuning itself to the rhythm of the work. Plant after plant being upturned.

— Good spuds these...

Losing himself to the rhythm of the spade. Trying to forget the loneliness of the digging. Moving up the row leaving potatoes strewn in the furrow. His heart racing, the sweat beginning to bead his face. And an aching beginning in his bending body. Alone in the paddock. A solitary speck amid the expanse of furrows out into the earth. Alone. Alone under the hot sun.

And then the spade slips to cut into the roots of a plant and slide into the potatoes beneath. And with despair, Rongo grasps them and flings them at the sun. And the rhythm of this man to the land is destroyed.

Witi Ihimaera, Whanau, 1974

headquarters at Aniwaniwa, east of Lake Waikaremoana (64 kilometres, or 40 miles, northwest of Wairoa), is a good starting place for a combination of beautiful lake walks. Be sure to take plenty of insect repellent.

The **Lake Waikareiti** track starts 200 metres (yards) from the park headquarters and climbs through fern-filled beech forest to picturesque Lake Waikareiti, dotted with forest-covered islands. There are toilets and a day hut. Rowboats stored here can be hired from the park headquarters before setting out. The popular 3.5-kilometre (two-mile) walk takes one and a quarter hours to the lake, or two hours round trip.

The track to **Lake Ruapani** starts at the same place, 200 metres (yards) from the park headquarters. After an hour it reaches Waipai Swamp, known for orchids, sundews and other carnivorous plants. A further hour's walking through red and silver beech forest brings you to little Lake Ruapani. Allow two hours from the park headquarters to the lake, or four hours for the round trip.

For an excellent full day's walk, make a circle by taking the connecting track from Lake Ruapani to Lake Waikareiti. This three-hour link trail passes a delightful series of forest ponds and skirts the western shore of Lake Waikareiti before ending at the day hut. The downhill track back to Aniwaniwa takes less than an hour. Allow six hours for the circle.

Hawkes Bay is best known for its vineyards and the gannet sanctuary on **Cape Kidnappers**, named for an incident on Captain Cook's first voyage. Between late October and March, the activities of these large, yellow-headed seabirds on the tip of the cape give added purpose to a good beach walk. The eight-kilometre (five-mile) walk (one way) can be accomplished only at low tide. Tide times are available at the information centre in Napier or Hastings, or from the office at Clifton Domain (21 kilometres, or 13 miles, south of Napier and 18 kilometres, or 11 miles, east of Hastings), where you get a free permit to visit the bird sanctuary and start the two-hour walk. You can start three hours after high tide. The sandy beach runs beneath towering cliffs of stratified rock to Black Reef, where a rest hut provides water and toilets. (Do not walk directly under the cliffs, because there are occasional rock falls.) A path leads up from Black Reef to the plateau for a close look at the gannets. Start back along the beach no later than one and a half hours after low tide. Allow five hours for the whole trip.

Urewera National Park spreads across the least-populated region of the North Island. Its rivers and lakes all offer excellent trout fishing, but the sparkling waters of 55-square-kilometre (21-square-mile) **Lake Waikaremoana**, set in primeval forest, are the most renowned. The park headquarters at Aniwaniwa, at the eastern end of the lake, provide adequate facilities.

Of the many streams flowing east from Urewera National Park to join the

Wairoa River, the favourite of several knowledgeable fishermen (and one they would prefer to keep secret) is the **Ruakituri River**. A small road follows the river upstream from its junction with the Wairoa River at **Te Reinga**. Near the river's source the road loops south to join Highway 38 about 15 kilometres (nine miles) from the park. Te Reinga is a hospitable Maori village. The marae provides beds, showers and flush toilets, and you can rent bedding. There is a kitchen, but you need to bring your own food. Telephone the marae ahead of time at (0724) 6809, or call George Niania, the marae chairman, at (0724) 8918, because if a *tangi* (funeral) or other ceremony is being held visitors may not be able to stay. There is no charge for spending a night, but Maori custom requires you to offer a *koha,* or gift (a modest sum of money is appropriate). This is a pleasant way to get acquainted with a modern Maori community far from the tourist track. Introduce yourself, smile, talk to people, and you will be warmly welcomed.

Hawkes Bay, around Napier, may have good river fishing for people coming down the coast from Wairoa, depending on the time of year. For information on local rivers and fishing conditions, phone River Information (070) 750–152.

Gisborne has two very nice courses. **Gisborne Park Golf Club**, south of the city on Cochrane Street in the Park Domain, is a pleasant, fairly flat, well-treed course with springy turf. Phone 79–849. **Poverty Bay Golf Course**, near the airport on Awapuni Road, is a well-cushioned links course with a fine view over the bay. Phone 74–402.

Hawkes Bay is another strong golfing centre, with four good 18-hole courses. **Napier Golf Club** at Waiohiki is a shortish course with many trees and good greens in pretty country just south of Taradale, which is just southwest of Napier. It is gently undulating with several doglegs. Par 72. Phone 447–913. **Maraenui Golf Club**, on Te Awa Avenue, at the south end of Marine Parade in Napier, is a flat, well-treed links course. Par 72. Phone 358–273.

Four kilometres (2.5 miles) west of Hastings is **Bridge Pa Golf Club**, a flat, lush, windy course that is fast and challenging. Par 72. Phone 797–206. **Flaxmere Golf Club**, on Valentine Road in suburban Flaxmere, west of Hastings, is considered one of New Zealand's notable up-and-coming courses. It is also one of the country's longest — and very enjoyable. Par 72. Phone 798–890.

Gisborne is the centre of the largest commercial wine-producing region in New Zealand. However, on 7 March 1988, a devastating tropical cyclone caused so much damage to the land and soils that it may take years to restore some of the vineyards. Grapes, mainly Müller-Thurgau, are grown here in volume by major wine companies such as

Montana, Corbans, Cooks and Villa Maria, then trucked to Auckland fresh, or processed by crushing and fermenting plants in Gisborne. Only two small wineries in the area grow their own grapes and see the wine right through to bottling.

Matawhero Winery, on Riverpoint Road south of Gisborne, first gained an international reputation for its Gewürztraminers. Denis Irwin and his Swiss winemaker, Hatsch Kalberer, produce mainly white wines, concentrating on Riesling-Sylvaner, Gisborne's only truly dry white, which is slowly replacing Müller-Thurgau. Their red wines are also enjoyable. The estate, which suffered no direct damage from the cyclone, is open year round. Phone 88–366.

The **Millton Vineyard** on Papatu Road in Manutuke, 16 kilometres (ten miles) south of Gisborne off Highway 2, is one-quarter the size of Matawhero. It is the only organic vineyard in New Zealand, formerly the hobby of James Millton but now his full-time business. It produces a variety of interesting dry white wines and very successful sweet, Germanic, botrytized wines. Annie Millton produces house plants and dried flowers from a garden beside the vineyard. The winery is closed from July to October, but the Milltons will open by appointment. Phone Manutuke 690.

Hawkes Bay is New Zealand's most important and longest established wine region. The climate here is drier than Gisborne's, similar to Bordeaux's. Fruit and vegetables thrive here. The area's wine reputation rests on top-quality Sauvignon Blanc, Chardonnay and Cabernet Sauvignon, but many other excellent wines are now produced, including New Zealand's best reds. A series of takeovers by large wine companies seems to have run down. As an old vine-worker remarked, 'Those small, family-run boutique wineries—it's a way of life, not a means of living. They'll never sell out. Good thing.' The 14 small to moderate-sized Hawkes Bay wineries (and one other large one) are all within 50 kilometres (30 miles) of one another. Their brochure, entitled 'Taste Our Tradition', is available at information centres and hotels throughout the region. It gives all their cellar hours and sales data and includes a good map. Afternoon wine tours by minibus are run from Hastings and Napier by Dan and Jenny Stothers' Bay Tours. Phone (24 hours) (070) 436–953.

At Taradale, Napier's southwestern suburb, **Mission Vineyards**, on Church Road, is the region's oldest winery, dating from the 19th century and still managed by monks of St Mary's Seminary. Its strengths are Sauvignon Blanc and Tokay d'Alsace. Reds are light-styled. Phone 442–259.

Taradale Winery Cellars is close by, also on Church Road. Formerly named McWilliam's, it merged with Cooks in 1984. Wine-making operations are in two locations; the cellar is in the original winery. Its strengths are Chardonnay and the 1983 Private Bin Cabernet Sauvignon. Phone 442–087.

Brookfields Vineyards, run by Peter Robertson, is on Brookfields Road at Meeanee, about four kilometres (2.5 miles) east of Taradale. Small and dedicated to quality, its strengths are Cabernet Sauvignon and Chardonnay. Phone 442–471.

Small **Sacred Hill Winery** is on Dartmoor Road in Puketapu, about six kilometres (four miles) west of Taradale. It is open by appointment only. Phone 444–852 or 444–964.

Driving from Taradale to Hastings on Highway 50, you pass two small, new wineries that deserve attention. **C J Pask Winery** is on Korokipo Road, north of Fernhill and about ten kilometres (six miles) south of Taradale. Phone 797–906. **Alan Limner**, opened in 1988, is on Mere Road, two kilometres (a mile) south of Fernhill. Phone 356–807.

The oldest winery at Hastings, dating from 1905, is **Vidal of Hawkes Bay**, at 913 St Aubyn Street East. It is owned by Auckland's Villa Maria but uses only Hawkes Bay grapes. Under talented winemaker Warwick Orchiston, the winery's strengths are Cabernet Sauvignon/Merlot and Fumé Blanc. Its bottle-fermented Vïdal Brut ranks with New Zealand's best *méthode champenoise* wines. The winery has an attractive restaurant and wine bar. Phone 68–105.

Ngatarawa Wines, on Ngatarawa Road near Bridge Pa, six kilometres (four miles) west of Hastings, was founded in the early 1980s, with highly skilled Alwyn Corban, of Auckland's celebrated Corban wine family, as its winemaker. Its strengths are Stables Red (a Cabernet) and Sauvignon Blanc. Phone 797–603.

Even newer is **St George Estate Winery**, on St Georges Road, just south of Hastings, the first vintage of which is 1985. Its best wine is Cabernet/Merlot. There is a very nice restaurant at the winery. Phone 775–356.

At Havelock North, the most famous cellar is **Te Mata Estate Winery**, on Te Mata Road, a company started in 1892 with vines supplied by the mission monks. The best wines, both reds, are named after its two separated vineyards—Coleraine Cabernet/Merlot and Awatea Cabernet Sauvignon. The top wines are exported and often hard to find in New Zealand. Phone 774–399.

Lombardi Wines, also on Te Mata Road, follows Italian wine-making traditions and produces mainly Italian vermouths and liqueurs. Table wines are Riesling-Sylvaner, Pinotage and Baco Bianco. Phone 777–985. A new winery, opened in 1988, is **Akarangi Wines** on River Road. Phone 778–228.

At Eskdale, north of Napier towards Taupo on Highway 5, **Eskdale Winegrowers** is Hawkes Bay's smallest vineyard, run since 1973 by Canadian scholar Kim Salonius. His small range of highly individual wines are aged in oak and worth a visit to obtain. They are Chardonnay, Gewürz- traminer, Cabernet Sauvignon and sometimes Pinot Noir. Phone 266–302.

One kilometre (half a mile) nearer to Napier at Bay View, on Highway 2, is **Esk Valley Estate Winery**, formerly called Glenvale. The name was changed when the winery was taken over by Villa Maria in 1987 (like Vidals

in Hastings), but family management by Robbie and Don Bird continues. Its strengths are Cabernet/Merlot and Sauvignon Blanc. Phone 266–411. A new winery that opened nearby in 1988 is **Crabs Farm Winery**, at 125 Main Road North in Bay View. Phone 266–678.

The West

 The western part of the North Island, running from south Auckland down to the lone volcano on the rounded Cape Egmont, or Taranaki, has a widely variegated landscape and a violent history going back more than a century. The rolling Waikato Plain, a fertile, green expanse south of Auckland, is perhaps the richest area of New Zealand. Towns and villages dot the plain, its main metropolis of Hamilton threatening to supplant the South Island port of Dunedin as the nation's fourth biggest city. Mineral springs support a Victorian-style spa at Te Aroha. Around Cambridge, stud farms breed and train thoroughbred racehorses on the lush pastureland, and everywhere dairy, vegetable and fruit farms instil a sense of peace and prosperity. But this scene of fruitful splendour is a phenomenon of the 20th century, following decades of bloody, bitter fighting in the Land Wars.

The Waikato was once communally owned by Maori tribes, who resisted the tide of European settlement. At first they had willingly traded with the settlers and accepted their Christian religion. But the subsequent flood of settlers, which threatened to drive the Maori from their lands and extinguish their culture, provoked the tribesmen into war in the 1860s. It took 20 years for the British and colonial forces to put down the rebellious Maori, which allowed them to occupy the Waikato lands, either by outright confiscation or by stealthier, pseudo-legal means.

One effort of the Maori to withstand the foreign onslaught was the King Movement, in which a powerful, respected Waikato chief attempted to unite all the tribes. Though some tribes joined him, others sided with the British, believing they saw in the powerful newcomers a chance to trounce traditional tribal enemies. The paramount king was installed by his followers at Ngaruawahia, near Hamilton in 1858, but the Waikato wars soon forced him to flee south from the rich plain to a mountainous area around the modern towns of Otorohanga, Te Kuiti and Taumarunui, which is still called the King Country. There the Maori succeeded in keeping out Europeans (thus preventing them from building roads or railways) while lengthy negotiations dragged on. The Auckland–Wellington Railway was not linked up in the King Country until 1908, finally opening the way for European settlement. Even today, forests cover more than half of the King Country, and the area remains thinly populated.

The Waitomo Caves, one of New Zealand's greatest attractions, are located between Te Kuiti and Otorohanga. Kilometres of subterranean limestone caverns, many still unexplored, are illuminated by thousands of glow-worms that twinkle in the darkness like stars, and a long-established tourist industry flourishes here.

Taranaki is a roughly circular region south of the King Country, on the North Island's western bulge. It is known for its rich, sometimes unique, plant life. A central snowcapped volcano, solitary and symmetrical, dominates a flat landscape of dairy farms with well-fed cows grazing in the fields. Local Maori tribes named the sacred volcano (and themselves) Taranaki and gained fame by waging the first major battles in the Land Wars. Captain Cook named the volcano Mount Egmont after England's first lord of the admiralty. Small, circular Mount Egmont National Park preserves the last of the region's native forest on the lower slopes of the mountain, which has now been renamed Mount Taranaki, a change effectively drilled into schoolchildren but lost on the older generation. Maori myth links it closely to the three volcanoes on the horizon in Tongariro National Park, but it is less active than they are, having last erupted in around 1636. New Plymouth, on the cape's north coast, is the main port and hub of Taranaki. Hawera is the largest town in the south. Highway 45 follows the coast around the cape, rejoining Highway 3, the main west-coast road, in these two principal towns.

The long Wanganui River runs southward from Tongariro National Park, through the King Country and into the South Taranaki Bight, forming the unofficial boundary of the western lands. Wanganui National Park was created in the mid-1980s to preserve the historical sites and natural beauty of this navigable waterway, which long served as the only route into the interior. At its mouth stands the comfortable, attractive port city of Wanganui, one of New Zealand's oldest towns.

Hamilton and Environs

A military post in 1864, Hamilton has grown into a thriving industrial, farming and agricultural-research centre and is now New Zealand's largest inland city. It is nicknamed the 'Fountain City', but its pleasant parks and gardens bordering Hamilton Lake and the Waikato River, which meanders leisurely through the city, could earn it other equally poetic names.

Getting There

Air New Zealand connects Hamilton with all major cities, and Eagle Airways flies throughout the North Island. 16 kilometres (ten miles) to the north. Airport Transport Ltd meets all planes, providing a bus service to the city. New Zealand Railways runs daily trains to Hamilton from Wellington and Auckland. The station is on Queens Avenue. Intercity (NZRR) Services and Newmans Coachlines join Hamilton with towns in all directions, operating

Maoritanga

Maoritanga means 'the Maori way of doing things', the daily exercise of a unique Polynesian culture that was nearly lost forever. A hundred years ago, reeling under the impact of European civilization, the Maori faced the tragic prospect of dying out as a people. Today their numbers are increasing, their birthrate almost twice that of the Pakehas (European New Zealanders). It is hard to count the Maori, as intermarriage has left few, if any, full-blooded Maori, and New Zealanders with only one-sixteenth Maori blood can and do claim their Maori rather than their European ancestry. The best estimate places the Maori population at 12–15 percent of the New Zealand total, or roughly 400,000 individuals. What is certain is that Maoritanga is enjoying a renaissance, and New Zealand is consciously moulding a bi-cultural society, trying hard to set right some of the wrongs of the past.

The Maori's rich heritage was passed down through stories and songs, which were reinforced by the symbolic carvings that stood in for a written language. The Maori traditionally trace their ancestors, and all life on earth, to the gods. In the beginning, they say, all was primeval darkness, in which Ranginui, the sky father, and Papa-tua-nuku, the earth mother, were locked in an eternal embrace. Their children, the gods, longed for light and struggled to separate their parents. The god of war would have killed them, but the eldest brother, Tane, god of the forest, prised them apart, creating night and day.

Ranginui wept so copiously for his wife that his tears, falling from the sky, formed the oceans. After many battles among the gods, peace descended and Tane created a woman out of clay. Through his daughter, the dawn maiden, Tane became the father of mankind.

Later, the myths recount, there was born the human hero Maui, a character common to the mythology of all Polynesians. Maui was so small and weak that he was tossed into the sea. The gods rescued the infant, and Ranginui nursed him to maturity. Maui returned to his family blessed with magic powers, which he used to benefit his people. He slowed the sun on its journey across the sky to make more daylight for gathering food. He unlocked the secrets of fire. He set out in his canoe and formed new lands by fishing up out of the ocean the islands of Polynesia. He created Aotearoa—the Land of the Long White Cloud, as the Maori know New Zealand—by fashioning the South Island from his canoe, Stewart Island from its stone anchor and the North Island from a great fish. Finally, Maui tried to win immortality for mankind but failed in this last quest and perished, as all men must.

Most Maori can trace their ancestry to the chiefs of Hawaiki (an unidentified island probably near Tahiti), who migrated southward by canoe four centuries after the great explorer Kupe discovered Aotearoa. Tribes took their names and identities from the seven or more canoes that carried them across the Pacific Ocean in around 1350.

Each sub-tribe had a hereditary chief whose *mana* (a god-given quality of prestige and honour) was drawn from his ancestors. A *tahunga,* or specialist, had priestly functions. His powers were derived from his special skill, such as carving, and his special knowledge of rituals, sacred lore, tribal history and the secrets of the gods, which had been passed down from older *tahungas.* In Aotearoa, the Maori brought stone-age technology to a high point, using sharpened nephrite, the hardest of jades, to work beautiful carvings.

The Maori settlers had brought with them the kumara, the Polynesian sweet potato that thus remained their staple food. When the kumara-growing season was over, the Maori engaged zestfully in tribal warfare, a perennial struggle based on the principles of mana and *utu* (retribution); an insult to one man's mana was an insult to his whole sub-tribe, and utu inevitably followed. In war season, people left their temporary farming settlements and gathered in the strategically located *pa,* a village fortified with pallisades, ramparts and trenches. Inside were dwellings, decorated storehouses and a finely carved meeting house in an open courtyard, or *marae.* The rules of warfare were well understood. Warriors gained fame for valour and cunning, while dances and elegantly carved weapons added lustre to the fray.

The Maori way of life was distorted and finally overwhelmed by European colonization. Muskets, introduced by the first traders, brought havoc to the ritual tribal warfare and threatened the Maori with self-inflicted genocide. Missionaries brought new hope but hastened the crumbling of traditional life. The land that provided each tribe's identity and mana was seized by the new settlers and broken up into farms. By 1900, the devastation of the Maori was

(continued next page)

nearly complete, their numbers having dwindled to 40,000, and they were generally regarded as a dying race.

Several factors brought a turnabout. Against all odds, many surviving Maori clung to their cultural roots. Distinguished Moari political and religious leaders arose to give their people pride and hope. Their influence in the 20th century has helped to bring about more enlightened government policies towards the Maori minority.

Maori communities live by their old traditions, and the marae remains the focus of community life, the locale for social, political and ceremonial events. The meeting house is built to represent the human form, named for an ancestor and carved with symbols recalling tribal myth, thus unifying the group. The open ground in front symbolizes the ancient lands of the tribe and its mana. The marae is run on democratic principles evolved from strict, traditional codes of behaviour.

Multi-tribal maraes, adapted to modern circumstances, function as community centres in the cities where Maori workers have migrated. Many urban Maori have become political activists, fighting poverty and discrimination and refusing to allow their culture to be debased as a mere lure for tourists or entertainment for visiting royalty. Organized protests and marches now focus more and more on Maori land rights and the disputed, unratified Treaty of Waitangi (see page 54).

In the 1970s, Britain joined the European Common Market, ending its favourable trade relationship with its former colony and effectively severing New Zealand from its last British apron strings. This caused a great identity crisis. Maori culture suddenly assumed new importance as something genuinely New Zealand's own. Students of both races started studying the Maori language, and many adults formed biracial groups, or 'families', to learn Maoritanga. Several bilingual schools were approved, and a dramatic Maori initiative sparked the setting up of over 400 kindergartens, called *kohanga reo,* where Maori language, customs and values can be passed on to pre-school children before the elders are all gone. Nightly news programmes in Maori are now broadcast on television, and regular commentators set a good example to the nation by pronouncing Maori place names correctly, instead of using the customary Anglicized abbreviations. Maoritanga is becoming the birthright of all New Zealanders.

from the NZR Travel Centre at the corner of Ward and Anglesea streets. Highway 1 connects Hamilton with Auckland, 129 kilometres (80 miles) to the north, and with Wellington, 525 kilometres (326 miles) to the south.

Information and Orientation

The New Zealand Visitor Information Centre is in the Irvin & Stern Building on Barton Street. Phone (24 hours) 392–065. The Waikato Visitors Information Centre is at 865 Victoria Street. Open weekdays 9 am–4.30 pm and weekends from 9 am to 12 noon. Phone 393–3660. The NZTP Travel Office is also situated on Victoria Street, the main downtown thoroughfare. Phone 80–959.

Sights

Hamilton is not a tourist centre, but it is nevertheless a pleasant city with interesting sights and makes a good base for visiting the surrounding areas. The **Waikato Museum of Art and History**, on Grantham Street, is definitely worth a visit. The modern, spacious building has an excellent collection of historic and contemporary Maori art centred around a superb war canoe built in the 1830s. The painting exhibits are often outstanding, and there is a restaurant in the building. The **Founders Memorial Theatre**, at London and Tristram streets, is the cultural centre, with a wonderful **Centennial Fountain** nearby. Other pleasant fountains are found in parks and gardens throughout the city, especially **Gerden Place**, on Victoria Street.

Cambridge, 24 kilometres (15 miles) upstream on the Waikato River, is a quiet, pretty town with tree-lined avenues, English-style gardens and a village green where men in white play cricket. Church bells peal, transporting the visitor to the uncomplicated England of another era. Along Highway 1 between Hamilton and Cambridge, racehorses graze in the emerald fields of stud stables.

Ngaruawahia, 19 kilometres (12 miles) downstream from Hamilton on Highway 1, was the capital of the Maori King Movement and is still the official residence of the present Maori queen. **Turangawaewae Pa**, a fortified village, is open to the public on occasional weekends, which are advertised locally and about which it is well worth making inquiries at the information centre in Hamilton. This marae contains a splendid meeting house, much fine wood carving and the queen's residence, which has a five-sided tower on one corner.

In mid-March, on the Saturday nearest St Patrick's Day, a unique carnival, the **Ngaruawahia River Regatta**, is held at the Point, the confluence of the Waikato and Waipa rivers. Events include traditional Maori canoe races, horse swimming, tribal dance competitions and a parade of great war canoes, with a spectacular salute to the Maori queen and her guests.

Te Aroha, 53 kilometres (33 miles) northeast of Hamilton on Highway

26, was a gold-mining town and fashionable spa at the turn of the century. The **Te Aroha Tourist Domain** is a swath of manicured lawns dotted with quaint Victorian gazebos and pavilions over drinking fountains of mineral water. The modern complex of spa pools is open daily 10 am–9 pm. Phone 48–717 for information and bookings.

Raglan, 48 kilometres (30 miles) west of Hamilton on Highway 23, at the mouth of picturesque, many-armed Raglan Harbour, is the city's nearest seaside resort. The main street is lined with palm trees, and the beaches at nearby Whale Bay and Manu Bay are famous among surfers for their long, rolling breakers.

Near Te Mata, 21 kilometres (13 miles) south of Raglan on the main road to Kawhia, a track is signposted to **Bridal Veil Falls**. A ten-minute walk through dense forest leads to a plummeting waterfall that drops 60 metres (200 feet) down sheer cliffs to a deep pool below. A ten-minute climb down a steep path brings you to an even more dramatic vantage point at the foot of the falls. Beyond the falls is strange **Lake Disappear**, which occupies an elevated valley in wet weather but disappears completely through cracks in the rocks during dry spells.

Kawhia Harbour, at the end of the road, is a remote corner of the King Country, forgotten by time. This is the best natural harbour on the west coast and was once a major trading centre, but when Europeans fled the King Country in the 1860s, history passed it by. Railways and main roads went elsewhere, and the area remains a time capsule of an earlier New Zealand. At **Te Puia Hot Water Beach**, beyond the tiny township of Kawhia, hot springs seep up through the sand, like those at Hot Water Beach on the Coromandel Peninsula. At low tide you can relax in a hot soaking pool scooped out of the sand with your own hands.

Waitomo

The remarkable Waitomo Caves lie beneath rugged hills 74 kilometres (46 miles) south of Hamilton, near Otorohanga and Te Kuiti in the northern King Country. They can be reached by car or Intercity (NZRR) Services from Hamilton, Rotorua and many other towns. This is one sight not to miss.

Waitomo village exists to serve tourists, with a post office, general store, museum, tavern, luxury THC hotel and other (but limited) accommodation. The **Waitomo Museum of Caves** (open daily) has excellent information about the caves, including displays, fossils and an audio-visual presentation.

Three main caverns are open to the public. **Waitomo Cave**, also called the Glow-worm Grotto, is entered near the carpark 500 metres (0.3 miles) from the museum. Every hour, groups of 50 are taken on a 45-minute guided tour of the cave. A well-constructed walkway leads through awe-inspiring limestone formations, but the high point is a boat ride in a flat-bottomed punt into a vaulted cavern twinkling with the blue-green lights of thousands of tiny glow-worms. In fact, these radiant creatures are not worms, nor do they resemble fireflies, which light up to attract mates. They are the tiny larvae of a fly and use their lights to attract food to the sticky threads they dangle like fishing lines. The hungrier they are, the brighter the light. When a flying insect is snagged, the larva hauls it in. The adult fly has no mouth and lives only long enough to mate, lay eggs and be eaten by a new generation of glow-worms.

Ruakuri Cave is the largest, a complex of caverns whose fantastic formations are lit by coloured lights and echo with the rushing of waterfalls. Tours go every two or three hours, depending on the season, beginning at 10 am. **Awanui Cave**, the smallest and prettiest, with delicately fluted stalactites and stalagmites, is also well lit. Tours go mornings and afternoons. Inquire at the museum for exact tour times of both caves.

Black water rafting is by far the most impressive way to see the caves, if you are adventurous and do not suffer from claustrophobia. You are provided with a wetsuit, a hard hat with a lamp and an inner tube, then experienced guides take you in small groups for a practice session above ground in the Waitomo River. That done, they lead you underground to follow a stream, later a river, to its exit through caverns and grottoes festooned with glow-worms. It is the experience of a lifetime to float down the silent river in a fairyland spangled with a myriad lights. When you emerge, a guide drives you to a hot shower and a bowl of soup. The trip takes about three and a half hours. Make arrangements through the museum, and try to book ahead, especially for holidays and weekends. Write to the Waitomo Museum of Caves, PO Box 12, Waitomo Caves, New Zealand, or phone (0813) 87–640.

Ohaki Maori Village, on the entry road to Waitomo Village, is worth a stop, in spite of the tourist-trap sign at the entrance and the mass-produced goods in the little shop. It is a part of a genuine weaving village, run by members of the Te Kanawa family, which includes not only the world-famous opera singer but also one of the greatest living Maori weavers. Local Maori crafts people demonstrate their skills here. A reconstructed, palisaded *pa*, or fortified village, is open for inspection, and there is a delightful, instructive walk through the forest to Opapaka Pa (see *Focus*, page 113).

Three natural wonders can be seen during a half-hour drive along Te Anga Road, which leads west from Waitomo Village. **Mangapohue Natural Bridge**, signposted 26 kilometres (16 miles) along the road, and then a ten-minute walk away, is a remarkable double limestone arch standing 15 metres (50 feet) high in a forested gorge—the eroded remnant of an ancient, collapsed cave. **Marakopa Falls**, signposted 32 kilometres (20 miles) along Te Anga Road, is formed by a fault that sends the Marakopa River bounding down a series of steps before it plunges a spectacular 36 metres (118 feet) down a forested cliff. A ten-minute walk on a good track leads to the base of the falls. Close by, **Piripiri Cave** is a big cavern containing giant fossil oysters some 30 million years old. Take a flashlight.

Taranaki

The map of Taranaki is a study in concentric circles. In the centre is the snowy peak of Mount Taranaki/Egmont's symmetrical cone. Girdling the mountain is circular Egmont National Park, around which lies a flat plain of dairy farms accessible by numerous little roads radiating from the volcano like the spokes of a wheel. Larger roads form a slightly lopsided outer circle, like the wheel's rim: Highway 45 describes a semicircle on the rounded coast of the cape, and Highway 3 arcs inland, connecting to the coastal road at New Plymouth and Hawera.

Getting There

New Plymouth Airport is served by Air New Zealand, Eagle Airways and Nationwide Aviation. Intercity (NZRR) Services operates a regular service from Wanganui and Wellington. Newmans Coachlines connects the city with Waitomo, Hamilton and Auckland and runs sightseeing tours in Taranaki, up the mountain and around the coast. The New Plymouth City Transport buses also cover much of the local terrain. For those driving, Highway 3 veers southwest from the King Country to the coast before cutting inland of the mountain and continuing along the southern coast to Wanganui.

Sights

New Plymouth, Taranaki's port and only big town, is the export centre for the region's agricultural produce and the management centre for the offshore natural gas fields hidden beyond the horizon. For a sense of the city's layout and a spectacular view of the sea, the coast and the volcano, drive or walk to **Mount Moturoa Lookout**, which perches atop a rocky prominence behind the port, near the huge smokestack of the gas-run power plant. Mount Moturoa is the relic of an ancient volcano much older than Taranaki/Egmont. You can get a city map, brochures about all the region's sights and other travel information and assistance from the New Zealand Visitor Information Centre at 81 Liardet Street. Open weekdays 8.30 am–5 pm and weekends and holidays 9 am–1 pm.

New Plymouth is a charming, hilly city with outstanding parks and gardens and good beaches nearby. **Pukekura Park** is considered New Zealand's finest city park. Its attractions include mossy avenues, fernery and begonia display houses, waterways with black swans and other waterfowl and a coin-operated, illuminated fountain. The park is at the upper end of Liardet Street, a ten-minute walk from the information centre. A rainy half-day can be happily spent at the **Taranaki Museum**, at the corner of Brougham and King streets, one of the best provincial museums in the country. It has a splendid collection of early Taranaki Maori art in stone and wood and exhibits on colonial and natural history. Open weekdays 10.30 am–4.30 pm and weekends 1–5 pm.

Pukeiti Rhododendron Trust, 20 kilometres (12 miles) southwest of New Plymouth on Carrington Road, is a beautifully sited botanic garden internationally famous for its rhododendrons and azaleas. Open daily from dawn to dusk.

Poukaiti Wildlife Reserve, at 590 Carrington Road, has lakeside walks where you can see a variety of exotic and ornamental birds, a walk-through aviary and several kinds of animals, mostly of the hoofed variety. Open daily.

Weather permitting, the 179-kilometre (111-mile) drive around the mountain makes a nice day trip rewarded with ever-changing views. From **Pungarehu**, 40 kilometres (25 miles) south of New Plymouth, a five-kilometre (three-mile) detour leads to the lighthouse on Cape Egmont, the most westerly point in Taranaki. Curious conical mounds remain from *lahars* (mudslides) let loose during periods of volcanic activity.

Hawera, the main town of South Taranaki, has two main points of interest. **Turuturu-mokai Pa** is a pre-European Maori fortress with earthworks cunningly designed for hand-to-hand tribal warfare. **Tawhiti Museum**, on Ohangai Road near the Ohangai–Tawhiti crossroads, is a marvellously imaginative recreation of Taranaki history, the private brainchild of Nigel and Teresa Ogle. Don't miss it! Open four days a week, Friday to Monday, 10 am – 4 pm. The New Zealand Visitor Information Centre is on High Street, near the water tower.

Eltham is the self-proclaimed 'Cheese Capital of New Zealand', offering opportunities to taste its produce (see *Focus* on wine-tasting, page 116).

Egmont National Park (described for walkers in the *Focus* on page 113) has access roads on the north from Egmont Village, on the east from Stratford and on the southeast from Eltham. The North Egmont Visitors Centre, open daily 9 am–5 pm, has maps, information, exhibits and good advice on visiting the park.

Wanganui

Spreading through a valley on the west bank of the estuary of the Wanganui River, Wanganui is one of the North Island's most pleasant cities. In its early days, the port handled international shipping and served as a gateway to the interior for canoes and river boats. It saw terrible, bloody battles over European settlement during the 1840s but was largely unaffected by the later Land Wars in the north; on one occasion the local Maori even saved the settlement from attack. Wanganui has mellowed into a friendly city of big trees, old houses and comfortable gardens.

Getting There

Air New Zealand flies twice daily from Wanganui to both Auckland and Wellington, and Eagle Airways connects the city with Hamilton and Auckland. The railway carries freight but no passengers. Intercity (NZRR) Services has a regular service to all major cities, and Newmans Coachlines has routes to many smaller towns. For those travelling by car, Highway 3 runs through the middle of Wanganui from New Plymouth in the north and Palmerston North in the south. Highway 4 runs south from Tongariro National Park and the King Country and intersects with Highway 3 at Wanganui.

Sights

Wanganui is a good city to explore on foot (see *Focus,* page 113). Maps, brochures and good advice are available at the Hospitality Wanganui Information Centre at the corner of Guyton and St Hill streets.

Queen's Park, a block from the main crossing of Victoria Avenue and Guyton Street, is the cultural centre of the city. It occupies a high, grassy knoll, the site of an early military stockade, and includes the stately War Memorial Hall, a modern public library, the domed Sarjeant Art Gallery, and, at its foot, the very famous **Wanganui Regional Museum**, one of the best and largest in the country. Its great Maori-style hall boasts splendid displays of greenstone and whalebone weapons, jewellery, feather cloaks, tattooing methods and a war canoe that held a crew of 70 and still has bullets embedded in its hull. Upstairs in the natural history section are the reassembled skeletons of several species of moa ranging in size from tiny to enormous.

Drurie Hill, directly across Wanganui City Bridge, has the unique feature of an elevator that rises from the inner end of a tunnel through a 66-metre (217-foot) -long shaft cut through bedrock to the summit. A carved Maori gateway marks the entry to the tunnel. (A road also leads to the top.) The War Memorial Tower, built of fossilized seashells, gives an unparalleled panoramic view of the city, the river, the coast as far as Kapiti Island and the distant volcanoes.

Virginia Lake, on the Great North Road, 1.5 kilometres (a mile) north of the city, is a lovely, quiet, park-like area of gardens, walks, bird-filled woods, fountains and the tranquil lake itself. The place is imbued with Maori legends.

Wanganui National Park stretches along parts of the Wanganui River between Wanganui and Taumarunui, in the King Country. A mostly unpaved road branches west off Highway 4 north of Wanganui and follows the river for 80 kilometres (50 miles) to Pipiriki, where the navigable stretch of river ends. It passes by Maori hamlets and an abandoned flour mill that dates from 1854 but looks as if it could still work. From Pipiriki, where there is a ranger station, a gravel road crosses over mountains to rejoin Highway 4 at Raetihi.

The most spectacular part of the river is north of Pipiriki and best seen by jet-boat. Operations at tiny Pipiriki are still sketchy (the park being quite new), and you may or may not find boats to sights such as the Drop Scene and the Bridge to Nowhere, so confirm arrangements before leaving Wanganui. In any case, a variety of well-organized jet-boat tours operate out of Tau-marunui, at the junction of Highway 4 and scenic Highway 41, which runs east to Lake Taupo and Turangi. Phone (0812) 6235. You can also ask at the helpful New Zealand Visitor Information Centre on Hakiaha Street. Phone (0812) 7494.

Focus

In **Waikato,** halfway from Auckland to Hamilton, Highway 1 skirts a vast swamp known as the **Whangamarino** (or **Waikato**) **Wetlands**. Here lives New Zealand's largest breeding population of bittern, as well as heron, egre shag, spotless crake, kingfisher, pukeko, shining cuckoo and many other species. Among the waterfowl on the Whangamarino and Maramarua rivers are a few brown teal, New Zealand's rarest indigenous duck. The wetlands can be reached by leaving the main road at Meremere or Te Kauwhata.

At **Otorohanga**, 46 kilometres (29 miles) south of Hamilton, near the Waitomo Caves, the Kiwi House and Native Bird Park, operated by the Otorohanga Zoological Society, is a famous kiwi-breeding centre. The first artificially incubated kiwi eggs were successfully hatched there in 1977. In the Kiwi House, kiwis forage by artificial moonlight. Outdoor cages and enclosures and a walk-through aviary hold an assortment of native birds. Open every day except Christmas, 10 am–5 pm, except from June through August, when it closes an hour earlier.

Taranaki's **Mount Egmont,** of all New Zealand's splendid national parks, is the most disappointing for birdwatchers. An early naturalist-explorer wrote in 1839 that 'birds are everywhere scarce, and too small to be worth powder and shot'. He and other explorers noted several species that neverthe-less have since vanished from the volcano. Common forest species such as tui, bellbird, pied tit, pigeon and fantail are found in the dense lower-level bush. Grey warblers breed in the higher sub-alpine scrub. The self-introduced silvereye is probably the most common bird in the park.

Some 15 kilometres (nine miles) west of **Wanganui** on Highway 3 is Kai-iwi, from where you travel north eight kilometres (five miles) to arrive at **Bushy Park**, a magnificent native forest administered by the Royal Forest and Bird Protection Society. Many types of bush birds can be seen from the forest paths. A pioneer's mansion and its grounds also grace the park.

Waitomo Caves has an interesting cave walk that can be taken as a short hike or as a half-day full circle. Start at the museum, where you should ask for the brochure describing the dramatic landforms. The trail takes you through a narrow river gorge—ancient stalactites creeping down its steep cliffs—to the **Ruakuri Natural Bridge**. When the river is low you can climb down inside the arch and look for fossils. For this part of the walk, allow one hour return. The longer walk continues across the Okohua River, which emerges from Ruakuri Cave, and leads through limestone formations and remnants of the great rain forest that covered 90 percent of the North Island only 150 years ago. The walk ends at the carpark 500 metres (0.3 miles) from the museum. Allow three and a half hours.

Ohaki Maori Village is the starting point of a lovely little walk to Opapaka Pa, the hilltop site of an old fortified village. A gravelled path leads steadily upward through a fine forest in which many Maori medicinal plants are labelled and described. The round trip takes about 45 minutes.

Taranaki-Egmont National Park, the circular national park moulded around the perfect cone of a volcano, can be approached from three sides:

North Egmont, 26 kilometres (16 miles) south of New Plymouth (turn off Highway 3 at Egmont Village), has a modern visitors centre with information and a snack bar. Veronica Walk and Veronica Track are both good, well-marked circular walks starting at the western edge of the upper carpark. Get a map at the visitors centre before starting out. Allow one and a half to two hours for Veronica Walk, which leads through forest up the mountainside to a high ridge with grand views. Veronica Track is easier but longer, branching from the Veronica Walk after 20 minutes. Allow about three and a half hours.

East Egmont, 14.5 kilometres (nine miles) west of Stratford, is served by Stratford Mountain House, which provides meals, luxury accommodation, maps and information. The delightful Patea Walk (marked yellow) starts at the lodge and goes through a moss-filled 'goblin forest', crisscrossing the Patea River. Allow about two hours.

South Egmont, accessible from Highway 3 by turning off at Eltham and continuing east to Kaponga and then north on Manaia Road, is served by alpine-style Dawson Falls Tourist Lodge. The short and popular Kapuni Walk (marked pink) starts from Manaia Road just below the lodge and follows the bank of Kapuni Stream through the forest to 18-metre (60-foot) -high Dawson Falls. A steep path leads down the side to the base of the falls. Another short path leading off before the falls crosses the stream to a fine lookout. The main track emerges lower down Manaia Road. Across the road, clearly marked Cossey's Track is a ten-minute hike through rain forest back to the lodge. The whole walk takes about an hour.

Wanganui is an agreeable city with a particularly fine city-and-river walk along the Wanganui River. Start at the Wanganui Museum, follow Victoria

Avenue across the Wanganui City Bridge and turn left. Across the road is the carved Maori gateway to Drurie Hill. Go into the tunnel, take the elevator through 66 metres (217 feet) of rock to the summit and climb Drurie Hill Memorial Tower for a breathtaking view. Return to the river by the road, turn right and follow the river to the next bridge. You will go through James McGregor Kowhai Park, a scenic natural reserve, and see the imaginative Kowhai Children's Playpark. Cross Dublin Bridge and turn left along Somme Parade. Turn away from the river on Bates Street, then at Moutoa Gardens cross Ridgeway Street and climb to the top of Queen's Park, with the Sarjeant Art Gallery and Alexander Library. From here you look down on to your starting point at the museum. Allow two to two and a half hours.

       The **Waikato** area south of Auckland has fish in all its rivers, but this densely populated area is generally less rewarding than some remoter spots in the western region. By a tragic accident, the long **Waikato River** itself has been invaded by koi carp, which were introduced in far-off Napier in the early 1980s to control water weeds. They have since multiplied, threatening the river's original species.

    Between **Wanganui** and **Taranaki** there is a large new lake that does not yet appear on most maps or in any guidebook, except this one. **Lake Rotorangi**, 45 kilometres (28 miles) long, came into existence in 1987 behind a hydro-electric dam on the **Patea River** in the little-travelled Taranaki outback. When Lake Rotorangi was first stocked with rainbow and brown trout, fingerlings got out through the flood gates and have since established themselves below the dam in the river's deep holes. The resulting excellent fishing is one of the best-kept secrets of the region. Turn inland from Highway 3 at Manutahi or Kakaramea (both of which are between Hawera and Patea) toward Alton. A good unpaved road goes from Alton to Hurleyville, where signs lead to Lake Rotorangi, 11 kilometres (seven miles) further. A carpark and camping facilities are near the dam. Houseboats can be rented on the lake from Houseboat Holidays, Box 236, Stratford.

 Hamilton has two very fine golf courses. **Hamilton Golf Club** at **St Andrews**, just north of the city, occupies a picturesque, undulating site beside the Waikato River. Par 72. Phone 492–069. **Lochiel Golf Club** is a nearly flat, tree-lined course near the airport at Rukuhia, about ten kilometres (six miles) south of the city. Par 72. Phone 436–898.

In **Wanganui**, the Wanganui Golf Club's **Belmont Links** is a beautiful championship course—very challenging and enjoyable. Par 71. Phone 44–481.

In **Taranaki**, **Ngamotu Golf Club**, on Devon Road in New Plymouth, offers an excellent championship links course with views of snowcapped Mount Taranaki/Egmont and the Tasman Sea. As at all seaside courses, the wind is an important source of interest and challenge. Par 72. Phone 70–424. **Westown Golf Club**, on Mangorei Road, is an inland course surrounded by native forest and offering good views of the volcano. Par 72. Phone 86–933. Rolling **Te Ngutu Golf Club**, at Normanby, five kilometres (three miles) north of Hawera off Highway 3, also has fine views and claims to be the best 18-hole course in south Taranaki.

Vineyards are rare on the west side of both islands, but the North Island does have a few interesting places to visit. Waikato has the one big winery in this region, which is **Cooks**, located at Te Kauwhata, 53 kilometres (33 miles) north of Hamilton on Paddys Road, off Highway 1. Cooks recently merged with McWilliam's, another giant, taking on an associated winery in Hawkes Bay. The large Te Kauwhata vineyard was planted in 1969, but a lot of Cooks' grapes are now drawn from the Gisborne area. Cooks was the country's first winery to invite public investment. Its Chardonnay and Cabernet Sauvignon are among New Zealand's best. The winery itself is a high-technology structure of glass and steel on the Te Kauwhata skyline. Visits are by appointment. Phone TUW–63–602 or 63–603.

The government's main wine research is also done at Te Kauwhata. The **Te Kauwhata Viticultural Research Station** was set up in 1897, but for several decades it suffered violent ups and downs under erratic government policies and the efforts of prohibitionists to close it. Serious research and experimentation with vine varieties took off in the 1970s, and in 1981 the administration of the facility was moved from the Department of Agriculture to the Department of Scientific and Industrial Research. Visits are by appointment only and are confined mainly to groups with a special interest. Phone Te Kauwhata 21.

The Taranaki town of **Eltham**, the cheese centre of New Zealand, is recommended for those with a taste for cheese as well as wine. This small town, eight kilometres (five miles) south of Stratford on Highway 3, lies in the heart of the flat dairyland around Egmont National Park. The New Zealand Co-op Rennet Company makes a dozen excellent French cheeses from Raclette to Bleu de Bresse to Pyrénées, with production supervised by a Swiss and a French cheesemaker. There is a viewing gallery at the factory and a display centre for tasting and buying at the town's main crossroads. Phone (06634) 8008.

Just north of Wanganui is the only operating vineyard in the entire southwest region, **Holly Lodge Estate Winery**. This tiny, pretty vineyard is reached by a 15-minute drive along the Wanganui River's western shore, or better by jet-boat—or, better still, by the 1907-vintage paddleboat that leaves the city marina at the end of Victoria Avenue daily at 10 am (three hours return). Holly Lodge is run by Norman and Alza Garrett, partly as a winery and partly as a tourist enterprise that includes an amusing pack-rat museum and other entertainments. They grow mainly Müller-Turgau and a little Pinot Noir for table wine, augmented by Palomino and American hybrid grapes for sherry, port and fruit liqueurs. Their small production of 40,000 bottles a year is sold entirely to visitors on the premises.

The South

The blunt southern point of the North Island is dominated by big, busy Wellington, the nation's capital, located on a fine harbour at the southwestern tip. A rugged mountain chain runs north–south, dividing Wellington from the Wairarapa, a peaceful, prosperous plain to the east, with its centre at Masterton. The Wairarapa boasts some three million sheep, which makes the ratio of sheep to people in this area almost as great as that in the South Island. It also has the distinction of being the North Island's only region of peace during the 20-year-long Land Wars of the last century. On the west side, the mountains come steeply down, leaving only a narrow strip bordering a sandy coastline, which sweeps northward from Wellington to Wanganui in a series of seemingly endless beaches.

The south is well populated wherever the land is flat enough for habitation. Wellington has two satellite cities at Lower and Upper Hutt. Along the west coast, opposite Kapiti Island Bird Sanctuary, many towns and villages are strung along Highway 1 as it threads its way north between the mountains and the sea to the broad, built-up triangle whose corners are Levin, Bulls and Palmerston North. The people on this side of the mountains are mainly suburbanites—a different breed from the farmers of the Wairarapa.

Wellington

The capital's excellent, hill-encircled harbour was first discovered by Kupe, the great Polynesian explorer, according to Maori legend. When Captain Cook sailed by in 1773, Maori settlements lined the shore. The local Maori tolerated the English colonists who arrived in 1840 because they appeared less dangerous than some of their neighbouring tribes, and the city took root as a trading centre. A massive earthquake in 1855 raised the coast and harbour floor by as much as one and a half metres (five feet), making it relatively easy to reclaim land for building, a process that is still going on. Wellington was chosen as the capital in 1865 (to the chagrin of the residents of Auckland) in recognition of its central location, convenient to both islands. It is now New Zealand's second-largest city.

Wellington is often compared to Chicago as one of the world's windiest cities. It stands in the path of the Roaring Forties, which funnel through Cook Strait at 90 kilometres (56 miles) per hour an average of 40 days a year. These strong winds, blowing mostly in spring and autumn, are credited with keeping the air fresh and smog-free. The city is also compared to San Francisco for its beautiful setting on hills around a harbour, its cable cars, and its frequency of earthquakes. But Wellington is very much itself. Old buildings jostle with contemporary concrete and glass structures up the hillsides, and the downtown business centre is forever changing its appearance as new flat land is drained and built up, leaving the original quays further and further from the present docks.

A large part of the population works in the government or in businesses with head offices in the capital, which makes the downtown scene more homogeneous, formal and 'citified' than many other New Zealand centres. Foreign embassies provide a cosmopolitan flair. Yet this attractive city is small enough to walk around and get acquainted with quickly.

Getting There

There are plans to expand Wellington's airport, eight kilometres (five miles) south of the city, into a true international gateway. It is currently served by Air New Zealand from all major cities and Eagle Airways from points in the North Island. Guthreys Coachlines runs a regular shuttle between the city and the airport.

New Zealand Railways has train services to Wellington from Auckland, Gisborne and points in between. The railway station is at Waterloo Quay and

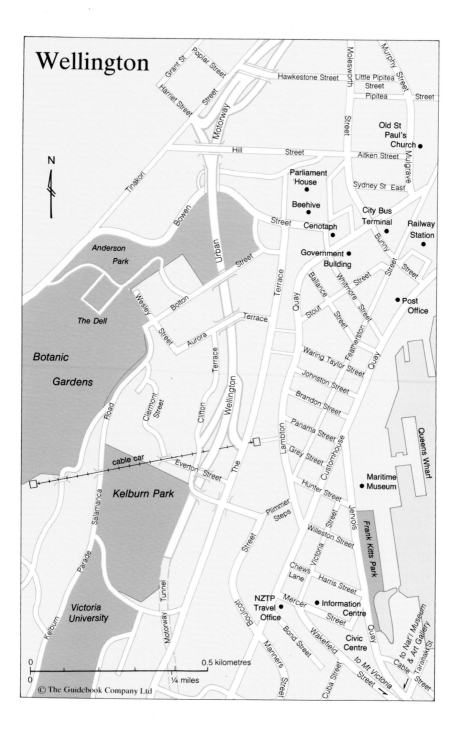

Bunny Road. Trains connect with Christchurch and the South Island via the Cook Strait Rail Ferry. Two large ferryboats carry passengers, cars (but not rental cars; see page 35) and trains three or four times a day, depending on the season, between Picton, on the South Island, and Wellington's Aotea Quay. The crossing takes about three and half hours. Bus service from all directions is provided by Intercity (NZRR) Services, Newmans Coachlines or Mount Cook Line. Cruise liners tie up at the Overseas Passenger Terminal in the harbour. Car rental companies have offices in downtown Wellington, at the airport and at the ferry terminal.

Information and Orientation

The **New Zealand Visitor Information Centre** is at the intersection of Mercer and Victoria streets in the Civic Centre area. It can provide all kinds of maps, information, bookings and advice. Open 9 am–5 pm. Phone 375–063. The **NZTP Travel Office**, a block away at 27–31 Mercer Street, is another good source of information, tours and travel help. Open 9 am–5 pm. Phone 739–269.

There is a very good city bus service, with most lines starting at Courtenay Place or the railway station. Newsstands sell a bus map with timetables. The City Bus Information Centre on Featherstone Street is glad to answer questions. Open weekdays 7.30 am–4.30 pm. Phone 856–579 during office hours and 873–169 after hours and at weekends.

Wellington's downtown shopping area of department stores, restaurants and boutiques runs for almost two kilometres (1.2 miles) from Lambton Quay, the original waterfront in pre-earthquake days, along Willis and Manners streets, with a detour on Cuba Street, to Courtenay Place. Be sure to get a city map from the information centre or a newsstand, as it is quite easy to get lost. The hills cause streets to run at unexpected angles, and the different levels are often connected by flights of steps. Sometimes you enter what you think is a low building on one side, ride down an elevator, and come out at the bottom on the other side to find it is a skyscraper!

Sights

Mount Victoria, which rises 194 metres (636 feet) above a pretty, old residential district near Courtenay Place, offers the best view of the whole city and harbour. Drive up the winding road, or take bus number 20 to the summit. On a clear day, the panoramic view stretches all the way to the northern tip of the South Island. Several paths lead back down to Courtenay Place for a nice half-hour walk.

Another way to appreciate the city's spectacular setting from above is to take the sleek red cable car up to **Kelburn Lookout** from Cable Car Lane, off Lambton Quay, opposite Grey Street. It makes three stops and passes through three short tunnels in the course of the five-minute ride. At the top is the entrance to the **Botanic Gardens**, which are beautifully laid out over 26 hectares (64 acres) with formal gardens, wild native forest, shrubs and flowers. Near the entrance, **Lady Norwood Rose Garden** contains not only thousands of sweet-scented roses that bloom from November to April, but also a camellia garden, a begonia house, a sunken garden, a waterfall, a tea house and many lookouts over the city. The ivy-covered buildings and manicured campus of **Victoria University** overlook the city from the hilltop south of the Botanic Gardens, an easy walk from the cable car's Salamanca Road stop.

Wellington Harbour, a source of city pride, is a deep, circular basin protected by the hills and opening into Cook Strait by a narrow channel. A walk on the waterfront along Jervois Quay (see *Focus,* page 125) gives a taste of the busy harbour life. The fine old Wellington Harbour Board building on Queens Wharf is now the **Maritime Museum**. Its upper floor is full of boat models, charts and relics from wrecks, all of which chronicle the port's history. Open weekdays 10 am–4 pm and Saturdays 2–5 pm.

Government Centre, the political heart of New Zealand, sits on top of a park-like knoll near the north end of Lambton Quay. The most striking building is the **Beehive**, a circular 11-storey structure that serves as the Parliament's executive wing. It was formally opened by Queen Elizabeth II in 1977. Dignified **Parliament House**, built of marble and granite in 1922, is less eye-catching, though it occupies the central position in the grounds. If the flag is flying, the House of Representatives is in session. The building was once shared by the Legislative Council, an appointed upper house modelled on Britain's House of Lords, but the body was abolished in 1950 as ineffectual, and it was never replaced, making New Zealand one of the world's very few democracies with a unicameral legislature. The stone, Gothic-style **General Assembly Library**, built in 1897, completes the ensemble of Government Centre. It serves as the parliamentary research library and repository for all New Zealand books and publications. Free conducted tours of the Parliament buildings are given on weekdays. Phone 749–199 for tour times or ask at the information centre.

The **National Museum** and **National Art Gallery** share a handsome building on a rise overlooking the city and harbour on Buckle Street, at the opposite end of town from Government Centre, accessible on bus numbers 3 and 11. A large tower in front, which can be seen from most parts of the city, has a carillon and the Hall of Memories, the national war memorial. The country's only government-controlled museum ranks with (but not ahead of) the splendid museums of Auckland, Wanganui and Christchurch. The best feature is its Maori Hall, which contains many fascinating articles including a meeting house built in the Gisborne area in 1867, undoubtedly the finest surviving example of its kind. A number of relics of Captain Cook's voyage are here, along with the fine Pacific Hall, the Bird Gallery and many other exhibits. The National Art Gallery, above the museum, has a large collection, mostly of European and Antipodean 19th- and 20th-century works, including painting, sculpture, photography, drawing and graphic art. The Museum Coffee House serves light refreshments. The building is open daily 10 am–4.45 pm. Admission is free.

The Hutt Valley

The Hutt Valley lies just east of Wellington, tucked between the Tararua Mountains and the Rimutaka Range, at the head of Wellington Harbour. The cities of Lower and Upper Hutt sprawl up its length beside the Hutt River until a steep gorge blocks the way. Wellington's first European settlers landed at Lower Hutt and would have established their city there if the Hutt River had not flooded and persuaded them to move further around the bay. For a while the valley served as Wellington's hinterland, with market gardens planted on its rich alluvial soil to feed the city. As the population grew, the city had nowhere but the Hutt Valley to expand into, and new housing projects created suburban bedroom communities. Manufacturing enterprises and research institutes soon followed, the market gardens vanished, and the communities swiftly grew into important industrial and commercial cities in their own right. They are attractively laid out with trees, parks, racecourses and golf clubs. Especially in Upper Hutt, residences are so luxuriantly land-scaped that they create the illusion of being far from any city.

The Kapiti Coast

This stretch of coastline northwest of Wellington is famed for its golden, sandy beaches and lined with city-dwellers' beach cottages. **Kapiti Island** itself is described below for bird-watchers (see *Focus*, page 124).
Paekakariki, about 30 kilometres (19 miles) north of Wellington, has a safe swimming beach strewn with shells, as well as two museums of old ve-hicles—the Engine Shed, featuring retired steam locomotives, and the Wellington Tramway Museum, which displays antique trams and fire engines.

   Paraparaumu, about ten kilometres (six miles) further north, is the main commuters' town, with a fine swimming beach and a world-famous golf course (see *Focus*, page 128). The Kapiti Information Centre, in the Coastlands Shopping Centre Carpark, has maps and brochures on the region and is helpful for hiring boats to Kapiti Island. For antique car buffs, the Southward Car Museum on Otaihanga Road merits a visit.

   Otaki, 74 kilometres (46 miles) north of Wellington, has several fine potteries on the south side. The sight to see here is the carving in Rangiatae Maori Church. Though unadorned on the outside, the church has an interior elegantly decorated with finely worked wooden panels whose simplicity

contrasts dramatically with the ornate embellishments of most Maori churches.

The Wairarapa

This wide, sheep-filled plain at the eastern foot of the mountains is a world apart from the sophisticated west coast, looking more like a smaller version of the South Island's Canterbury Plain. **Masterton**, the main town, on Highway 2, is a tree-lined agricultural centre with a beautiful park, but its claim to fame is the annual Golden Shears Sheep-Shearing Contest, held amid carnival exuberance for four days in the first week of March. New Zealand teams vie with Australians, as the best of the country's 8,000 professional shearers show their speed and accuracy through elimination heats to the final contest for the coveted championship. Thousands of sheep lose their fleeces in the process, some in the course of barely a minute, and oceans of beer are drunk as hordes of spectators gather to watch the excitement.

Mount Bruce National Wildlife Centre, north of Masterton towards Palmerston North on Highway 2, is a fascinating stop for any nature lover (see *Focus,* page 124).

Martinborough is an intriguing little town south of Masterton, halfway to Upper Hutt, off the main road on Highway 53. (Take a good road map with you.) Its main square was designed in 1870 in the shape of the Union Jack, with eight streets converging to form the crosses of Great Britain's patron saints. The old post office on the square has been turned into a delightful little restaurant, the Zodiac, and the town has suddenly gained fame as the centre of an excellent new wine-producing region (see *Focus*, page 128).

Nearby **Greytown**, on Highway 2, is worth a stop for its Cobblestone Museum, on the main road. This early-settlers' museum on the site of the town's first stables is full of memorabilia from the days of stagecoaches.

Palmerston North

The North Island's fourth largest city can be reached quickly from Wellington via the west coast on Highway 1 or more pleasantly through the Wairarapa on Highway 2 as far as Woodville, then west on Highway 3 through the magnificent Manawatu Gorge. Palmerston North is a major communications centre on the level Manawatu Plain. It is an attractive, low-profile city with a large green park in the middle of its commercial district. Gardens and parks abound. Massey University is renowned for veterinary and agricultural sciences. There are no outstanding tourist sights, but it is a nice place to stop, relax and look around.

Focus

Around **Wellington**'s harbour you may see reef herons and flocks of shearwaters. Take the ferry across **Cook Strait** to Picton and look for giant petrel, diving petrel, cape pigeon, varieties of shearwater, prion, albatross, mollymawk and gull. It is surprising that with such a wealth of seabirds New Zealand has only three species of gull. The large Dominican gull is widespread in the southern oceans. The red-billed gull is a maritime bird found also in Australia and South Africa; the black-billed gull, usually found inland, is strictly endemic.

Enchanting **Kapiti Island**, with sloping forest on the east and steep cliffs on the west, ranks second only to Little Barrier Island (see *Focus,* page 62) as a sanctuary for rare native birds (though possum and rat predators have so far defied eradication) and it is easier to visit. The pride of Kapiti is its great variety of bush birds, among them whiteheads, North Island robins, pied tits, grey warblers, tuis, bellbirds and—best of all—a good population of the strictly nocturnal little spotted kiwi, the rarest of the three species. Water birds frequent the shores and the lagoon at the northern tip. A few rare brown teal hide in the swamp near the ranger's house, and blue penguins nest all over the island. A permit to visit Kapiti Island can be obtained from the Department of Conservation, 59 Boulcott Street, Wellington. Phone (04) 710–726. Visitors cannot stay overnight, and only 50 people are permitted on the island each day, so apply early for your permit. It will be issued for the date you want (if it is available) without charge. Two companies in Paraparaumu charter boats to Kapiti.

Mount Bruce National Wildlife Centre lies about 130 kilometres (80 miles) northeast of Wellington, between Masterton and Eketahuna on Highway 2. Founded in 1962, it continued the efforts of an individual bird-lover who devised a method for fostering rare takahe chicks with bantam hens. Today Mount Bruce enjoys an international reputation for the management, study and captive breeding of endangered species. The large aviaries and enclosures set in native bush allow bird-lovers to see rare species that they are unlikely to find in the wild. Mount Bruce is open every day except Christmas day 10 am–4 pm.

Wellington, in spite of its hills, is a good city to see on foot, with many stairways and footpaths between street levels. The streets run at odd angles, so be sure to get a free street map from your hotel, a visitors centre or the NZTP office. There are several one-and-a-half- to two-hour guided walks conducted by Walking Tours of Wellington that leave the James Cook Hotel carport on the Terrace, opposite the cable car entrance. For a city walk at your own pace through the heart of the capital, start at the Citizens War Memorial (Cenotaph) at Lambton Quay and Bowen Street. Cross the Parliament grounds, with 'the Beehive', a statue of Richard John Seddon (who was prime minister 1893–1906), Parliament House and the General Assembly Library. Walk to the top of Molesworth Street and take the underpass to Murphy Street, where there is a small garden area planted as a memorial to Katherine Mansfield, the New Zealand born writer. Visit Old Saint Paul's Church on Mulgrave Street and continue past the Family Court and the Government Printing Office to Lambton Quay. End up opposite the War Memorial again, at the huge Government Building, the second-largest wooden building in the world, after Todaiji Temple in Japan. This walk can take up to one and a half hours.

For a harbour walk, start at the NZTP Travel Office and go down Mercer Street, with its Rotary Garden Court, to the waterfront and Frank Kitts Park. Follow Jervois Quay to the Maritime Museum at Queens Wharf and on to Customhouse Quay. A left-hand turn into any side street will take you to Lambton Quay and the heart of Wellington. Allow 45 minutes.

Two longer walks outside Wellington are well worth doing.

Colonial Knob is at **Porirua**, 20 kilometres (12 miles) north of Wellington on Highway 1. The 7.5-kilometre (4.7-mile) circular trail starts at the carpark at Broken Hill Road, passes a reservoir in a scenic reserve and then climbs through pastoral farmland to Colonal Knob Radio Station (for civil aviation). The track is steep in places, but the reward at the top is a spectacular view as far as Mount Taranaki/Egmont to the north and the Marlborough Sounds of the South Island, across Cook Strait, to the west. Allow three to four hours for the round trip.

Cannon Point is on the outskirts of **Upper Hutt**, 32 kilometres (20 miles) northeast of Wellington. The ten-kilometre (six-mile) circular walkway starts behind Totara Park subdivision, north of the Hutt River. It provides a pleasant walk through regenerating vegetation and native bush to the top of a prominent ridge with a splendid view over the Hutt Valley. Allow two to three hours. A shorter walk of five kilometres (three miles) can be followed directly to the stone trigonometric survey marker known as Cannon Point Trig, taking one and a half to two hours.

The **Wairarapa**, the region to the east and northeast of Wellington, would be considered a good fishing area anywhere in the world, but in New Zealand it is outclassed by other, better places. The main river in the region is the **Ruamahanga**, which empties into a coastal lagoon called Lake Onoke. The river above Martinsborough has a shingly bed, as do most of its tributaries. Brown trout are fairly abundant. If you feel like a change from trout, angle for perch. Near the river's mouth are whitebait and, occasionally, flounder.

From the Brink of Extinction

In 1980 the rarest bird in the world was incontestably the Chatham Island black robin. Only five of the bright-eyed little bush birds remained on earth. That New Zealanders were aware of the impending loss—and cared—was due to a tragic irony. New Zealand had once been the exclusive realm of bird life, a paradise without predators, where many birds forgot how to fly. For millions of years species unknown elsewhere in the world lived in peace in the forests and grasslands. A thousand years ago, human beings arrived bringing rats, cats and other bird-destroying animals—and fire. Since then, fully half of New Zealand's native birds have become extinct, and many more perch precariously on the brink today. Awareness came almost too late.

Officers of New Zealand's Wildlife Service took their first census of the Chatham Island black robins in 1972. They climbed the forbidding cliffs of a tiny islet off the remote Chatham Islands, 800 kilometres (500 miles) east of Christchurch, to a small patch of deteriorating forest known to be the last refuge of the black robin. The men counted only 18 individuals and marked each bird with a coloured leg band. Four years later there were only seven. With infinite care the wildlife team caught the robins, wrestled their cages down the cliffs and ferried them by rubber boat to a bigger, better-forested island nearby. There, the two remaining breeding females, named Old Blue and Old Green for their coloured leg bands, each raised chicks, but the older birds died one by one. Time was running out. The wildlife team took up residence on the forsaken, windswept island and, in desperation, decided to try a technique called cross-fostering. As soon as Old Blue or Old Green laid eggs, they were whisked away to the nests of warblers, who were known to make good foster parents. Saddened to find their nests empty, the robins laid again, and once more the eggs were given to warblers. Ten eggs were hatched by the warblers, but only four chicks survived. The warblers were not able to feed the babies sufficiently, and the robin population fell to five.

Southeast Island, 15 kilometres (nine miles) away, was a nature reserve. Its forest included tits, who are close relatives of the black robin. This was the last chance. Old Blue was now the only remaining female. She had lived almost 13 years, twice a normal lifespan, but she kept laying. The wildlife team mustered the help of fishermen, who ferried each newlaid robin's egg across open sea in a tiny incubator. Within two hours it was on Southeast Island, placed in a nest under a warm mother tit. When Old Blue died in 1984, there were 19 black robins—six of which were her children and 11 of which were her grandchildren. Today there are more than 60, all descended from valiant Old Blue.

Cross-fostering, using specially trained bantam hens as adoptive mothers, saved the takahe from certain extinction in the 1950s, and a number of them now live under official protection. Little Barrier Island and Kapiti Island, guarded by the vigilant Department of Conservation, serve as a last refuge for nearly vanished species such as the stitchbird, saddleback, kakapo, black petrel and Cook's petrel. Other rare birds are carefully monitored and protected in the national parks.

Wellington has 22 golf courses within an hour's drive, two of which rank among the top five in New Zealand. **Paraparaumu Beach Golf Club**, 78 kilometres (48 miles) north of Wellington off Highway 1, at 376 Kapiti Road, is a classic, sand-based links course, which Gary Player ranked as one of the 12 best in the world. It is an absolute must on any serious golfer's itinerary. The course is exposed to the winds of the Roaring Forties, making it one of the greatest challenges anywhere. Par 72. (Bob Charles, New Zealand's great left-hander, once shot a 62 here.) Phone 84–561.

Opposite in style but almost equal in quality is the **Wellington Golf Club** at **Heretaunga**, 32 kilometres (20 miles) from the city, between Lower and Upper Hutt. This is a long, picturesque, park-like course with beautiful trees and clear streams. Interesting contours put a premium on accuracy. A casual visitor must be invited by a member to play, but a letter of introduction from your home golf club will assure you a welcome on weekdays. Par 72. Phone 284–590.

Two other courses near Wellington are well worth noting. The **Hutt Golf Club**, on Military Road in the middle of Lower Hutt, is an excellent inland course, mainly flat but attractive. Par 71. Phone 674–722. **Manor Park Golf Club**, in the countryside between Lower and Upper Hutt, shares some of the characteristics of nearby Heretaunga, though Manor Park is lower down the valley. It is a very fine course. Par 72. Phone 638–558.

At **Palmerston North**, the national-championship **Hokowhitu Golf Club**, on Centennial Drive, is an excellent inland course beside the Manawatu River. Difficult and windy, it is characterized as 'unrelenting'—a real challenge. Par 72. Phone 78–793.

The **Wairarapa**, the sleepy farming region northeast of Wellington, has sprung into prominence with a new, very promising wine area around **Martinborough**, 50 kilometres (31 miles) from Wellington on Highway 53. Five small wineries entered the market at the top-quality, high-price level with their first significant vintage in 1986 and have earned an immediate reputation. Their production is still small and quickly absorbed by Wellington, so it is often hard to find these wines elsewhere in New Zealand.

Warm summers, dry autumns and gravelly soils—not to mention the hopes held out by New Zealand's revitalized wine industry—drew viticulturists to this area in 1979. The following year saw the planting of grapes suited to making premium wines: Gewürztraminer, Sauvignon Blanc, Riesling, Chardonnay, Pinot Noir and Cabernet Sauvignon. The operators of the five new wineries were confirmed in their opinion that the region could be successful and unique. They formed the Martinsborough Winemakers Association, which delineated the limits of the area in the expectation of establishing its own appellation and laid down regulations against contract grape-growing, which is widely practised elsewhere. The secretary of the association is Rosemary Chifney. Phone 69–495.

The five members, devoted to quality above all, are expanding slowly. As the vineyards develop and business settles down, more wine will be cellared. At present, by financial necessity, most of the wine is sold either at the winery or by mail order as soon as it is bottled.

Four of the five are located on Huangarua Road (turn off Highway 53 at St Anthony's Church, about two kilometres, or a mile, from Martinsborough). They are **Ata Rangi Vineyard** (Phone 69–570), **Chifney Wines** (phone 69–495), **Dry River** (phone 69–388) and **Te Kairanga Wines** (phone 69–122). All except Dry River are open to the public from Monday to Saturday. **Martinborough Vineyard**, on Princess Street (phone 69–955), may be emerging as the foremost winery of the region.

South Island

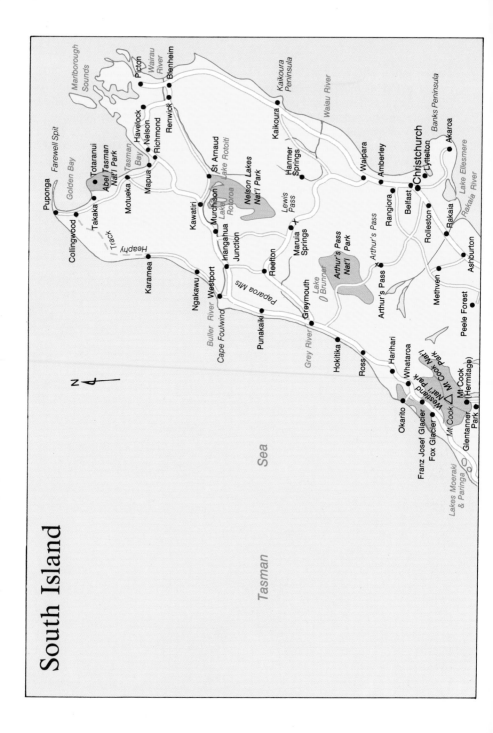

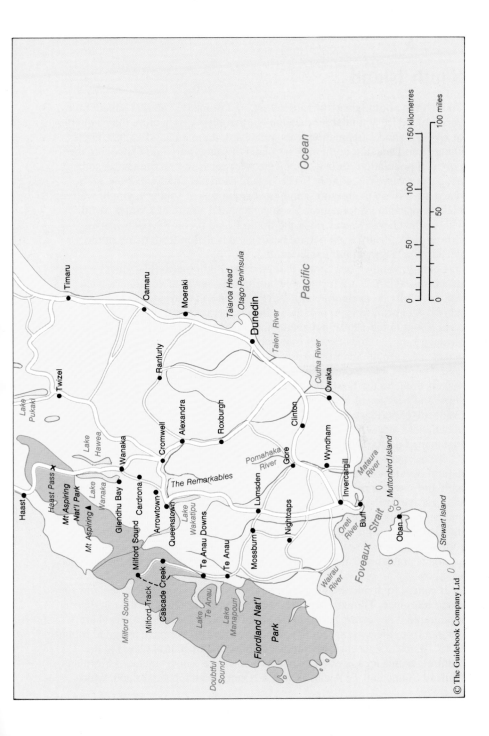

© The Guidebook Company Ltd

South Island

Though the South Island, at 150,460 square kilometres (58,093 square miles), is nearly a third again larger than the North, only slightly more than a quarter of New Zealand's population lives in its hard, dramatic landscape. Christchurch and Dunedin, in the rich farmland of Canterbury and Otago, are the only real population centres. Along the west coast and on Stewart Island, people are very scarce indeed. The North Island has always exerted a magnetic pull on the brightest and most ambitious of southern youth, who see it as the place to go for action, advancement and a taste of a wider world. Those who choose to stay on in the South Island prefer the open spaces, slower pace, unsurpassed natural beauty and isolation from many of the outside world's most intractable problems.

Choppy, windy Cook Strait, though only 23 kilometres (14 miles) wide at its narrowest point, is a formidable barrier between the two islands, which will not really be overcome until New Zealand can afford to build a bridge or tunnel. A car-rail ferry to link the islands' separate railway systems finally came about in the 1960s, but even today winemakers in Christchurch find it cheaper to have empty bottles transported a couple of thousand kilometres across the Tasman Sea from Australia than across Cook Strait from Auckland. People move more easily than goods, however, and hordes of holidaymakers come to the South Island every year. They come to enjoy the sunshine and beaches of Nelson, the grandeur of eight national parks and the chance to experience an untouched, carefully protected wilderness that nonetheless offers the safety and convenience of ranger stations, well-maintained tracks and overnight huts.

For overseas visitors, the South Island is more than a wonderland of natural beauty—of a rocky coastline softened with sandy coves, of glaciers amid the snowcapped Southern Alps, of deep, still fiords in the southwest. It is an escape from the hassle and stress of daily life. Despite speedy planes and helicopters that can whisk sightseers to remote spots, and good roads that make all parts of the island easily accessible, South Islanders tend to stay rooted in their own regions, in love with the land. Their sincere caring for strangers and warm smiles speak of a kinder, more generous era than the one we know.

It is hard to divide the long, thin South Island into convenient sections for ready reference. Though the north, west and east are fairly distinct in their topography, the 'centre' is far to the south around Queenstown, yet sharply distinct from the extreme south around Invercargill. We have assigned Mount Cook, Wanaka, Queenstown and the countryside of central Otago to the 'centre', as this area is often visited as a unit. The 'south' includes Fiordland, Milford Sound and Te Anau, as well as Dunedin and its hinterland, which share the same latitude on the east coast. The deep south and Stewart Island naturally appear in this section, too.

The North

 The beautiful northern part of the South Island, facing Cook Strait, is often bypassed by foreign visitors, who rush straight down the east coast to Christchurch. They do not know what they are missing. This region of superb scenery, intricate waterways, golden beaches and the sunniest weather in the whole country is treasured by New Zealanders as their favourite holiday place. Abel Tasman National Park and Nelson Lakes National Park preserve a magnificent coastline and a forested mountain wilderness around deep glacial lakes. Orchards and vineyards grace the green valleys and hillsides sloping down to the sea. The people are creative, friendly and easy-going, as befits the benevolent climate. The north is divided into two provinces—Marlborough on the east, around the town of Blenheim, and Nelson on the west, around Nelson township.

Getting There

The most pleasant way to travel from the North Island is by ferry from Wellington to Picton, a journey of three hours and 20 minutes. There are at least four services a day. The ferries are large ships, with several lounges, a ship's store and deck space for walking around. They carry passengers, motorbikes and cars, but not rental cars (see page 33). Ferry tickets become sold out during heavily travelled holidays, so book ahead of time. Keep warm clothes handy because Cook Strait can be very windy and chilly.

Train service is coordinated between the two islands, as the ferry is operated by the railway. Air New Zealand flies to Blenheim and Nelson from all the major cities.

For those coming from other parts of the South Island, Newmans Coachlines serves Nelson, Blenheim and Picton. Air New Zealand flies from Christchurch to Nelson, and the railway connects Christchurch with Picton and other towns along the line. There are two main roads to the north, Highway 1 from Christchurch to Blenheim, and Highway 6 from Westport to Nelson.

Marlborough

This province, the sunniest in New Zealand, includes a flat plain on both sides of the Wairau River, where Blenheim is located, and mountains to the north. The South Island's northeast corner is composed of the Marlborough Sounds, a half-submerged mountain range revealed as a convoluted labyrinth

A Land of Sheep

Viewed from the air, much of the South Island looks like a sesame bun, with countless sheep sprinkled like white sesame seeds over a golden-brown crust of tussock grass. One million people share the island with 60 million sheep. Wool is important item in New Zealand's economy—as has been mutton ever since the first refrigerated ship sailed to England with a cargo of frozen meat in 1882. Sparks from the cooling mechanism set fire to the sails, and in another incident the captain almost froze to death, but the meat arrived in good shape.

Adorable lambs start dotting the hillsides in September, the early spring. Soon their tails are lopped off for cleanliness, the males are castrated, and identification tags are stapled to their ears. A few are spared this treatment and raised unblemished for shipment to North Africa in the care of a shepherd. There, as sacrificial lambs, they meet their end in the Muslim ceremony of Id al-Adha.

Most sheep graze through the summer on 'runs' (ranches) that may measure tens of thousands of hectares in the South Island's high country. At the end of April a great 'muster' (round up) takes place, and the sheep are brought below the snowline for the winter and sheltered in huge paddocks while the grass regenerates up above.

Muster time is sheep dogs' glory. Descended from border collie stock, they are bred not for blood lines but for ability. These working dogs are of two kinds. Heading or 'eye' dogs work silently, gathering and directing the scattered sheep. Raucous 'huntaways' control the great flocks by barking and chasing them into the valleys. One man can manage half a dozen dogs, guiding them with whistles and motions of his stick—a great boon in terrain too rugged for riding a motorbike or horse. A big run may use as many as 30 dogs. They eat once a day when they are working (every other day when they are not), and 30 dogs will go through six sheep carcasses in a week. Their work in the high country is over by the age of seven. Most dogs are then sold to lowland sheep farms, where the work is easier and the dogs can carry on until they are 12.

Sheepshearers are the aristocrats of sheep men. A good one may shear by hand more than 50,000 sheep in a season. Early in March each year, a competition called Golden Shears takes place in Masterton, northwest of Wellington, to determine the national champion. Hundreds are eliminated before six finalists struggle to shear 20 sheep to perfection as quickly as they can, which, at this level of the competition, takes little over a minute per animal.

But sheep farmers are in trouble. New Zealand has had to find new market for its farm products since Britain joined the European Common Market in 1973. Much mutton now goes to the Middle East, where mutton is the preferred meat. At freezing and packing plants, the sheep are often slaughtered according to *halal* (the Islamic equivalent of kosher) requirements, the process closely supervised by Iranian mullahs no less strict than New Zealand health inspectors. Where the land can be adapted, farmers are turning from sheep to lucrative kiwi fruit or to grapes for the new and burgeoning wine industry.

of waterways, inlets, coves, bays and islands. The result is a marvellous recreation area for boating, swimming and fishing. The loveliest areas are protected in Marlborough Sounds Maritime Park, comprising many small reserves interspersed with private land.

Picton, the terminus for the Cook Strait rail ferry, is the main town of the Sounds. This pretty little port at the head of Queen Charlotte Sound is backed by steep hills and opens to a superb view of forested mountains rising dramatically from the sea. Ship's Cove, in Queen Charlotte Sound, was Captain Cook's favourite anchorage, to which he returned for rest and safety again and again. Picton's harbour berths the ferry and handles its freight at its western end, reserving a lively marina in the east for small craft. Between the two ends is a palm-studded park backed by London Quay, which shares much of the town's tourist activity with High Street, at right angles to it. The **ASK Information Centre**, at the corner of London Quay and Auckland Street (phone 1341), supplies maps, information on tours, walks and local events, and help with accommodation and bookings.

The **Smith Memorial Museum**, on London Quay, is the best sight in town, with fascinating displays recalling Picton's early whaling days, interesting Maori antiquities and a hodge-podge of curiosities. Every kind of boat ride, cruise and fishing expedition on the Sounds is available along the harbour. 'Flightseeing', popular all over the South Island, offers a stunning aerial view of the Sounds, the cost depending on how long you stay aloft. Float Air Picton has offices by the ferry terminal. Phone 37–606.

Havelock, 70 kilometres (43 miles) west of Picton, is a peaceful, long-established fishing village at the head of Pelorus Sound. A fishing fleet brings in mussels and scallops, and a scheduled mail run, operated by Glenmore Cruises, takes mail and supplies to isolated homes and settlements scattered throughout the Sounds. The full-day Wednesday run to the Outer Sounds is recommended for bird-watchers (see *Focus*, page 140). If you are a good driver with enough time, **Queen Charlotte Drive**, a narrow, winding coast road connecting Picton and Havelock, will reward you with lovely views of coves and bays. It is faster, though further, to reach Havelock from Picton via Blenheim on Highways 1 and 6.

Blenheim is Marlborough's largest town, a tidy commercial and agricultural centre with parks and gardens standing on an open plain. In Blenheim's early years, the local settlers raised sheep, like most South Islanders, and had a little river port on the Wairau. The Second World War brought light industry to the region. But the biggest change has happened in the last 15 years with the blossoming of a major wine industry here, further south than it had been thought grapes could ripen (see *Focus,* page 143).

On the east coast, the **Kaikoura Peninsula** juts out into the Pacific Ocean at the southern edge of Marlborough. Here the high Seaward Kaikoura Mountains come right down to the sea, and the views from the craggy promontory are magnificent. There are good walks (see *Focus*, page 141) and a chance to see hundreds of fur seals playing on the rocks at its tip. For hundreds of years, the peninsula was a Maori stronghold well supplied with seafood, as shown in the name *Kaikoura*, which means 'eat crayfish'. Europeans turned it into a whaling station. Today, the small resort town of Kaikoura still depends on fishing for export, especially of crayfish. Along Highway 1 are many handmade signs advertising crayfish and rock lobster for sale. A Maori meeting house has been rebuilt at **Takahanga Marae** as the central point of local Maori social and cultural life. It is on Takaranga Terrace, next to the hospital. **Fyffe House**, at 62 Avoca Street, is an early whaler's house, constructed partly of whale bones and the timbers of shipwrecks.

Nelson

Overlooking V-shaped Tasman Bay, right in the middle of the north coast, Nelson is the one real city in the South Island's north. It spreads gracefully over green hills that drop down to sandy beaches—an attractive, white-painted, spacious, sunny city. The surrounding countryside is famous for fruit, especially apples. There are also vineyards (see *Focus*, page 144), hop fields and some tobacco patches. Many craftspeople have come to live around Nelson, drawn by the sunshine and the pleasant, relaxed way of life.

Getting There

Air New Zealand connects Nelson with Christchurch, Wellington and Auckland, Newmans Coachlines with Christchurch, Picton and Greymouth, and Highway 6 with Blenheim to the east and Westport and Greymouth to the southwest. The road from Havelock to Nelson, following the valley of the Rai River through the Richmond Range, takes about two and a half hours— longer than one might expect from looking at a map. The road twists through beautiful forests with an enticing stream bounding beside it. Fishermen may be sorely tempted to stop and try their luck.

Information and Orientation

Nelson has a fairly compact city centre around Trafalgar Street, dominated by a modern Anglican cathedral built largely of local Takaka marble. A busy, natural harbour is formed by a slim boulder bank 13 kilometres (eight miles) long and still lengthening. The old lighthouse on the bank, dating from 1862, was put out of business by a new, land-based light in 1982. Suburbs stretch out on all sides. Some, like Richmond, appear on maps as separate towns, but on the ground it is often hard to tell where one town ends and another begins. It helps to get a large city map at the **New Zealand Visitor Information Centre** at the corner of Trafalgar and Halifax streets.

Sights

Those interested in art should see the **Suter Art Gallery**, in a Tudor-style building adjoining Queen's Gardens on Bridge Street. This active gallery has a very good permanent collection, including a painting of Ship's Cove by one of Captain Cook's official shipboard artists, and stimulating current exhibitions. A pleasant restaurant serves lunch, and a crafts shop sells high-quality wares, weavings, pottery and prints by local artists. A stroll around Trafalgar Square, Nile Street and Collingwood Street will take you past colonial houses and many more craft exhibits. The most-noted historic houses from colonial days include **Isel Park**, off Marsden Road in Stoke, a landowner's mansion full of antiques and surrounded by a park with century-old trees, rhododendrons and azaleas. Beside it, **Nelson Provincial Museum** has a small but excellent Maori collection and interesting displays about Nelson's early history. **Broadgreen**, dating from 1855, is a colonial cob (clay-and-chopped-straw) house completely furnished with artifacts from the period. For sun and sea, **Tahunanui Beach**, at the end of Rocks Road, is the city's safe, sheltered seaside playground.

Among the craftspeople drawn to the area by the sun and the informal, relaxed way of life, Nelson's potters are renowned as the best in the South Island— many people think in the whole country. New Zealanders in general do not relegate fine pottery to the display shelves of connoisseurs. Average families commonly use it on a daily basis, much as people in other countries

use plastic ware. Various superior clays and minerals for glazes occur naturally near Nelson, and a profusion of small potteries with showrooms dot the back roads and small valleys of its hinterland. A free brochure called 'A Tourist Guide to Nelson Potters', available at the information centre, tells you how to find them. One place to see a whole variety of crafts in the process of creation is **Craft Habitat**, at the Stoke end of the Richmond Bypass. Established by well-known British potter Jack Laird, a guiding light in Nelson's pottery industry, it expanded into a cooperative community including weaving, wood- and metal-working, glass-blowing, jewellery, basketry and Maori crafts, as well as the original pottery. A coffee house rounds out the imaginative *mélange*.

Abel Tasman National Park

On the headland between Tasman and Golden bays is one of the smallest— and loveliest—of all New Zealand's national parks, and the drive to Abel Tasman National Park from Nelson is as enjoyable as the park itself. Highway 60 leaves the main Highway 6 at Richmond and branches northwest to run parallel to the coast of Tasman Bay. Out in the country, smaller roads lead to the shoreline around Mapua and Ruby Bay, the heart of the apple district—which includes an attractive little vineyard (see *Focus,* page 144). Orchards are in full blossom in October and laden with ripe fruit in March. At Motueka, the road is lined by fields of hops trained along wires and tobacco.

Beyond Riwaka, a side road on the right leads to the beach at Kaiteriteri and then on to the southern entrance of the national park, where it ends. The main park information office is about 50 kilometres (30 miles) further along Highway 60 at Takaka, perched between a looming marble mountain and the beaches of Golden Bay. From here you can drive 33 kilometres (20 miles) to **Totaranui** along the only road that actually enters the park. It passes along a sweeping coastline of cliffs and forests, with safe, beautiful beaches at Pohara, Ligar Bay and Tata, beyond which the road has a gravel surface. Totaranui has a splendid beach and a park information office with maps and advice. There are splendid short walks and the unbeatable Coastal Track (see *Focus*, page 141).

Beyond Takaka, Highway 60 continues to Collingwood, where it ends. Here you can hire a four-wheel-drive vehicle to take you by a tiny road out to the beginning of Farewell Spit, a bird sanctuary with no access. This wild region is scarcely populated. Southwest from Collingwood, the Heaphy Track crosses an utter wilderness of forest, red tussock, rivers, valleys and giant sandflies to the west coast above Westport.

Nelson Lakes National Park

This inland park covers a remote, untamed area at the northern end of the Southern Alps, incorporating long, tranquil Lakes Rotoiti and Rotoroa. **St Arnaud**, its sole village, is reached from Blenheim (103 kilometres or 64 miles) by Highway 6 to Renwick and then west along Highway 63, or from Nelson (119 kilometres or 74 miles) by Highway 6 to Kawatiri, 22 kilometres (14 miles) before Murchison, and then east along Highway 63, which follows the Buller River upstream to Lake Rotoiti. St Arnaud, beside the lake, has the park headquarters and a visitors centre. Phone St Arnaud 806. Lake Rotoiti is somewhat developed, with sailing, water sports, no-frills skiing in winter and good walks around the lake through pristine scenery. By contrast, Lake Rotoroa, a fisherman's joy (see *Focus*, page 142), is hardly touched by civilization.

A dramatic and beautiful way to leave the north and arrive on the west coast is to drive or bus along the big **Buller River** through two spectacular gorges to its mouth at Westport. The Buller flows west out of Lake Rotoiti deep and swift, already a fully formed river that teems with fish for its whole length (see *Focus,* page 142). Take Highway 6 to Murchison, 130 kilometres (80 miles) southwest of Nelson. The **Upper Buller Gorge** begins west of this pleasant, placid town tucked away behind a ring of mountains. The river's green waters plunge between cliffs overhung with evergreen and fern, while the road hugs it closely, crossing the century-old Iron Bridge, where a punt once ferried horses and coaches over the water. A major tributary joins the Buller in an area of limestone caves near Inangahua Junction, halfway between Murchison and Westport, gathering force for the **Lower Buller Gorge**. Even more magnificent than the upper gorge, under its canopy of emerald rain forest, the lower gorge funnels the cascading river under crags and past old gold-mining settlements to the coast. There are pull-off places all along the road, and short, well-marked paths to lookouts or waterfalls.

Focus

In **Marlborough**, east of **Blenheim**, the Wairau River estuary forms lagoons where royal spoonbills nest and can be seen through the summer. White-faced heron, pukeko, South Island pied oyster-catcher, duck, teal and other waders and waterfowl also gather in the area.

The **Marlborough Sounds** are a haven for sea birds. Take the mailboat *Glenmore* from **Havelock** on its Wednesday trip to the outer sounds. It leaves Havelock Wharf at 9.30 am and returns at 6.30 pm, which allows for plenty of bird-watching. Tickets cost about NZ$30, obtainable from Glenmore Cruises in Havelock. Phone 42–276. There are many shore and sea birds to be seen in the outer sounds. The rare king shag breeds on Duffers Reef in Forsyth Bay and Sentinel Rock beyond the Chetwolde Islands.

In **Nelson**, shore birds and waders are found around the city's river estuaries. The mud flats of **Mapua** are a good spot. **Abel Tasman National Park** has forests with plenty of bush birds—kaka, weka, pigeon, bellbird, tui, yellow-breasted tit, robin, brown creeper and rifleman.

Farewell Spit is a 35-kilometre (22-mile) -long sandbar at the west end of Golden Bay. Its tidal mud flats welcome huge numbers of waders, especially godwits, knots and turnstones. Rare migrants such as whimbrel are frequent visitors. Black swan and several kinds of duck share the area. Many land species such as pipit, goldfinch and California quail frequent the plants among the sand dunes. A sparsely inhabited shore road leads from Collingwood past Pakawau to its end beyond Puponga. You can walk 2.5 kilometres (1.5 miles) along the inner beach, or four kilometres (2.5 miles) along the outer beach to the start of the spit itself, which is a nature reserve off limits to the public. Sightseeing trips to the lighthouse by four-wheel-drive vehicle are run by Collingwood Safari Tours (phone 48–257) but they go too quickly for most bird-watchers.

In **Marlborough**, on the east coast, the **Kaikoura Peninsula**, 127 kilometres (79 miles) south of Blenheim and 191 kilometres (119 miles) north of Christchurch, is an important wildlife habitat for fur seals, birds and marine life. It offers two invigorating **coastal walks**, one on the cliff tops, the other at the shoreline. Easy access from Highway 1 is either via Kaikoura township or South Bay. The walks start at the carparks where the roads end. The 3.7-kilometre (2.3-mile) clifftop walk gives panoramic views of the coastline and a distant look at the seals and sea birds on the rocks below. Allow one hour one way. A return by the 4.5-kilometre (2.8-mile) shoreline walk around the tip of the peninsula gives a close-up view of breeding colonies of terns and gulls and a large winter colony of fur seals. Allow one and half hours one way. An old whaler's track at East Head links the highest point of the cliffs with a small bay on the shoreline below.

In **Nelson**, small **Abel Tasman National Park**, between Tasman and Golden bays, protects a spectacular coastline made up of sandy coves, headlands, reefs, lagoons and sparkling beaches backed by rugged hills. The park can be reached at either end from Highway 60, either by turning off the highway after Riwaka toward Kaiteriteri and continuing to the road's end at Marahau, or by leaving the highway at Takaka and driving 33 kilometres (20 miles) to Totaranui. The best of all walks is the Coastal Track, which you can take as far as you wish from either end. The easy, year-round tramp takes two and a half to five days to complete in its entirety. Follow it for a while through lovely forest glades, explore a few coves, swim and then come back. Or make use of the daily launch service between Marahau and Totarunui that can drop or pick you up at Bark Bay or Torrent Bay, further along the track. Get the launch timetable from the information centre at Kaiteriteri or Takaka, or make arrangements with a water-taxi service run by John Wilson at Motueka. Phone 87–801.

In **Marlborough**, the **Wairau River**, which flows into Cloud Bay, near **Blenheim**, affords good fishing along its whole length, as well as on its tributaries. Sea-run trout frequent its mouth, and a recent draft drive on the Upper Wairau near Nelson Lakes National Park showed 25 fish per kilometre (40 per mile). There are roads along both sides. Highway 63, on the south bank, connects Blenheim to the Nelson Lakes. It gives access to several tributaries, but at holiday times it is a noisy, bustling route. Many fishermen recommend the quiet little north-bank road that peters out after about 40 kilometres (25 miles).

In **Nelson**, the mouths of rivers and creeks along the north coast between Havelock, Nelson and Motueka all provide good fishing, and there are streams by the roadside worth stopping at.

Remote **Nelson Lakes National Park** has magnificent fishing throughout its lakes and rivers. Quiet, unpopulated, crystal-clear **Lake Rotoroa** is most favoured by fishermen for its abundant brown trout, lack of powerboats and water-skiers, and relative lack of sandflies. (Take plenty of insect repellent nonetheless.) There are rainbow trout in the lake, but they are no longer being restocked. The very best fishing is by boat near the mouths of the Sabine and D'Urville rivers, at the south end of the lake. Smaller streams entering the lake on both sides are all full of fish. The tiny settlement of Rotoroa is hardly more than a fishing lodge. **St Arnaud**, on Highway 63 at Lake Rotoiti, is the main centre of activity and amenities.

The **Buller River**, the west coast's biggest, is a fisherman's delight along its whole length. It flows from Lake Rotoiti to Westport, closely paralleled by Highway 6. **Murchison** stands on a small plain at the junction of the Upper Buller and Matakitaki rivers, with fine trout streams in all the valleys around it. The Mangles River, close to Highway 6, and the nearby Tutaki River are especially worth fishing. Ask about the best localities from local people in Murchison. At Inangahua Junction, turn south on Highway 69 to **Reefton**, the remnants of a gold-mining boom town and now the centre of Victoria State Forest, the swift, boulder-strewn rivers of which teem with brown trout. Be sure to ask landowners' permission when crossing private property and leave all gates as you find them. Highway 7 follows the well-stocked Grey River (see *Focus*, page 192) to Greymouth.

The season for rivers in and around Nelson Lakes National Park is usually 1 October to 30 April, except for the Buller River, which is open all year.

In **Marlborough**, 15 kilometres (nine miles) north of Blenheim on the main road, **Rarangi Golf Club** is an attractive, well-groomed links course, flat and well-treed with a lovely shoreline view. Par 72. Phone 25–709. The **Marlborough Golf Club**, six kilometres (four miles) southwest of Blenheim at Fairhall, is a partly undulating, pretty, park-like course. Par 71. Phone 87–646. Visitors are very welcome.

The **Nelson Golf Club** is a challenging links course with fine trees. It overlooks Tasman Bay from the seaside close to Nelson Airport. Par 72. Phone 85–029. **Greenacres Golf Club**, further out of town off Lansdowne Road, is noted for its beautiful scenery. Phone RD–48–420.

Marlborough is the third biggest wine region of New Zealand, after Gisborne and Hawkes Bay. The centre is Blenheim, 27 kilometres (17 miles) south of Picton, which is the ferry landing from the North Island. Wine-making began here only in the 1970s, as everyone assumed until then that Marlborough was too far south to allow grapes to ripen. In fact, Blenheim often records the highest number of sunshine hours in New Zealand. It is not intense sunshine, however, so it gives the grapes a long, slow ripening period. Dry summers and low humidity mean that far less spraying is needed than in the North Island. A lot of contract growers truck their grapes to the North Island, but half a dozen local wineries have developed their own style and do their own bottling. Marlborough is well aware of its attraction as a wine centre and welcomes visitors. Wine tours can be made by coach or minibus from Blenheim, and a brochure has maps of the winery locations. Everything is available from the New Zealand Visitor Information Centre on Arthur Street in Blenheim. Phone 84–480.

Marlborough's one huge operation is **Montana Wines**, New Zealand's biggest wine company and, many say, its best. Montana began as a small winery in the Henderson Valley in 1943, founded, like so many others, by a Yugoslav family from Dalmatia. Thirty years later, two sons were producing millions of gallons of wine, much of it from Gisborne contract grapes. In 1973, they planted a new vineyard in Marlborough on the advice of two grape experts from California—for which they were roundly ridiculed by the New Zealand wine industry. The first vintage was taken north to Gisborne for crushing and fermenting, then on to Auckland for bottling. The next year, Montana established a full winery on Highway 1 at Riverlands, just east of Blenheim. Montana now has three major vineyards, one of them the largest in New Zealand, plus local contract growers. The winery is well set up for visitors, with hourly conducted tours and tastings. Phone 82–099.

Montana's success immediately attracted others. **Hunters Wines**, on Rapaura Road, three kilometres (two miles) north of Blenheim, is a very attractive winery with a wine bar and restaurant beside a swimming pool. Run by Ernie Hunter, originally from Ireland, and German winemaker Almuth Lorenz, it created a sensation with its first vintage, which earned six medals at the National Wine Competition. A slump followed, but the winery's fortunes have been rising steadily, and its wines have a strong following in New Zealand and abroad. Phone 28–289 or (for the restaurant) 28–803.

Small **Cellier Le Brun**, on Terrace Road, 3.5 kilometres (2.2 miles) north of Renwick, off Highway 6 towards Havelock, is the creation of Frenchman

Daniel Le Brun, whose family in Champagne has been making wine since 1640. He uses the classic grapes of Champagne to make the excellent *méthode champenoise* sparkling wine that is his speciality. As a further distinction, he owns the only underground cellar in New Zealand. Phone BM–28–859.

The Maori name of tiny **Te Whare Ra**, on Anglesea Street, off Highway 63 beyond Renwick, means 'House in the Sun'. A Maori motto inscribed in the winery's leaded window, *Na Te Ra Nga Mamahi*, means 'By Sun and Hard Work'. Run by Joyce and Allen Hogen, Te Whare Ra is a distinctive and charming place known especially for its Cabernet Sauvignon, Gewürztraminer and very good botrytized dessert wines. Phone 28–581.

Cloudy Bay Winery, on Jackson Road, in Rapaura, is owned by a Western Australian company, Cape Mentelle, and has had considerable success. Most of its product is exported. The winery is open for sales only.

A new winery called **Merlin Wines** has recently opened near Blenheim. Knowledgeable wine followers say it definitely bears investigating.

Nelson is even more blessed in its weather than Marlborough, having less rain at harvest time. Vineyards are usually irrigated. This small wine area is the most beautiful of any in the country, surrounded by orchards and green hills. The industry here is unlikely to expand, however, because of difficult transport over the mountains to Blenheim. A brochure called 'The Nelson Winemakers', available in Nelson, has more information and a good map.

Weingut Seifried, on Sunrise Valley Road, in Upper Moutere, is the oldest and biggest of Nelson's three full-time wineries. Austrian Hermann Seifried established it in 1973, and he is still planting new vineyards to find new soils for different varieties of wine. The Rhine Riesling, Chardonnay, Cabernet and Beaujolais have all won acclaim. The winery is open from Monday to Saturday year round. Phone UMO–32–795.

A very small and friendly vineyard nearby, on Neudorf Road, in Upper Moutere, is **Neudorf Vineyards**, started in 1978 by Tim and Judy Finn. The winery, two-time winner of the Easter Cup for champion South Island wine, produces mainly dry wines. Its Cabernet Sauvignon is outstanding. Much of the wine is sold on the spot. A pleasant wine and lunch bar is open from December to the end of February. Visits are by appointment during the rest of the year. Phone UMO–32–643.

Korepo Vineyard is Jane and Craig Gass's small family vineyard on the coast at Ruby Bay, 34 kilometres (21 miles) west of Nelson near Mapua, off Highway 60. Their production is small but of high quality, the Sauvignon Blanc and light reds being especially notable. Much of it is consumed at the winery's popular outdoor wine bar and luncheon restaurant, which are open during the summer. Visits are by appointment during the rest of the year. Phone MPX–22–825.

The East

 The fertile region of Canterbury makes up much of the South Island's east side, rising slowly from the Pacific coast to the Southern Alps. It is the largest area of flat land in the whole of New Zealand. In its natural state, the Canterbury Plain, which lies in the rain-shadow of the mountains, was relatively treeless, covered instead with grey-gold tussock grass, feathery toi-toi, flax and scrub. The plain's stark contrast to the narrow, wet, lushly forested west coast or the hilly, green north made it an obvious site for agricultural development by European settlers. Also, the Maori were not numerous here, having been decimated in tribal warfare, so sheep runs, for wool production, were soon leased all the way to the high country. The draining of swamps, the irrigation of dry areas and the discovery of refrigeration for meat brought about changes that led to a more diversified, intensive form of agriculture. The plain became New Zealand's granary, adding to the produce of sheep and dairy farms. From the air on the approach to Christchurch the ground looks like a patchwork quilt of green and gold.

Christchurch

Ranked the third-largest city and second most important industrial centre in New Zealand, Christchurch dominates the east coast. Just south of the city, Banks Peninsula juts into the Pacific Ocean like a fat thumb, breaking the even coastline and forming an excellent harbour at Lyttelton. Christchurch is often called the most English city outside of England, but, if so, the city belongs to an England that no longer exists except in nostalgic memory. It manages to hum along, the undisputed hub of the South Island, without the ugliness, congestion and hustle-bustle that characterize other modern cities, in England or anywhere else. It has enviable space for leafy parks and flower gardens. It has time for music, lunch hours in the open air and a variety of top-quality cultural pursuits. The active role of citizens' groups in every phase of city life gives it the feeling of a small town in which people care a lot about their community. The perplexing problems of other metropolises worldwide seem barely to have raised their head in Christchurch, making it one of the most pleasant places of escape on earth.

Getting There

Christchurch's convenient international airport, 15 minutes from the centre of town, is well arranged, with international and domestic terminals. International connections with Australia, North America, Southeast Asia and Europe increase every year, and frequent domestic flights by Air New Zealand and others join Christchurch to all the country's major towns. Since 1955, the airport has also been the base for the US's Operation Deep Freeze, which

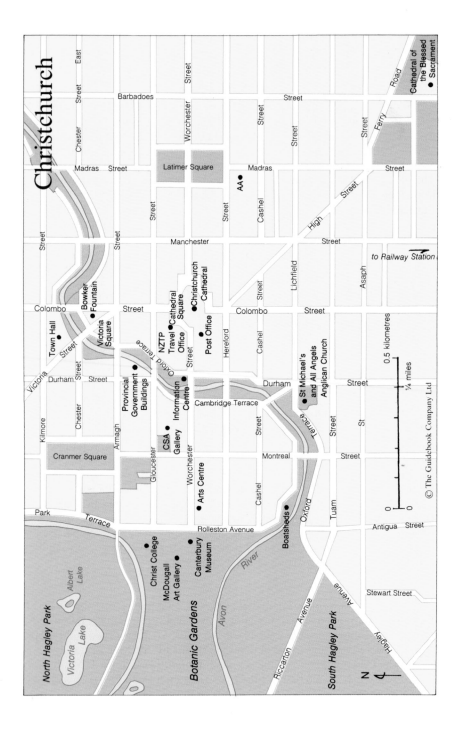

flies about 1,500 scientists and others non-stop to McMurdo in Antarctica every year. American sailors live at the airport to support this activity. A large American Indian totem-pole on the road to the airport is America's token of thanks for Christchurch's hospitality.

New Zealand Railways connects Christchurch with Dunedin and Invercargill in the south, and with the North Island by way of the car-rail ferry between Wellington and Picton. Four long-distance bus lines connect the whole of the South Island with Christchurch—Intercity (NZRR) Services, Newmans Coachlines, Mount Cook Line, and H & H Travel Line. Those travelling by car usually arrive on Highway 1, which runs the length of the east coast.

Information and Orientation

For city maps and information about accommodation, restaurants, trips, excursions and entertainment, consult the **Canterbury Information Centre**, 75 Worcester Street, at the corner of Oxford Terrace. Open weekdays 8.30 am–5 pm and weekends 9 am–4 pm. Phone 799–629. Similar information, as well as help with travel arrangements to other parts of New Zealand, can be found at the **NZTP Travel Office**, at 11 Cathedral Square. Open weekdays 8.30 am–5 pm and Saturdays 9 am–12 noon. A third information centre is at the airport.

Christchurch has an excellent city bus system that takes in the outlying suburbs. It also runs scenic Red Bus Tours. A red **information kiosk** in Cathedral Square provides timetables, maps, tickets and much helpful information, including a free brochure called 'Buses Can Take You Walking'. Open every day. Phone 794–600 day or night. Christchurch seems made for bicycles, with its flat landscape and open spaces. Many roads have special cycle lanes for the city's numerous bikers. You can rent all kinds of bicycles at **Christchurch Rent-A-Bike**, 82 Worcester Street, in the Avon Carpark Building. Phone 64–409 or, after hours, 856–085.

Sights

The large heart of Christchurch, **Cathedral Square**, is for pedestrians only— a place where people meet, sit, snack, show off, sightsee, people-watch or deliver orations from the free speech area. It is dominated by **Christchurch Cathedral**, planned even before the Canterbury Pilgrims arrived in 1850 to found their Anglican colony, though it was not completed until 1904. A 133-step climb up the bell chamber to the balconies on top of the tower is rewarded by a magnificent view of the city, plain and mountains. Choral Evensong takes place in the cathedral on Tuesdays and Wednesdays at 5.15 pm, and a boys' choir sings on Fridays at 4 pm during the school term.

Around Cathedral Square, the streets of the central city are set out in an orderly grid, broken by the **Avon River**, which meanders between grassy

Cathedral Square

Christchurch Anglican Cathedral stands in the middle of a broad square set precisely in the centre of Christchurch, in accordance with a plan devised long before the first Anglican pilgrim left England.

Christchurch was the brainchild of an earnest and deeply religious young Tory aptly named John Robert Godley, who feared that the Church of England, like society itself, was collapsing under the new egalitarian ideas current in England towards the middle of the 19th century. Godley hoped to see the old values regenerated in the pristine newness of the southern hemisphere—much as people today dream of utopian colonies in space.

To launch his plan, Godley helped to found the Canterbury Association in London, whose 53 members included archbishops, members of Parliament and peers. He then journeyed to New Zealand to study the terrain with his own eyes and select a site for the settlement, deciding in the end on this place on the Canterbury Plain, on the banks of the Avon River.

Four ships set sail in 1850 with the first carefully selected Canterbury Pilgrims on board. All were under the age of 40, and all bore letters from their vicars certifying them to be 'sober, industrious and honest'. When the pilgrims landed in December 1850, Christchurch was born. (Ancestry traced to a First-Four-Shipper is as much boasted about in Christchurch as a forebear aboard the Mayflower in Boston, Massachusetts.)

By 1855 over 3,500 well-screened immigrants had arrived. The town took shape and farms were established, but building the cathedral proved to be more complicated than anyone anticipated; more clergymen turned up than the community could support, there was a mix-up about bishops, and other urgent, but easier, matters (such as establishing a cricket club) were dealt with first. The impressive stone cathedral was not completed until 1904, 40 years after construction began, and even then it never escaped its scaffolding for long, as earthquakes shook the spire off no fewer than three times.

Yet even before the cathedral was built, spacious Cathedral Square had become the hub of civic activity. It was the site of the post office, the Four Ships Court (which recorded the names of the first pilgrims engraved on marble slabs), a Maori memorial and the offices of *The Press,* Christchurch's first newspaper, to which the famous author Samuel Butler contributed articles on Darwinism while running a successful sheep farm in the 1860s. (The articles were recast for inclusion in his satirical work, *Erewhon.*) Trams shunted in the square, and parades, crowds and traffic jammed it. Finally, it was planted with trees, handsomely paved and restricted to pedestrians.

Now the square is livelier than ever. Social action groups, many of them church sponsored, carry on public information campaigns under the trees. Radicals protest. Office workers eat their lunch on benches around flower-filled planters. Tourists listen for the chiming cathedral bells. Pigeons snatch crumbs or follow the half-blind Birdman, a picturesque local fixture who promenades with one seagull perched on his shoulder and another on his hat.

Orators in the Speakers' Corner, near the cathedral steps, draw responsive crowds.

The Speakers' Corner is relatively new, dating from the early 1970s, and owes its existence to a flamboyant character calling himself the 'Wizard' who was determined to establish the square as a free-speech area, like Hyde Park Corner in London. Born Ian Brackenbury Channell, the Wizard was a sociologist (some say psychologist) from Leeds University in England who arrived in Christchurch via Australia. He held forth on any and all subjects in the square, only to be arrested for his trouble, such speechifying in the square then being illegal. Undaunted, he had himself carried to the square in a box and, when the police came to arrest him, proclaimed his innocence, pointing out that he was speaking in the box, not the square. This argument failed to impress the arresting officers. Then he delivered an hour-long soundless tirade in mime, which drew an enthusiastic audience. Exasperated but outwitted, the City Council agreed to delineate a free-speech area. The Wizard is still around, considered by some a loony demagogue. He turns up most days at 1 pm in one outlandish costume or another—a long black robe and cap, sheik's outfit, sackcloth and ashes—and harangues the crowd from a stepladder.

The very Englishness of Christchurch makes it tolerate, even cherish, its eccentrics. One colourful denizen of the square is the Bible Lady, an evangelist converted to Christianity from Judaism who carries on a comic dialogue with her faithful flock and, in the tradition of Henny Youngman, accompanies her message with crazy ditties on the violin. Another regular is Ray Comfort, an ex-drug addict in a business suit who preaches on the evils of drugs and pre-marital sex. Others, too, offer their spiel to anyone prepared to listen—a young man in a frenzy of political fervour, a Maori woman who has found Jesus.

But like the living heart it is, the square has shame and sorrows, too, in that Christchurch, for all its serenity and order, has not been able entirely to escape the problems that plague big cities worldwide. Around the edges of the square are the unemployed, the unwanted and teenagers with nothing better to do than hang out (except when the policeman stationed there to watch them is away from his kiosk, when they erupt into some spectacular break-dancing). Most of the youths are Maori or Polynesian, and many of them get into trouble. Drugs are not as great a hazard as sniffing glue.

Some of the kids yearn for a better life—for themselves and for their friends. In the cavernous cathedral to one side is the Pacific Chapel, a small, intimate space. Here, the Lord's Prayer is written on the wall in Maori and English. A letter in a childish scrawl and addressed 'Dear God' is tacked to a bulletin board. 'Please pray for Hube not to go to youth prison,' the letter begins, 'and for all my friends to be safe and happy and become nomarl [sic] and lead nomarl lives and please make Michelle and Nick give up sniffing. Love, Mitz.'

In a time of turmoil Mitz took his woes to the cathedral, the symbol of the Canterbury Pilgrims, who believed they could make a utopia at the other end of the earth.

banks, shaded by weeping willows and oaks. Children are allowed to fish for trout from the Victorian stone bridges, and ducks paddle peacefully around. **Worcester Street** leads from Cathedral Square to the quiet, neo-Gothic former campus of Canterbury University. (The new, modern campus is in the western suburb of Ilam.) In 1982 the campus was turned into the lively **Arts Centre of Christchurch**, which includes three theatres, a cinema, shops, restaurants and the studios of craftspeople, rug weavers and painters. On Saturdays and Sundays in summer (Sundays only in winter), an open market spills from the quadrangle into Worcester Street, at which is sold everything imaginable, while musicians and jugglers stroll by and booths sell delicious-smelling ethnic food from a dozen countries. In one corner of the quadrangle, the den of the great physicist Ernest Rutherford is preserved intact, showing where he made his first experiments in magnetism with primitive instruments in 1894, before going on to England to split the atom and win the Nobel Prize in 1908.

The **Canterbury Museum** is a few steps further across Rolleston Avenue. Its remarkable collection of birds, historical reconstructions, oriental art and early Maori culture is topped by the unbeatable Hall of Antarctic Discovery, which records the whole story from Scott and Shackleton to the present. A large, revolving relief globe is tilted to show the southern hemisphere, jolting visitors from northern countries with a new perspective on the world. Restoration and extension work on the museum will be completed in 1990. The **McDougall Art Gallery** is behind the museum, in a beautiful location overlooking the Botanic Gardens. It is the chief art museum of the region, with frequently changing exhibitions and an important permanent collection that includes classic paintings of the Maori by the noted artists Lindauer and Goldie. For a look at the work of current New Zealand artists, walk around the corner to the **Canterbury Society of Arts (CSA) Gallery**, at 66 Gloucester Street. Three floors hold rotating exhibitions of modern work of all sorts, as well as musical concerts. The Selling Gallery has interesting art works and crafts for sale. Just north of the museum is **Christ College**, an exclusive Anglican boys' school established in 1850 in imitation of Eton and Harrow. The boys can be seen on the campus or bicycling around town dressed in their school uniform of striped blazers and straw boaters. Many of them hope to serve as government officials or diplomats.

Victoria Square, two blocks north of the cathedral, is presided over by a statue of Queen Victoria. Opposite her stands Captain Cook, backed by the Bowker Electric Fountain, dating from 1931, which features coloured-light shows at night. Adjacent, at the corner of Armagh and Durham streets, the Gothic **Canterbury Provincial Government Buildings** recall a time when Canterbury ran its own provincial government in these premises. The interior is a replica of Westminster, full of detailed mosaics and stone carvings. It

now houses the law courts. The corner building is the ornate Provincial Council Chamber, open daily 9 am–4 pm. Free guided tours are given on Sundays at 2 and 3 pm. Bordering the river on the other side of Victoria Square, the handsome and modern **Town Hall** offers a total contrast. Opened in 1972, it is the centre of Christchurch's cultural and civic activities, with a concert hall, theatre, auditorium and restaurant in the building. A superb modern fountain facing the square makes water sculptures that complement the Town Hall's façade.

An architectural gem slightly off the main track is the Roman Catholic **Cathedral of the Blessed Sacrament**, at Barbadoes Street and Ferry Road, near the railway line. Banished to an unsavoury site near the gasworks by the Anglican city fathers, the Catholics nevertheless·completed in 1905 a five-domed basilica of white Oamaru stone, in High Renaissance style, with a mosaic floor and coffered ceilings. George Bernard Shaw upset the Anglicans in 1934 by declaring it the treasure of Christchurch. A fine organ and impeccable accoustics make it a favoured location for concerts.

The gardens and greenery of Christchurch have earned it the title of 'Garden City'. Private suburban flower gardens seen from the road often look like competing showpieces. Best of all is the **Botanic Gardens**, set in a loop of the Avon River at the end of Worcester Street, by the museum. In fine weather, an open, motorized vehicle, dubbed the 'Toast Rack', carries visitors who do not feel like walking through hectares of gorgeous gardens, flowering trees and lawns. The Cockayne Memorial Garden is devoted entirely to native New Zealand plants. Canoes and pedal boats can be hired by the hour on the river, and a restaurant serves smorgasbord lunches. Across the river from the Botanic Gardens is enormous **Hagley Park**, which is crisscrossed by walking, jogging and cycling tracks. It includes various sports grounds (including even a 12-hole golf course) and, in the middle, Victoria Lake, which is the meeting place for racers of remote-controlled model yachts. The City Council stages outdoor concerts and fireworks displays in summer.

The **Port Hills** lie directly southeast of Christchurch, separating the city from the port of Lyttelton. Summit Road winds for 26 kilometres (16 miles) along the crest, starting in the seaside suburb of Sumner. The view is magnificent, looking northward over Christchurch to the Southern Alps and eastward to Lyttelton. Two historic roadhouses along the route are named the Sign of the Takahe and the Sign of the Kiwi. They were built in the 1930s in old English style and make convenient, scenic stops for light refreshments or lunch.

Banks Peninsula

This knob of land beyond the Port Hills is all that remains of two huge volcanoes. Their craters, drowned by the sea, now form two deep ports. Formerly an offshore island, the peninsula was joined gradually to the mainland by silt and gravel from the Southern Alps, deposited by Canterbury's rivers. **Lyttelton**, the South Island's leading port, stands at the joint. The two-kilometre (1.2-mile) -long tunnel that now connects it to Christchurch is the longest in New Zealand. Wooden houses along steep streets climb the abrupt hills surrounding the harbour, overlooking the much-revered spot where the 'First Four Ships' landed with carefully picked Anglican colonists in 1850. The route followed by the Canterbury Pilgrims over the high hills to the flat Canterbury Plain is known as the Bridle Path. Every year in December, hundreds of their modern descendants make a pilgrimage over the Bridle Path to commemorate the landing, while the old stone signal tower in Lyttelton raises nautical flags to simulate the sighting of the first ship.

Quail Island, the cone of an extinct volcano, protrudes from the middle of Lyttelton Harbour, dominating the smaller islands. The scene of several shipwrecks, it has served, at different times, as a quarantine station for migrants, a leper colony and a staging post for the Antarctic expeditions of Shackleton (1907) and Scott (1910). Launches take visitors to Quail Island every half hour in summer. An easy walkway around the island (about two hours) gives a view of the ships' graveyard, the lepers' graves and the kennels that housed Scott's dogs.

Akaroa is a picturesque, French-flavoured village near the tip of the peninsula. It was settled in 1840—the first and only attempt of the French to found a colony in New Zealand. If communications had been better and if the French had not dawdled on the way, New Zealanders might be speaking French today. On arrival, the French found to their dismay that the Treaty of Waitangi had been signed in the North Island, that the Union Jack was flying and that hastily assembled British law courts were in session. The British had arrived on Banks Peninsula exactly five days before them. The French stayed anyway and left their mark. They had intended to make their settlement into a base for French whalers in the Pacific and perhaps a French penal colony, but instead they built a Catholic church and turned their efforts to farming. The sponsors in France sold the colony to the New Zealand Company in 1849.

Some of the streets still have French names. The wooden Church of St Patrick and the museum attached to the Langlois-Eteveneaux Cottage are well worth a visit. The latter houses an information centre. A trip around Banks Peninsula by New Zealand Railways Road Services bus or the more luxurious Town and Country Tours makes a very enjoyable day's outing from Christchurch.

Waitekauri Every Time!

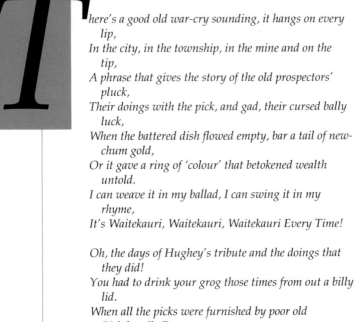

*T*here's a good old war-cry sounding, it hangs on every
    lip,
In the city, in the township, in the mine and on the
    tip,
A phrase that gives the story of the old prospectors'
    pluck,
Their doings with the pick, and gad, their cursed bally
    luck,
When the battered dish flowed empty, bar a tail of new-
    chum gold,
Or it gave a ring of 'colour' that betokened wealth
    untold.
I can weave it in my ballad, I can swing it in my
    rhyme,
It's Waitekauri, Waitekauri, Waitekauri Every Time!

Oh, the days of Hughey's tribute and the doings that
    they did!
You had to drink your grog those times from out a billy
    lid.
When all the picks were furnished by poor old
    Pick-handle Dan,
And Harry Skene retorted in a broken frying pan.
When the dirt went fifteen ounces, and every now and
    then
They used to weigh the bullion not by troy weight, but
    by men.
I can swing it in my ballad, I can weave it in my
    rhyme,
Waitekauri, Waitekauri, Waitekauri Every Time!

They never growled at road or track, or at the county
    groan,
With a compass and a slasher they would travel on
    their own.
I used to pack the tucker to the 'Perseverance Push',
And the only road I knew of then was blasphemy and
    bush.

There was no Rae nor Ryan, but the boys could get
    their fill
At the shanty in the ti-tree, up at Paddy Sheehy's hill.
Ah, the tears come in my ballad, and the sadness in my
    rhyme,
Those times 'twas Waitekauri, Waitekauri Every Time!

But now they've got a boarding house, a lock-up and a
    cop,
And a milkman, and a parson, and Good Gawd, a
    barber's shop!
John Bull he owns the country, and he snaffles every
    find,
And the poor old-timer—well, he gets the dust that blows behind.
Perhaps it's for the better, but somehow it seems to me,
That up there at the Beehive they ain't what they used
    to be.
There isn't just the accent as they howled it in their
    prime,
When the ranges used to echo—Waitekauri Every Time!

I think of those vast aisles of bush and fern where I
    have heard
The whistle of the tui and the screeching of that bird,
The gloomy, lonesome kaka, whose gloomy lonesome
    ring
Breaks the solemn silence where no other songsters
    sing.
He's dead, the bush is fallen, and there's no dust and
    cyanide,
And syndicates and companies, and God knows what
    beside.
Well, it's in the way of all things—you must climb and
    climb and climb.
Anyhow, we'll yell the chorus—Waitekauri Every Time!

Edwin Edwards, circa 1890

North Canterbury

Going north from Christchurch, Highway 1 runs parallel to the east coast towards Marlborough, while Highway 7 curves inland at Waipara, heading towards the Lewis Pass and the west coast through hilly country with big sheep runs and open views along the Hurunui and Waiau rivers. The charmingly old-fashioned spa of **Hanmer Springs** lies in a high alpine setting just off Highway 7, some 136 kilometres (85 miles) north of Christchurch. A great forest, hot springs and comfortable accommodation make it a favourite retreat from urban life in Christchurch.

Originally bubbling up from bare tussock-covered land, the thermal pools developed in the 1890s into a fashionable spa where the wealthy flocked to take the cure. The first forest plantation was established in 1902, using convict labour, to supply Christchurch with timber from pine and fir trees. It has grown to cover 17,000 hectares (42,000 acres) and lends a beautiful backdrop to the little town. When fashions changed, Hanmer Springs became a quiet holiday resort, although many people still come here to treat arthritis and rheumatism with a regime of thermal baths. It is neither as dramatic nor as extensive as the famous thermal areas of the North Island, but it is full of charm.

A large public pool area has changing rooms where bathing suits and towels can be rented for a small fee. Three pools, ranging in temperature from 37° to 40°C (99° to 104°F), have healing waters rich in sodium chloride, sodium borate and lithium. Their built-in underwater benches make them seem like giant hot tubs. It is especially enjoyable to soak in the comfortable heat and enjoy the view of the mountains and forest when the air is crisp. A 25-metre (82-foot) -long swimming pool is kept at 28°C (82°F) for exercise and cooling off between soaking sessions, and a safe, shallow paddling pool is provided for children. Walks in the bird-filled forest, an excellent scenic golf course and good fishing in the nearby rivers make Hanmer Springs a top-quality excursion from Christchurch.

South Canterbury

The richest farmland of the Canterbury Plain lies south of Christchurch. The rural scene includes long fields of grain, thousands of white sheep cropping the green grass, cattle browsing, red deer grazing (Germany and Austria provide hungry markets for venison), broad, shingly riverbeds and tidy small towns. **Timaru**, midway between Christchurch and Dunedin on Highway 1, at the junction with Highway 8 (which leads to Twizel and Mount Cook), is a busy port and popular seaside resort. Timaru's artificial port, protected behind a long breakwater, ships out much of the province's meat and grain and serves as the base for a fishing fleet. A fine sandy beach on Caroline Bay, north of the port, draws thousands of holiday-makers in December for a three-week carnival lasting until the New Year. The **Aigantighe Art Gallery**, at 49 Wai-iti Road, is one of the nation's best provincial galleries, open afternoons except Monday and Friday. The **Botanical Gardens** are lovely. Timaru can be reached by Air New Zealand, New Zealand Railways or any of the major bus companies.

Focus

Christchurch provides interesting bird-watching in the **Avon-Heathcote Estuary**, between the suburbs of New Brighton and Sumner. Here you find migrant waders in summer and a good number of coastal residents. An easily viewed colony of spotted shag occupies the cliff top above Sumner. Take Scarborough Road up from the waterfront and turn left at the top. A grass path opposite the pine trees leads to the edge of the cliff. Other spotted shag colonies can be found around the cliffs of **Banks Peninsula**.

Lake Ellesmere, a huge, shallow lagoon about 20 kilometres (12 miles) south of the city, is an outstanding bird habitat. The main road between Christchurch and Akaroa passes close to its northern end, where pukekos, black swans and a good assortment of ducks can often be seen from the roadside. The lake's west shore has wide mud flats where rare waders sometimes gather. With luck you might see golden plover, pectoral sandpiper, curlew sandpiper, sharp-tailed sandpiper, greenshank, red-necked stint or wrybill among the more common waders. Be sure to take a road map, as it is easy to get lost in the small roads around the lake. The outlet of the lake and nearby Lakeside Domain are good places to see welcome swallows.

The middle and upper reaches of the wide riverbeds crossing the Canterbury Plain are home to a variety of birds. The most accessible spot is the **Rakaia River**, where you may find banded and black-fronted dotterels and wrybills.

Christchurch offers no better way to see its leisurely city centre than a walk along the winding **Avon River**. Start at the Cashel Street bridge, which commemorates the soldiers of the First World War, and take Oxford Terrace downstream along the river bank through the bustling centre of town, stopping to look at the old provincial government buildings at the corner of Armagh and Durham streets. Catch a bus back from Victoria Square, with its statues of Queen Victoria and Captain Cook, and the old, electric Bowker Fountain. Or walk back past St Michael's and All Angels Anglican Church, noting its old campanile dating from 1860. Go beyond the Montreal Street bridge and look for some boatsheds across the river. Cross the footbridge here and bear left. On your left is the entrance to the Botanic Gardens, another beautiful walk. Or follow Rolleston Street to the mellow buildings of the old Canterbury University campus, which now house the Arts Centre of Christchurch and the Canterbury Museum. Allow one and half hours either way.

Banks Peninsula, formed by two extinct volcanoes, has a **crater rim walk** in the Port Hills, southeast of Christchurch. Begin at the **Sign of the Takahe,** a historic Tudor-style inn just off Dyers Pass Road. A short walk up Victoria Park Road leads to a sign by some stone steps. The good clay track follows Dyers Pass Road to the **Sign of the Kiwi,** another old, but smaller, roadhouse at the junction of Dyers Pass and Summit roads. This first leg of the walk takes less than one hour. Across the road from the Sign of the Kiwi, the trail runs through a forest under the mountain summit topped by a TV tower. There are great views of Lyttelton Harbour. Follow Mitchells Track across grassland and forest to Witch's Hill, by Summit Road above the harbour. The second leg takes one and a half hours. A third leg leads through scenic reserves to the Bridle Path, near the junction of Summit Road and Highway 74, where the Canterbury Pilgrims first came inland.

In **North Canterbury,** lovely **forest walks** and soaks in open-air thermal pools should attract any walker to **Hanmer Springs,** 136 kilometres (85 miles) north of Christchurch, just off Highway 7 about two-thirds of the way to Lewis Pass. A number of excellent walks, some with panoramic views, thread through a huge, 90-year-old forest of pine and fir. They range in time from 30 minutes to five hours. The Forest Park Information Centre, on Jollies Pass Road, one kilometre (just over half a mile) from the Hanmer Springs Post Office, has maps and information about all the walks.

Rakaia Gorge, off Highway 72, 100 kilometres (62 miles) west of Christchurch and 11 kilometres (seven miles) north of Methven, offers a superb **river walk.** The Rakaia River funnels through a dramatic, steep-sided ravine whose terraces record seven glacial advances—a geologist's delight. The five-kilometre (three-mile) -long trail starts at the Rakaia Gorge Bridge and follows the rim past the cottage of a ferryman who hauled passengers across the river in a rope-pulled punt in 1851 and past the portals of a long-abandoned coal mine. It ends at a high point with a fine, broad view. The return trail loops towards the river before rejoining the main trail near the coal mine portals. A side route from the loop goes to a boat landing from which you can take a jet boat back to the bridge. To arrange for a boat, phone Glenroy 574 or 862. Allow one and a half to two hours for the walk one way.

In **South Canterbury, Peele Forest Park,** 51 kilometres (32 miles) west of **Ashburton,** is an oasis of greenery and waterfalls that offers a **forest walk** off the main tourist track. At least half a dozen trails, most about one and a half hours long, lead through the fern-filled native forest. The visitors centre at tiny Peel Forest township (phone Arundel 826) has details and maps of all the walks.

The snow-fed rivers flowing to the South Island's east coast are famous for salmon fishing. Quinnat salmon (known as chinook in North America) are well established from the Clutha River in the south all the way to the Wairau in the north. Hatcheries release fingerlings annually.

The mouth of the broad **Rakaia River** is 60 kilometres (37 miles) south of Christchurch. **Rakaia**, a town on the south bank, fronts a stretch of water renowned for its salmon. Take Highway 1 south, crossing the river on New Zealand's longest bridge. The century-old Rakaia Hotel on the river bank has canning and smoking facilities on the premises, and the owner is an expert guide to the river. Phone (053) 27–058. The bigger town of **Methven**, some 30 kilometres (19 miles) upstream, is also a centre for guides and organized fishing safaris, but you will need to book well in advance for the latter. Phone (053) 28–482.

Two lakes about an hour's drive from Christchurch offer very good trout fishing. **Lakes Pearson** and **Grasmere** lie three kilometres (two miles) apart beside Highway 73 (the road to Arthur's Pass) in open tussock land with a view of the mountains. Both are known for their brown and rainbow trout.

The season runs from 1 October to 30 April. Consult local fisherfolk about limits because regulations vary widely.

The Canterbury Plain has more golf courses per capita than any other region of New Zealand, and some of them are magnificent.

Christchurch alone has 11 golf courses within easy reach. The **Christchurch Golf Club** at **Shirley** (Bob Charles' home club) is one of the top courses in the country. The gracious, undulating course is given colour by yellow-blooming gorse and broom bushes under its pine trees. The club house resembles an old English manor. Visitors are welcome on weekdays. Par 72. Phone 852–739 or 852–738. **Russley Golf Club** is a city course bounded on three sides by roads and close to the airport at 428 Memorial Avenue. The challenging course is flat and tree-lined, with fine greens. Visitors are welcome on weekdays. Par 73. Phone 584–748.

Four other Christchurch courses are worth noting. **Waitikiri Golf Club** is an excellent, undulating course with flowering shrubs and beautiful trees. It is in the suburb of Burwood, on the north side of the city. Par 72. Phone 859–590. **Harewood Golf Club**, at the corner of Harewood and Pound roads in Harewood, west of the city, is another very good course. It is reputed to be the friendliest of Christchurch's clubs, where you will certainly find partners for an enjoyable game. Par 72. Phone 598–843. The **Coringa Country Club** is located near Harewood, eight kilometres (five miles) from the airport, in a relaxed country environment. Its flat, pleasant course is one of the longest in the region. Phone 597–172. Right in the centre of Christchurch, spacious **Hagley Park** contains a public 12-hole golf course (you play the first six over again to make 18 holes), so that even the most hard-pressed citizen can include a game of golf during a busy day in the city.

In **North Canterbury**, the one course among many that should not pass unmentioned is the 18-hole **Hanmer Springs Golf Club**, 136 kilometres (85 miles) north of Christchurch. Situated on Argelins Road in this quiet, forested spa, the course is especially scenic, being one of the highest in the country. Phone HP–7110.

Near **Timaru**, 164 kilometres (102 miles) south of Christchurch, the championship **Timaru Golf Club** at **Levels** is celebrated for its beautiful flowers and view of the Southern Alps. While the flat, green course looks easy, it is in fact very challenging, especially for long hitters. Par 72. Phone 82–012.

The **Canterbury** region, near Christchurch, boasted ten wineries in 1987 and now may have more. All have wine shops and tasting areas. A good brochure entitled 'Canterbury Wine Trail', available at all information centres and hotels, has maps of each winery. In 1973, some scientists at Lincoln College, in suburban Lincoln, planted the first grapevines for research into cool-climate viticulture. Over 60 varieties were tested. Austrian-born Danny Schuster succeeded in making wine commercially in 1977, and Canterbury was launched, against all expectations, as a promising new wine district.

North of **Christchurch** is the locale of Canterbury's first commercial winery, **St Helena Wine Estate**, on Dickey's Road off Highway 1, in suburban Belfast. Brothers Robin and Norman Mundy were looking for a new type of crop in 1978 after their potato farm suffered setbacks. Danny Schuster came as their winemaker and stayed for seven years. St Helena's Pinot Noir was awarded Canterbury's first gold medal at the 1983 National Wine Competition. Its finest white wine is Pinot Blanc. Open Monday to Saturday. Phone 23–8202.

Other vineyards quickly followed. Four-hectare (ten-acre) **Amberley Estate**, at Amberley, 50 kilometres (31 miles) north of Christchurch, was planted in 1979 by Jeremy Prater, who had spent four years studying winemaking in Switzerland, France and Germany. With his first vintage in 1984, he adopted a modified Swiss style. He hopes to double his acreage by 1990. Jeremy Prater is the moving spirit of the Canterbury Grapegrowers and Winemakers Association. His shop and tasting area is open from Tuesday to Saturday. Phone 48–409.

North of Amberley at Waipara (close to the Waipara School), John Mc-Caskey raises grapes at **Glenmark Wines**, part of the Glenmark family's sheep station where he was born. When irrigation became possible, much of the land was put into wheat and barley. The vineyard was planted in 1980, and the shearing shed became a winery. The first vintage in 1986 showed

great promise. Open Saturday or by appointment. Phone (050446) 828.

While you are north of Christchurch, do not fail to visit **Havill's Mazer Mead Company**, New Zealand's only commercial meadery, at Fernside, near Rangiora. Leon Havill took up the ancient art of making wine from honey (mead) in 1964 believing, like everybody else, that grape-growing in Canterbury was impossible. The wine is not sweet but nutty-flavoured, containing the same amount of sugar as dry table wines. It makes an excellent drink before dinner. Production is year-round, and storage is easy because mead never spoils. Exports go to Switzerland. Phone (0502) 7733.

Some 35 kilometres (22 miles) south of Christchurch is Burnham, where in 1981 three youthful brothers from Germany planted 25 hectares (62 acres) to start the **Giesen Wine Estate**, on Burnham Road. It is rapidly emerging, alongside St Helena, as one of the region's most important wineries. The Giesens work with energy, seriousness and strict professionalism to obtain the highest quality in their wine. Their strengths have been Chardonnay and Pinot Noir. Open Monday to Saturday. Phone 256–729.

Larcomb Wines was established in 1980 by John Thom, a veterinarian, on Larcombs Road, off Highway 1 between Templeton and Rolleston. It is a charming little winery (formerly a shearing shed) set in the vineyard with peacocks, ducks and geese wandering around on the lawn. An unpretentious restaurant serves lunch with wine under pine trees. Five wine varieties are produced, of which Rhine-Riesling and Pinot Noir are the stars. Open from Tuesday through Sunday during the summer or by appointment. Phone 478–909.

West of **Christchurch**, a number of small vineyards have come together to form **Torlesse Wines**, with Danny Schuster as the consultant winemaker. Their first vintage appeared in 1987. The winery is on Jowers Road, off Highway 73 before reaching West Melton, about 20 kilometres (12 miles) from Christchurch. Open on Saturdays. Phone 426–086.

The Centre

 Mount Cook is the most famous place in New Zealand. Towering 3,764 metres (12,349 feet) high in the middle of the South Island, its snowy peak can be seen from both coasts. The name Mount Cook is attached to so many products and companies that it is almost a national symbol, like the kiwi. But what makes the name stick most indelibly in the mind, the more so after a typically long wait for the clouds to clear, is the spectacle of this magnificent mountain viewed from up close.

South of Mount Cook lies the high country, a thinly populated land of sheep runs and deep, still lakes gouged out by retreating glaciers. Golden tussock grass, shady forests, sparkling water, and winter snow have made it a top vacation area. There are no big cities, but Queenstown, the region's lively, year-round resort, is the next-closest thing. Set like a jewel among lakes and mountains, it has something exciting to offer everybody, young or old—day or night. Many New Zealanders find the international razzmatazz of Queenstown a bit too much and prefer to visit other parts of Central Otago, as the lake country is officially called. Wanaka, nestled on a different lake, has a quieter charm and a beauty of its own. The river valleys, stamped by the sites and relics of the great gold rush of 1861, maintain the allure of their wild past, while the orchards around Cromwell and Alexandra present a sea of fruit blossoms or a feast of peaches, plums, apricots and nectarines, each in its own season.

Mount Cook

The pristine symmetry of Mount Cook tempted the imagination of mountain climbers almost as soon as Europeans learned it was there. Photography added to the enticement. The first to try to conquer the mountain, in 1882, were a young Irish clergyman and his two Swiss companions. Their first attempts to find a route up the mountain failed. A third try from the north, by the Haast Ridge, would probably have succeeded if they had not been overtaken by storms near the top and forced to turn back. The excitement generated by this attempt on their prized peak started New Zealanders on their long path to glory in the heady world of mountaineering. Twelve years later, when an English climber headed for Mount Cook, accompanied by an Italian guide and much publicity, some New Zealanders were ready. A trio named Fyfe, Graham and Clarke triumphantly reached the summit ahead of him, on Christmas Day, 1894. The disgusted Englishman had to be content with conquering three other peaks instead. Mount Cook became a favourite among international mountain climbers when it became known as the training ground for Sir Edmund Hillary, the first to ascend Mount Everest in 1953.

Mount Cook National Park is a long, narrow strip of land 65 kilometres (40 miles) long and only 20 kilometres (12 miles) wide, enclosing the highest crests of the Southern Alps. The main divide includes Mount Cook (3,763 metres, or 12,349 feet), Mount Tasman (3,498 metres, or 11,476 feet) and Mount Dampier (3,440 metres, or 11,286 feet). One-third of the park's total area is under eternal snow and ice; the rest is covered with alpine scrub, forests and tussock. The weather at Mount Cook is unpredictable, with a wide variation between its hottest and coldest periods. Fine weather can be marred by biting wind. The park can be fogged in for days—or sparklingly clear. In winter, snow stays on the valley floors for an average of 21 days.

The stark, treeless land from which the Mount Cook Range rises is named the MacKenzie Country, after James MacKenzie, a semi-mythical Scottish sheep thief. With the help of his clever dog, Friday, he kept his ill-gotten flocks out of sight of the law on this high, barren, uninhabited plain. When he was finally caught in 1855 (but later pardoned), others saw the area's possibilities and moved in with their own sheep. Twizel is New Zealand's newest township, built in 1969 for construction workers on a vast hydro-electric scheme to supply large parts of New Zealand with energy. The five reservoirs known as the MacKenzie Hydro-Lakes have changed the face of the once-harsh region and are being developed for recreation.

Accommodation at Mount Cook village is very tight at most times of the year, so before you set out to visit Mount Cook National Park be sure you have firm reservations (see below).

Getting There

However you choose to travel, getting to Mount Cook is interesting. Mount Cook Airlines flies from Christchurch, Queenstown and Te Anau; the fights offer stunning aerial views but are often cancelled in bad weather. All the big bus companies go to Mount Cook. One or two schedule it as a regular two-hour lunch stop on the run between Christchurch and Queenstown. Travelling by car, you need to get on Highway 8 to **Twizel**, either from Highway 1 at Timaru, between Christchurch and Dunedin, or from Highway 6 at Cromwell, between Queenstown and Alexandra. The access road to Mount Cook village runs for 60 kilometres (37 miles) up the valley of the Tasman River, much of the way beside man-made Lake Pukaki. In fine, windless weather its opaque, glacial water reflects a panorama of snowy peaks—an incredible sight.

Accommodation

Tiny Mount Cook village clusters at the end of the access road around the Tourist Hotel Corporation (THC) Hermitage, the most famous hotel in New Zealand. This is the third hermitage to enjoy the matchless, unbroken view of Mount Cook. The first hotel, opened in 1884 a kilometre (half a mile) from the present site, was washed away by a flash flood in 1913. The second, sensibly moved to higher ground, burned down in 1957. The present structure looks very solid, modern, luxurious—and fireproof.

All accommodation at Mount Cook, except the youth hostel, is owned by the THC. The luxury-class Hermitage offers gourmet meals, fireplaces and picture windows framing the fantastic view. The Glencoe Lodge is less luxurious but still elegant, and it serves meals. Individual chalets and a motel are equipped with cooking facilities, and there is a food shop in Mount Cook village. All of the above are comfortable, well-appointed and relatively expensive. Reservations for all, which should be made as far in advance as possible, are available through the Hermitage. Phone (05621) 809. The youth hostel, part of the nationwide YHA New Zealand, is very reasonably priced, fully carpeted and well managed by two West European couples. Communal facilities include bunk rooms of different sizes, a kitchen, TV room, washing

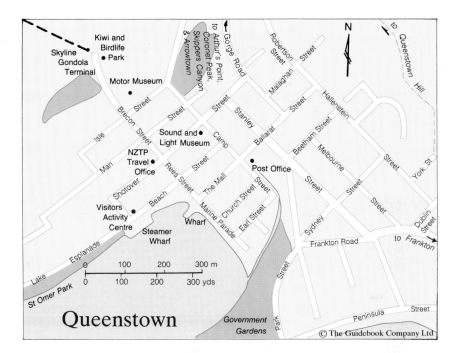

machines, ample showers and even a sauna. The hostel also requires booking well in advance. Phone (05621) 820. People who would normally stay in higher class accommodation often stay at the youth hostel at Mount Cook in order to stretch their money for heli-skiing, flightseeing, the THC restaurants or other expensive indulgences.

Another alternative is to stay outside the national park. Glentanner Park is a small centre 20 kilometres (12 miles) south of Mount Cook village on the shore of Lake Pukaki. It has a splendid view, its own store (which arranges a wide variety of tours and activities), a helipad and airstrip for excursions and a motor camp with accommodation ranging from bunkrooms to cabins and flats, with bedding for hire. Phone (05621) 855. Finally, one can stay at Twizel's sole hotel, which also houses the town pub.

Information and Activities

The excellent New Zealand Visitor Information Centre in Mount Cook village is also the Mount Cook National Park headquarters. It has maps of walks and trails, a great deal of other information and interesting displays. Alpine Guides sells and rents equipment for climbing, skiing and hard hiking and supplies experienced guides for mountaineering. The Hermitage and Glencoe Lodge have desks with free maps and brochures where bookings can be made for half-day and full-day excursions in the park. Phone 666. Avoid trying to get anything arranged around noon, as this is when the tour bus crowds are at their thickest.

Tasman Glacier can be reached either by the two-hour Tasman Glacier Guided Coach Tour, run by Alpine Guides, or by car. (Some rented cars are not insured for this rough route.) The rocky Ball Hut Road runs along the Tasman River for 12 kilometres (7.5 miles) past forests and a waterfall to the glacier. A 15-minute walk up the moraine wall gives a view over the Blue Lakes and the glacier's whole terminal area. Although the ice is over 600 metres (2,000 feet) thick, it is hard to see any of it under its layers of debris and moraine.

Flightseeing is possible by ski-plane or helicopter, from Mount Cook village or Glentanner Park, with or without a landing high on a glacier. These flights are expensive but worth it, offering breathtaking sweeps around snow-clad peaks and along spectacular glaciers. Similar flights go to Franz Josef Glacier and Fox Glacier, on the other side of the main divide.

Queenstown

This small, attractive resort town perches amid picturesque mountain scenery with its waterfront on **Lake Wakatipu**, a 77-kilometre (48-mile) -long lake shaped like an S. The bare face of a serrated mountain range called the Remarkables rises like a wall from the lake, and in the distance the peaks of the Southern Alps raise their eternally snowcapped heads. Queenstown sprang to life in the gold rush of 1862, like all the towns of Central Otago. As in its gold-rush days, the town is still small and bustling, but the modern source of gold is tourism.

Getting There

Mount Cook Airlines flies small planes daily to Queenstown Airport (in nearby Frankton) from Auckland, Rotorua, Christchurch and Dunedin. Newmans Air flies similar planes from the same cities, plus Mount Cook, Glantanner, Te Anau and Wanaka. A new airport able to handle medium-range jets is planned for the foot of the Remarkables, but the date for this expanded service is not yet set. Six major bus lines have regular coach services to Queenstown from other cities. Travelling by car, you need to get on Highway 6, the main road that runs the length of the west side of the South Island.

Information and Orientation

The hub of Queenstown is the junction of Marine Parade, which runs along the waterfront, and the Mall, a bustling, pedestrians-only, block-long strip geared to help, entertain or entice tourists. The well-supplied **NZTP Travel Office**, at 49 Shotover Street, has books, free pamphlets and a lot of information about almost anything you can imagine. Phone 143. Many other booking offices able to arrange accommodation and excursions are clustered near the Mall, where most tours start. The waterfront is horseshoe-shaped, with the wharf for the steamer *TSS Earnslaw* and the Fiordland Travel Office at one end, and beautiful Government Gardens on a peninsula at the other.

To get oriented, take a ride up the **Skyline Gondola** to Bob's Peak, 450 metres (1,476 feet) above the town. The Skyline Chalet's observation deck gives a glorious panoramic view of Queenstown, Frankton, Lake Wakatipu, the Remarkables and all the surrounding mountains. In addition to the observation deck, the chalet has a souvenir shop, coffee shop, restaurant and small, wide-screen theatre that shows a 23-minute film entitled 'Kiwi Magic'. The film takes you riding, flying, sledding, jet-boating and white-water rafting through all of New Zealand's greatest sights. (Besides inducing laughs and thrills, the film's overpoweringly realistic effects help you to decide which of those activities you may want to *avoid*.)

Activities

Queenstown bursts with rides, many with the accent on speed, others on the views. The **Visitors Activity Centre**, at the corner of Beach and Shotover streets, stays open daily 7 am–8 pm to give information and make book-ings—services offered by other tour offices as well. Several companies offer opportunities for hair-raising jet-boating with skilled drivers through the gorges and shallow rapids of the Shotover and Kawarau rivers. White-water rafting, lasting three and a half to seven hours, takes place along various stretches of the river, geared to different levels of proficiency and nerve. All the companies provide helmets and lifejackets, with hot showers and drinks at the end. Some include wet-suits as well. Milder tours around Lake Waka-tipu can be made by hydrofoil or on the venerable *TSS Earnslaw*, a perfectly preserved, coal-fired, twin-screw steamer built in 1912 to serve the sheep runs around the lake. The well-oiled engines are open to view below deck, while incomparable scenery glides past above.

Flightseeing is a must if you do not have time to visit Milford Sound. Mount Cook Airlines, Fiordland Airline and others offer spellbinding flights over the sound, Sutherland Falls, the Milford Track and the coast of Fiordland. Horseback riding on scenic half-day or day-long treks can be arranged from Queenstown or Arrowtown.

Queenstown also offers excellent golfing at Kelvin Heights Golf Course. There is fine fishing and walking nearby, apart from famous longer tracks, such as the Routeburn Track. Birds abound for bird-watching, and wine-tasting tours will no doubt be organized when the new Otago wine-growing district comes into its own (see *Focus*, page 179). In winter, Queenstown turns into a skiing town, with one of New Zealand's best skifields at Coronet Peak. Equipment can be hired on the mountain or in town. At this time of

year, accommodation is reasonable, and other prices are also lower than in summer.

Sights

While en route to or from Bob's Peak, catch the excellent **Queenstown Motor Museum** near the bottom of the cableway, with its collection of vintage and classic vehicles drawn from private collections all over the country. Open 9 am–5.30 pm. Also near the base of the cableway is the **Queenstown Kiwi and Birdlife Park**, where a number of native birds are displayed among 6,000 native trees. Kiwis can be seen feeding by artificial moonlight in a house in which day and night are reversed. Open 9 am–5 pm.

To orient yourself historically, visit the **Sound and Light Museum**, on Beach Street next to the health food shop. It recreates Queenstown's pioneering past in a 20-minute show using imaginative walk-through sets, old film clips and authentic dialogues. On the main jetty at the end of the Mall, **Queenstown Waterworld** lets you view gigantic trout, salmon and eels from a gallery five metres (16 feet) under the surface of the lake, as they knife through the clear water to automatic feeders.

For spectacular views of the Shotover River, drive to **Arthur's Point**, about five kilometres (three miles) north of town on the road to Arrowtown.

A country pub and restaurant, built in 1863 and rebuilt after a fire in 1880, retains its original colourful character. For the best view of Mount Cook and the highest peaks of the Southern Alps, continue two kilometres (a mile) further north to the turnoff on the left signposted for **Coronet Peak**. From the end of the road a chair-lift ascends to the summit. From June to September you can ski down, and from October to March you can career down the heart-stopping **Coronet Cresta Run**, a winding, 600-metre (0.4-mile) stainless-steel toboggan track. (You can also come down on the lift.)

Three high-country sheep stations across Lake Wakatipu from Queenstown welcome visitors to see sheep-shearing and observe sheep dogs in action. The **Walter Peak** tour includes a launch trip across the lake, demonstrations of wool-spinning and handicrafts, a close-up look at highland cattle, sheep and dogs—and tea. **Cecil Peak** offers a high-speed launch trip to the station, which retains its original stone cottage, and features horse-riding in addition to sheep and dogs. Accommodation is available, and there are plans to develop the station into a large-scale resort with a hotel. **Mount Nicholas** is reached aboard the grand old *TSS Earnslaw,* which lays over at the station's pier while passengers enjoy the programme of dogs and sheep.

The **Cattledrome**, at Arthur's Point, seven kilometres (four miles) from Queenstown along the road to Coronet Peak and Arrowtown, offers yet another display of herding skills. Twice daily, at 9.30 am and 2.30 pm, a multilingual audio-visual show is followed by a live cattle show put on by the same people who organized the Agrodome in Rotorua (see page 77). Visitors can learn to hand-milk a cow. Various bus tours include this stop in trips to Arrowtown.

Arrowtown is a quiet, well-preserved town dating from the days when the Arrow River served up seemingly endless quantities of alluvial gold. Buckingham Street, with its charmingly restored miners' cottages, century-old sycamore trees, expensive boutiques and restaurants would probably astonish the grubby, rough-and-tumble prospectors of old. The excellent **Lakes District Centennial Museum** is well worth seeing. The old gaol, a few churches and the Chinese quarter still exist, but **Ah Lum's Store** is one of the very few Chinese buildings to have survived intact.

Otago Goldfields Park, administered by the Department of Conservation, preserves a cross-section of about 20 sites scattered through Central Otago representing the life and technology of gold-miners. Tours are organized and guides provided during the summer months. Information is available from the Department of Conservation's information office on Ballarat Street. Phone 933. **Goldfields Town Museum Park**, three kilometres (two miles) from Queenstown on the road to Frankton, recreates an old gold-mining village from genuine buildings, fixtures and furnishings —authentic right down to the smell.

A trip to **Skippers Canyon** is a thrilling excursion for gold-rush enthusi-asts with nerves of steel. Skippers held the most fabulous gold diggings of the whole Wakatipu region, producing almost one ounce of gold per square foot of riverbed, and thousands of prospectors risked their lives descending the steep cliffs by a precarious bridle track. The narrow modern road follows the same track around the steep gorge past abandoned claims and other relics. There are no barriers at the edge of the road and few passing places. Do not drive there, as it is quite scary enough to take a half-day coach tour with an experienced driver, who will go only if weather conditions allow.

Wanaka

The small resort town of Wanaka, on the southern shore of clear, blue Lake Wanaka, lies in a gentler landscape than that of Lake Wakatipu. This resort is more sedate than Queenstown and devoted mainly to outdoor recreation — hiking and water sports in summer and skiing in winter at the Cardrona Skifields.

Getting There

There are two roads between Wanaka and Queenstown. Highway 6 goes by Cromwell and the Clutha Valley, a distance of just over 100 kilometres (62 miles), and then continues beyond Wanaka over the Haast Pass to the west coast. Highway 89 leaves Highway 6 at Arrow Junction, 18 kilometres (11 miles) east of Queenstown, and runs for 53 kilometres (33 miles) over the Crown Range, passing the ghost town of Cardrona and the famous skifields of the same name, to Wanaka. It is a steep, rough, marvellously scenic gravel road, but it is not recommended in bad weather.

Sights

Wanaka is the headquarters of **Mount Aspiring National Park**, named for its highest peak (3,035 metres, or 9,957 feet). The park visitor centre at the corner of Ballantyne and Main (Ardmore) streets has interesting displays and information about walks and drives. Boats can be hired at the waterfront. **Glendhu Bay**, on Lake Wanaka's south shore, is one of its most scenic points, looking across the water to snowcapped mountains. The **Maze and Puzzle Centre**, two kilometres (a mile) southeast of town towards Wanaka Junction, is an unabashed tourist trap but contains a fascinating three-dimensional maze of over-and-under wooden passages and bridges to challenge the wits of old and young alike.

Cromwell, at the confluence of the Clutha and Kawarau rivers, is a brand-new town built on high ground to replace the historic gold-mining town doomed to disappear (if it has not already) under the waters of Lake Dunstan as they back up behind the new Clyde Dam. The **Clutha Valley Development Information Centre**, on the Mall, displays models and has an audio-visual show about the Clutha Valley hydro-electric power project. The **Cromwell Borough Museum** shows the interesting past that is lost.

Focus

En route to **Mount Cook National Park** on the road from Twizel, watch for birds along the shore of Lake Pukaki. Besides many waterfowl you may see wrybill, pied stilt, white-faced heron and spur-winged plover. The dry, braided riverbed of the Godley River, which flows down to the lake, is a nesting place for banded dotterel and a known habitat of the black stilt, the rarest wader in the world. You may see chukors in rocky gullies up mountain slopes. Keep an eye out for falcons. Inside the park, keas sometimes come close enough to the hotel to do mischief. At night, listen for the call of the morepork and the little owl. Rangers at the park headquarters can be helpful with seasonal information on birds.

From **Queenstown**, the best bird-watching is at the head of Lake Wakatipu. Follow Glenorchy Road along the north shore of the lake to the broad shingle riverbeds where black-billed gull, black-fronted tern, banded dotterel, pied stilt and oystercatcher nest. Paradise shelduck, spur-winged plover and Canada geese are also common here. The road forks and continues for a few kilometres up the valleys of the Rees and Dart rivers to beech

The Curious Kiwi

Everybody knows the comical kiwi. You see it on tins of shoe polish and crates of Chinese gooseberries, now known as kiwi fruit, all over the world. It appears with increasing frequency as a symbol for New Zealand itself—modest, humorous and one of a kind—and New Zealanders proudly call themselves Kiwis.

Yet few have seen a live kiwi in the wild. For one thing, kiwis are nocturnal and, for another, they are quite rare. But in New Zealand there exist a number of kiwi houses, where day and night are reversed, allowing you to watch these strange birds by artificial moonlight as they stalk through the underbrush.

Unlike most birds, kiwis have weak eyes but a strong sense of smell. With nostrils at the tip of their long beak and sensitive cat-like whiskers at its base, they poke around purposefully in the dark for grubs, worms and berries. The female, bigger and stronger than the male, lays one enormous egg, up to 25 percent of her body weight. (An X-ray of a female about to lay is an astonishing sight.) In a hidden burrow, the male sits on the egg for ten weeks or more, sleeping away the time. The chick emerges fully feathered and with its eyes open, ready to leave the nest in a few days and start hunting with its parents.

When the first kiwi skin was brought to Europe in 1813, the scientific community flatly refused to believe that a wingless, tail-less bird could exist. When further proof trickled back, some scientists assigned the kiwi to the penguin family, others to the extinct dodo. It took 20 more years before a missionary with a scientific bent sent an accurate, eyewitness description of this 'most remarkable and curious bird' and correctly tied its hair-like feathers to those of the emu.

Today, scientists know that the kiwi is the last-surviving member of a family of flightless birds unique to New Zealand, cousins to the cassowary, emu, rhea and ostrich on other continents. The kiwi's ancient forebear, the moa, lost its ability to fly 80 million years ago yet was so well adapted to New Zealand that it existed until as recently as about 200 years ago. One species of moa stood 3.6 metres (12 feet) tall, making it the largest bird ever recorded. These ponderous giants grazing on the grasslands were easy prey for human hunters when Polynesians discovered New Zealand in around 900, and they were hunted to extinction.

Kiwis, however, were deemed sacred, called by the Maori the hidden children of Tane, the god of the forest. Only chiefs were allowed to eat or sacrifice them, and their tough, leathery skins, covered with warm, waterproof feathers, were treasured for chiefs' cloaks. It was the coming of Europeans that seriously endangered the survival of the kiwis. Their habitat was destroyed to create farmland, and they were slaughtered by the thousands to feed miners and bushmen, and by the tens of thousands to provide feather trimmings for ladies' hats. Today all kiwis are protected, but one of the three species, the little spotted kiwi, is still in danger of extinction, firmly established only on Kapiti Island.

forests full of bush birds. Here you may see the rare yellowheads. In Queenstown, you will almost certainly see a flock of black New Zealand scaup diving for food around the wharf.

Mount Cook National Park is not only for mountaineers. Some beautiful walks along fairly flat valleys give fine views of the glaciers and mountains. Brochures on all walks can be found at the visitor centre. **Kea Point** is an impressive walk to a spur of lateral moraine overlooking Mueller Glacier, with the ice face of Mount Sefton looming above. The path starts at the Hermitage and passes through two kinds of vegetation typical in the park—the tussock and scrub of the river flats and dense subalpine shrubbery higher up. Three peaks of Mount Cook can be seen above the rubble-strewn Mueller Glacier. Allow three hours return.

The **Hooker Valley** walk, which branches off the Kea Point track, is a glorious hike. The trail crosses the valley floor and after one hour reaches a swing bridge over the Hooker River, which it then follows upstream. After half an hour it recrosses the river by another swing bridge. Mount Cook, in all its splendour, comes into view around a spur of Mount Wakefield, and a shelter is reached amid alpine meadows. One hour beyond the upper swing bridge the trail ends at a small lake at the terminal face of Hooker Glacier. Allow a whole day for the round trip.

At **Queenstown**, there are many walks around Lake Wakatipu, but the leisurely 4.5-kilometre (2.8-mile) climb up **Queenstown Hill** provides the best panoramic view from its 902-metre (2,959-foot) summit. The walk starts and ends at Kent Street, 500 metres (0.3 miles) from the centre of town. Much of the trail is lined by pine, larch, sycamore and mountain ash. Higher up, in an area of burnt manuka, a plaque bears the hill's Maori name—Te Tapunui. There is a small alpine lake along the last stretch to the summit where wildflowers abound in the spring. Rocky outcroppings make splendid seats for admiring the ever-widening view. (Much of the track is on rock, so wear sturdy shoes.) Allow two and a half hours for the round trip.

The **Frankton Arm Walkway** is a flat, pleasant lakeside track between Queenstown and Frankton, which is across the water from Kelvin Heights. Take the walk from either end, starting at Peninsula Street in Queenstown or Frankton Beach, and return by bus. Allow one and a half hours.

The Southern Lakes District is deservedly famous for superb fishing against a backdrop of glorious mountain scenery. Rainbow trout, brown trout and landlocked quinnat salmon abound in its high lakes and rivers.

Unusual **Lake Wakatipu** has a depth over much of its area of around 377 metres (1,237 feet), is always cold and is subject to *seiches*, or rhythmic pulses that gently raise and lower the water level every 4.5 minutes, as

though the lake were breathing. The best fishing for both brown and rainbow trout is from a boat at the northern end of the lake, near the mouths of the Rees and Dart rivers. Boats and guides are readily available in **Queenstown**, which has all of the amenities for fishermen. The district around Wakatipu encompasses eight lakes and ten rivers or streams, all within easy reach by car or boat from Queenstown. Consult the sports shops for up-to-date information on the best spots. Fishing expeditions to remote valleys by helicopter can be arranged at the Queenstown Airport.

Lake Wanaka, to the northeast, is an even more popular fishing centre. It has good numbers of brown and rainbow trout, but a decreasing population of landlocked salmon. The best fishing is at **Glendhu Bay**, on the south shore, a lovely spot shaded by forests and with a fine view of the Southern Alps. You need waders if you are casting from the bank. Excellent fishing is also to be had on the **Upper Clutha River**, from its lake exit just north of Wanaka as far as Luggate. A very good free guide to the river is put out by the Department of Conservation in Wanaka, giving maps and details of some 20 exceptional fishing spots. The town of **Wanaka** is much quieter than Queenstown but well set up for fisherfolk. Boats are available for hire, and most people think it is advisable to take a guide around this lake.

Lake Hawea, across a neck of land from Lake Wanaka, is so deep that, though its surface is at an altitude of 345 metres (1,133 feet), its bottom lies 65 metres (213 feet) *below* sea level. It is rich in rainbow trout and salmon. The abrupt shoreline of the lake dates from 1958, when its level was raised 20 metres (65 feet) as part of an irrigation scheme. As there are no beaches and gentle banks, fishing is all from boats. The New Zealand Visitor Information Centre in the small town of Hawea, south of the lake, can help to arrange boat rentals.

The Southern Lakes fishing season is from 1 October to 31 May. The limit is six per day, of which no more than four can be salmon.

The Kelvin Heights Golf Course, on a small peninsula surround by the clear waters of Lake Wakatipu, is considered the top scenic course of New Zealand and a must on any golfing holiday. The short, demanding course undulates across the lake's Frankton Arm, east of Government Gardens in Queenstown, and can be reached by road or by jet-boat water taxi (for the latter, phone 647). Par 71. Phone 29–169.

Other towns in the region also have very good (though scenically less spectacular) 18-hole courses, which make a nice circuit from Queenstown. They are all beautiful, flattish and very pleasant to play. Visitors are warmly welcomed, and no reservations are needed. **Wanaka** is considered the most interesting course. **Alexandra**, in a less scenic area, is a well-maintained, green oasis, but you find yourself among dry stones and boulders if you stray from the fairways. **Roxburgh** has a lovely, nearly flat course with huge rocks that make for entertaining play. **Arrowtown**, only 20 kilometres (12 miles) north of Queenstown, also has a good 18-hole course.

Central Otago, centred around Queenstown, is the newest wine district to evolve in New Zealand and the southernmost in the world. In 1973, Montana's first vineyard in Marlborough was ridiculed by the wine establishment, as wine production in the South Island was considered impossible. As everyone now concedes, it is a howling success. Still further south, against all conventional wisdom Canterbury got into the wine business in the early 1980s. It, too, has surpassed all expectations. And now comes Otago, which, it turns out, has excellent soils and receives nearly as much sunshine annually as Marlborough.

The first wines make clear that the cool climate here can produce good— possibly great—wines with vines from Alsace and Germany. Otago grapes show a strong regional character and an intensity that is rare elsewhere. The industry is now out of the kitchen and close to commercial production, with new vineyards appearing. This is an exciting time to visit the informed, friendly pioneers who are making it happen.

Taramea Winery, on Speargrass Flat Road, near Arrowtown, is the brainchild of Anne Sly, a trained horticulturist, who experimented with 11 varieties of vine in 1976 before settling on northern European types. She hopes to start an Otago grape-growers' association and, with Alan Brady, is the nucleus of the new Otago wine industry. Contact her for information about the local industry.

Gibbston Vineyard, between Arrowtown and Cromwell on Highway 6, was planted in 1981 by Alan Brady, a former TV producer, and his wife, Denise. Four years later they received very strong encouragement from the Te Kauwhata Viticultural Research Station for the quality of their first vintage. They hope in time to open a wine-bar and restaurant. Phone 21–566. Another wine-grower, Rob Hay, has a ten-hectare (25-acre) vineyard that abuts Alan and Denise Brady's.

Rippon Vineyard, two kilometres (a mile) from Wanaka, is owned by Rolfe Mills. This may be the first Otago vineyard to reach full commercial production, targeted for 1989. Phone 8084.

Close to Queenstown, at Arthur's Point, on the road to Arrowtown, Andy Stevens has started a terraced vineyard on rocky land that required blasting with dynamite. It is still, by necessity, a part-time occupation, but he can be found in Queenstown c/o Shotover Jets. In Earnscleugh, five kilometres (three miles) west of Alexandra, Sue Edwards and Verdon Burgess have planted a vineyard, and there may be others by now.

Gold Rush

If you think New Zealanders are an unexcitable, well-regulated people by nature, take a look at their history. The glint of gold brought as much turmoil, craziness and change to the South Island of the 1860s as ever it did to California or Australia.

When the Californian and Australian gold rushes were in full swing, New Zealand was a dull backwater; many settlers pulled up stakes to seek wealth in the foreign goldfields. Among them was Charlie Ring, who left his sawmill up north near Coromandel to try his luck in California. When he got home again in 1852, a committee in Auckland was offering 500 pounds to anyone who could find a 'payable' goldfield in New Zealand. Within two days Charlie raced to Auckland with gold-bearing quartz from Coromandel to claim the prize. Unfortunately his find was not 'payable', requiring expensive machinery to extract the gold, but it was New Zealand's first recorded strike, and it set off an epidemic of gold fever.

Provincial governments in the South Island offered rewards for local finds, and prospectors fanned out. There was a short-lived rush to Golden Bay near Nelson. Then, in 1861, Gabriel Read, a miner from Tasmania, found gold in a gully in Otago, the wild hinterland of Dunedin. Read had experienced the brawling goldfields of California and Victoria and loathed the violence he had seen there. Hoping to set things on a better course in Otago, he generously made his discovery public, collected his prize money and set out to uphold decency and maintain law and order among the 11,000 prospectors who swarmed to 'Gabriel's Gully' by personally settling disputes, defending miners' rights and even paying to bring out a preacher.

Nobody else was so public-spirited. After Gabriel's Gully was mined out in 1862, two close-mouthed prospectors appeared in Dunedin with bags containing 1,392 ounces of gold. Bribery and sharp guesswork traced the new strike to Lake Wakatipu. A secretive loner named Fox was ferreted out on the Arrow River. Soon the mighty Clutha River and many of its tributaries were giving up hidden hoards, and 80 new goldfields mushroomed. Queenstown, Arrowtown, Cromwell and a host of smaller towns sprang into being. In two years the population of Otago increased fivefold.

The canny Scots of Dunedin harvested a fortune from the newfound business for their port, breweries and banks. They built a splendid stone city, the biggest and richest in New Zealand. But by 1865 Otago was fading. When news came of gold in remote Westland, half the miners in Otago swarmed over the Southern Alps at Arthur's Pass. Thousands more came by sea from Australia, helping to swell Westland's population from 800 to 30,000. The English and Scots deplored the Irish pouring in. The brawling, drinking miners despised and harassed the Chinese, whose vices were gambling and opium. Greymouth and Hokitika sprouted banks, shops, hotels—even an opera house. But the gold soon waned, and the rush turned north to Thames, on the Coromandel Peninsula, where gold fever had struck.

In a mere decade the gold rush was over. The European population of New Zealand had doubled, but the flow of gold, which had accounted for 70 percent of all exports in 1863, fell to a trickle. Wool now remained the only source of wealth. In 1882 an unexpected discovery saved New Zealand from depression and emigration—refrigeration! As soon as meat and butter could be shipped around the world safely, New Zealand came into its own, with a new source of prosperity that would last for a hundred years.

The West

The west coast is a long, narrow strip of lush, wild land between the forbidding ramparts of the Southern Alps and the rocky shoreline of the Tasman Sea. It follows the great geological rupture called the Alpine Fault, which runs along the base of the whole mountain range. Magnificent rain forests laced with waterfalls cover the lower slopes of the mountains and part of the narrow plain. The heavy rainfall on this side of the Alps produces a very different landscape from the tussock grass and toi-toi on the rain-shadow side of the divide. Natural beauty is protected in five national parks along the coast, starting with new Paparoa National Park in the north and ending with Fiordland, which takes in the whole southwestern corner of the South Island.

Highway 6 runs nearly the whole length of the coast through a landscape of rivers, marginal farmland, lakes, forest and glaciers. Small towns have an ephemeral look, perched precariously on an ancient, uncaring landscape. Life here is hard, and the people are few, but they are wonderfully warm and friendly. As a visitor you feel that you have somehow travelled back in time to another age and an uncontaminated world of staggering beauty.

Before the Europeans came, Maori tribes lived in small fishing communities on the west coast. Other tribes knew their way across the mountain passes to get precious greenstone, the fine jade found in riverbeds here, which could be shaped and sharpened to a keen, long-lasting edge, taking the place of metal in the Maori culture. Beautifully shaped fighting clubs and ornaments of all sorts were fashioned from greenstone. More valuable than gold, it was traded across the sea with tribes on the North Island.

The first Europeans on the west coast were whalers and sealers, who arrived soon after Captain Cook told about the rich southern land. They set up stations on the coast and slaughtered the seals nearly to extinction for fur and oil, but they did not stay to put down roots. When ill-prepared colonists came from England to hilly Nelson in 1843, hoping for flat farmland, they quickly investigated Maori rumours of plains to the south. Expeditions with Maori guides followed the Buller River and explored the west coast, but their findings were utterly discouraging. Almost casually the government bought the west coast from Maori tribes in 1860 for 300 pounds, but only one enticement succeeded in drawing Europeans here—gold.

Discoveries of the precious yellow metal grew apace four years later, and a stampede took off across the mountains and over the sea. The town of Greymouth sprang up around a Maori settlement at the mouth of the Grey River. New gold strikes further south brought Hokitika into being almost overnight, and it rapidly grew into the biggest, busiest port on the coast. Ships suffered wrecks with appalling frequency, but the brawling, boozing prospectors kept coming. New towns mushroomed, and in three years the population had grown to 40,000—12 percent of New Zealand's total at the time.

The gold rush ended when the easy gold was gone and new strikes were made in the North Island. The west coast kept producing gold until 1895, but the population declined. Today it has only 30,000 people—one percent of New Zealand's total. Nowadays, coal and timber are the mainstays of its economy.

Getting There

A rented car is by far the best way to see the west coast, because there are so many temptations to stop and explore. Air New Zealand flies to Westport or Hokitika from Christchurch or Wellington. The TranzAlpine Express, a luxury train with panoramic windows, makes the spectacular coast-to-coast journey between Christchurch and Greymouth daily. Newmans Coachlines runs to the west coast from Nelson, Intercity (NZRR) Services runs from Christchurch and Queenstown, and local coach services operate up and down the coast.

Three passes bring roads across the Southern Alps. The **Lewis Pass**, the most northerly, is the lowest and easiest. Highway 7, usually called the Lewis Pass Road, links Christchurch and the Canterbury Plain to Greymouth, with a second road breaking north to Westport from Reefton. Towns are few and far between. The road runs near delightful Hanmer Springs (see page 156) on the eastern side of the divide. There are picnic places and walks of varied lengths at the pass, but the scenery here is rather less spectacular than at the other two passes. On the western side of the pass, the road runs high above the Maruia River and soon comes to Maruia Springs, where a lone hotel provides a restaurant, a bar and hot mineral pools.

Arthur's Pass, straddling the middle of the Southern Alps, is the highest (922 metres, or 3,024 feet) but shortest route from Christchurch to Greymouth or Hokitika. The pass is named after Arthur Dudley Dobson, a surveyor and explorer who found the pass in 1864 and chose it as the best route for road and rail from the east coast to the west. He was knighted for his pioneering work—but not until 1931, when he was 90. Highway 73 climbs past lakes and tussock land to the spectacular mountain scenery of Arthur's Pass National Park. A very good New Zealand Visitor Information Centre at Arthur's Pass township displays one of the original stage coaches that regularly made the journey and shows an entertaining audio-visual pro-gramme on the building of the road and railway. On the western side of the pass, the road drops steeply by hairpin turns through the Otira River Gorge for several kilometres, while the train goes through an 8.6-kilometre (5.3-mile) -long tunnel that took 15 years to drill.

The **Haast Pass**, the most southerly, is in Mount Aspiring National Park. A gold prospector named Cameron was the first to cross it, while racing to the goldfields in 1863, but it was the Austrian geologist–explorer Julius von Haast who paused here long enough to name it after himself. The pass is now

What's In A Name?

I t is the last hour in the afternoon and the flowers and tears and brandy of the morning are long since left behind. I've completely forgotten all that. I've mislaid who I am. Sensuously and accurately I vibrate and respond to the multifold touch of my Little Ones, and to the Big Ones who invade at this hour. I am made of their thoughts and their feelings. I am composed of sixty-odd different pieces of personality. I don't know what I have been saying or what I will say next, and little of what I am saying at the time. It is a potent drunkenness, an exhilaration, and it is one that does not leave depression in its wake. Indeed it is not unlike, in its effect, the intoxication of Beethoven for three hours the night before.

"Miss Vorontosov," says Whareparita, a senior from the upper school, a calm, brown and beautiful girl, "Mr Reardon he sent me over to help you."

That's what I like about Whareparita; she can say the name my father left me. And that's whăt I like about the Head; he sends someone to help me and he chooses someone who can say this name.

"Miss Vottot!" cries little brown Ara, "Seven he's got a knife! He's cutteen my stomat!"

"Whareparita, disarm Seven."

That's another thing I like about a big girl to help me. They can take orders and smart ones.

"Miss Vontofoff," claims Waiwini, six and brown and girl, "I'm going to write a letter to Mr Reardon when I go to Health Camp."

I kneel to her level; it's the least of the courtesies. "I thought you would write to me, Waiwini."

"Your name's too long."

"Miss Voffa," inquires Twinnie, "how do you spell 'boko'?"
"What are you writing?"
" 'My twin she dong me on the boko'."
"What is a 'boko', Whareparita? Tame, use your handkerchief. Irini,
have you brought your fourpence for your pencil?"
Irini is half Chinese and very five. "My muvver she haven got
fourpen."
And this is the home where eighty-four pounds went down in drink
one night last week; the child allowance for a family of ten and all the
wool bonus for mothers.
"Miss Vorontosov," complains brown Matawhero, "I'm sicka
writing." A little Maori boy of six can say my name. I kneel to his level.
"Well write, 'I'm sick of writing.' "
"Miss Foffof," points out brown Wiki, all eyes and smiles and curls,
"you sayed I could play the piano when I camed in."
"That's right. Tuck in your shirt, Matawhero. Handkerchief, Blos-
som."
"Can I play it now?"
"Have you finished your reading, little Wiki?" I kneel again.
"No, that's why I hates readeen."
"Well, finish it, then you can play the piano. Really, Whareparita," I
say, standing again, "the things these children say I have said! The
things they say I have said!"
"You do say a lot of them, Miss Vorontosov."

Sylvia Ashton-Warner, Spinster, *1960*

crossed by Highway 6, this stretch of which opened in 1965. The road is paved part of the way through the pass and has a good gravel surface for the remainder. There are several one-way bridges. It is a beautiful route, with views of lakes, waterfalls, forests and snowcapped mountains, and numerous places to pull off the road for a picnic or a walk. There are no towns in the 146 kilometres (91 miles) between Wanaka and the tiny coastal village of Haast (population 200). The first accommodation is at Haast Junction.

A fourth way to reach the west coast by road is to take Highway 6 south from Nelson to Murchison, then follow the wonderfully fishable Buller River (see *Focus,* page 142) through Inangahua Junction on to Westport (226 kilometres or 140 miles).

Sights

There are three biggish towns on the west coast, all at the northern end. Further south, Highway 6 runs through sparsely populated districts and villages to the splendid Westland National Park.

Westport stands at the foot of the steep, coal-bearing Paparoa Mountains. where the mouth of the big Buller River forms a natural port. Out of it go timber (New Zealand's number one export), coal from the mountains and cement from the huge works nearby. When the gold petered out, coal was found to be the true wealth of Westport, and today the best sight in town is **Coaltown Museum**, which is housed in an 1890s-era brewery at the end of Queen Street South. The museum tells a tale of pioneering spirit and techni-cal ingenuity with relics, audio-visual shows and a realistic, walk-through coal mine. Open daily 9 am–4.30 pm. **Carters Beach**, five kilometres (three miles) west of the city, provides good surfing and safe swimming in summer. **Cape Foulwind**, 33 kilometres (20 miles) to the west and named by Captain Cook during a storm, is a high granite promontory with a lighthouse. **Tauranga Bay**, ten kilometres (six miles) by road further around the south side of the headland, has a lively seal colony on its offshore rocks. It can also be reached by an easy four-kilometre (2.5-mile), one-hour walk along the cliff tops from Cape Foulwind, with fine views on the way.

The road north from Westport ends after about 100 kilometres (60 miles) at the mouth of the Kohaihai River, just beyond **Karamea**. This little dairying centre, with a uniquely mild climate for the region, is backed by rugged, forested mountain ranges encompassing the whole northwest corner of the South Island—a wilderness that can be crossed only by a five-day tramp on the Heaphy Track.

Punakaiki, 56 kilometres (35 miles) south of Westport on the road to Greymouth, is the headquarters of Paparoa National Park, a good stop for bird-watchers and walkers (see *Focus* sections, pages 190–4). The sight not to be missed here is the **Pancake Rocks**, 30-million-year-old cliffs of thin limestone layers like immense stacks of pancakes, with mighty blowholes that boom in rough weather. The ten-minute **Dolomite Point Walk** leads from the highway through an enchanting tree-fern forest to the top of the cliffs.

Greymouth is the largest town on the west coast, a bustling commercial centre and important port without a great deal of charm. The Grey River, well known to fishermen, carves a cleft in the mountains (the Gap) which sometimes funnels into the city a cutting wind, appropriately called 'the barber'. Good views of the area can be seen near the Gap along a trail from Mount Street, near the railway station, up the hill through tree-filled **King Domain**. A major west coast attraction near Greymouth is **Shantytown**, a meticulously reconstructed gold-mining town of the 1880s, complete with gold-buying office, bank, church, hospital and gaol. A few of the buildings are original. A steam locomotive puffs into the bush taking visitors to the Chinese gold works, and an original Cobb & Co stage coach harnesses up for rides in summer. Shantytown is well signposted from Paroa, eight kilometres (five miles) south of Greymouth on Highway 6. Open daily.

Hokitika, which sprang to life with the gold rush, was known as the 'Capital of the Goldfields'. In its heyday it boasted grand hotels and an opera house. Prospectors poured in from Australia, and scavengers grew rich from the many shipwrecks dotting the beaches around this treacherous port. Hokitika has kept some of its old character, although the hotels are now B & Bs and prosperity comes from timber, not gold. The **West Coast Historical Museum**, on lower Tancred Street, shows all manner of gold-mining equipment, but those interested in the human side of the gold rush should go for the excellent 20-minute audio-visual show on Hokitika's early days. The **Greenstone Factory**, on Tancred Street, demonstrates how raw rocks of hard nephrite jade are converted into finely crafted, polished jewellery of Maori design. It is open daily, but workmen are there only on weekdays. A second greenstone factory is located two kilometres (a mile) east of town on Blue Spur Road, at the Vintage Farm Museum. At **Plane Table Lookout**, one kilometre (half a mile) north of town on the airport road, a panoramic view of the Southern Alps is augmented by a pointer and map identifying over 50 peaks.

The little town of **Ross**, 31 kilometres (19 miles) from Hokitika on the main road south to the glaciers, sits amid what were the richest alluvial goldfields and was able to keep going long after other boom towns had become ghost towns. The **Ross Historic Goldfields Visitor Centre**, in a restored miner's cottage, provides some colourful history. The biggest nugget ever discovered in New Zealand was found near Ross and bought by a tavern keeper for 400 pounds—100 pounds more than the purchase price of the whole west coast a few years earlier. The nugget was christened the 'Honourable Roddy', after the minister of mines, and eventually was presented to King George V, who had it fashioned into tableware for Buckingham Palace.

Ross is best in spring, when cherry blossoms line the main street and huge rhododendrons are out. An easy walk from the visitor centre leads to an old cemetery in which the dangerous life led (and lost) by west coast gold-miners is recorded on the gravestones.

Okarito is 96 kilometres (60 miles) south of Ross, 13 kilometres (eight miles) towards the sea from the Highway 6 town called The Forks. Okarito is simply a group of 'baches'—or tin summer cottages—but bird-watchers will probably see white herons on the tidal reaches of Okarito Lagoon (see *Focus*, page 190).

Westland National Park centres around Franz Josef and Fox glaciers, which are separated by 25 kilometres (15 miles) and surrounded by some of the most majestic scenery in the Southern Alps. The glaciers, together covering over 4,000 hectares (10,000 acres), are unusually big for such a low altitude, due to the heavy snowfalls dumped by prevailing westerly winds on the west face of the mountains. The weight of the snow presses the deeper layers into pure blue ice, which slowly creeps down the valleys. The terminal, covered with rock and rubble, steadily melts and runs off mixed with rock 'flour', which has been finely ground by the moving ice, in a stream that looks like dirty milk. Through history the glaciers have advanced and receded many times. During the past century the retreat has been very fast, interrupted by three or four short surges forward. Contradictory theories predict retreat and advance as the global climate warms due to the greenhouse effect.

The villages of Franz Josef Glacier and Fox Glacier (known locally as simply Franz and Fox) have food and lodging but tend to be badly over-crowded in summer, so book accommodation well in advance. Both villages have big, well-managed New Zealand Visitor Information Centres offering displays, information, maps of walks (see *Focus*, page 189) and advice. Both villages have small airstrips, and the visitor centres help to make arrange-ments for expensive but spectacular flights up the glaciers. A popular activity is 'heli-hiking', in which a helicopter lands passengers high on the glacier with equipment and a guide for a hike among dazzling pinnacles, blue-green ice caves and crevasses. (Take good sunglasses.) Flightseeing excursions of varying duration and price are available around the glaciers, Mount Cook and other mountain peaks. Several companies operate tiny planes from both centres, but the changeable weather makes cancellation a constant threat. Early morning and late afternoon *tend* to be clear (photographers take note), with clouds coming down in the middle of the day. March and April are *usually* the sunniest months.

Franz Josef Glacier is the more up-scale of the two villages, with a THC Hotel and pretty little St James Anglican Church, whose altar window once framed a perfect view of the glacier before it retreated out of sight. Franz Josef Glacier, named by Julius von Haast for the Austrian emperor in 1865, is 12 kilometres (7.5 miles) long, steeper and slightly shorter than Fox Glacier.

To reach it from the visitor centre, go about half a kilometre (0.3 miles) south on Highway 6 and turn left on Glacier Access Road immediately after the bridge (total distance six kilometres, or four miles). Signposts along the lovely, forested valley record the glacier's retreat and point to various short walks. The ten-minute walk to Sentinel Rock, four kilometres (2.5 miles) along the road, gives a magnificent view up the Waiho Valley to the glacier. From the carpark at the end of the road, a trail leads across the gravelly riverbed and several streams to the glacier's rubble-strewn face. Be sure to take a jacket and plenty of insect repellent. Allow at least an hour for the walk.

Fox Glacier is a bit more accessible. From the village, take Highway 6 south for about two kilometres (a mile) and turn left on Glacier Access Road, just before the bridge. The road follows the Fox River for about five kilometres (three miles) to a gravelly carpark. An easy, 20-minute walk across the riverbed leads to the grey terminal ice. Keep to the track and do not try to climb on the ice. Keas — cheeky grey-green mountain parrots—often frequent the carpark. They like to steal food and can be quite destructive to windshield wipers.

Focus

Paparoa National Park, opened only in 1988 with its headquarters at Punakaiki, includes much of the coast and mountain area between Westport and Greymouth. The birds in this park are typical of those found all down the west coast. Near the shore are yellow-breasted tit, tui, pigeon, bellbird, silvereye, grey warbler and others. Further inland are kaka, brown creeper, rifleman and yellow-crowned parakeet. You might see blue duck along mountain streams. Near **Barrytown**, about 15 kilometres (nine miles) south of Punakaiki, the rare Westland black petrel breeds in winter along the forest-covered cliffs of the Paparoa Mountains. The birds can sometimes be seen in flight along rivers and creeks at dusk in winter.

Okarito, about 115 kilometres (71 miles) south of Hokitika, or 60 kilometres (37 miles) north of Franz Josef, is the site of New Zealand's only white heron sanctuary. Permission from the Department of Conservation in Hokitika or the New Zealand Visitor Information Centre in Franz Josef is needed to visit it, which you must do in the company of a ranger. White herons can usually be seen outside the sanctuary by following the Okarito walkway to Three Mile Lagoon, a walk of about one and a half hours. (Watch out for quicksand if you go beyond the lagoon.)

The **Haast Pass** road over the Southern Alps provides a good opportunity to see bush birds of all sorts if you stop at Thunder Creek Falls or Fantail Creek Falls or take the 20-minute Makarora Bush Walk. The **Arthur's Pass** road passes right beside Lake Pearson and Lake Grasmere on the Canterbury side, where you are very likely to see crested grebes.

Some 32 kilometres (20 miles) northeast of **Westport** is **Ngakawu**, the starting point of the unforgettable **Charming Creek Walkway**, which follows the route of an old bush railway built during the early coal-mining days. The walk begins a short distance upstream from the Ngakawau Bins, where a carpark is provided. The path threads through a dramatic gorge with giant river boulders to Mangatini Waterfall, one hour along. (An S-shaped tunnel in the gorge area shows where construction crews, working from both ends, almost failed to meet.) The path continues over a suspension bridge above the falls, then through another tunnel to one of New Zealand's famous beauty spots, finally emerging on the road to Seddonville (three hours). Try to arrange in advance to be picked up here.

The area around **Punakaiki**, 57 kilometres (35 miles) south of Westport, combines limestone, sea and forest in several irresistible walks. Maps, brochures and information are available at the Paparoa National Park Headquarters in Punakaiki. The **Truman Track**, signposted on the main highway 2.8 kilometres (1.7 miles) north of the New Zealand Visitor Information Centre in Punakaiki, is one of the most beautiful 15-minute walks anywhere. An impressive forest with some giant trees leads to a magical section of the coast with blowholes, reefs and pools. At low tide you can continue the walk north past reefs, caves and waterfalls as far as Perpendicular Point.

Westland National Park is best known for its **glacier walks**. The park headquarters at both Franz Josef Glacier and Fox Glacier offer guided walks on the ice with experienced glacier guides at fairly reasonable cost. (It is dangerous to walk on the glaciers without a guide.) Walks leave daily at 9.30 am and 2 pm. Boots, socks, poles and transportation to the glacier are included in the price. Half-day or full-day 'heli-hikes' (see page 168) are also available, at considerable cost. Get the latest information from the park information centres in Franz and Fox.

At **Franz Josef Glacier** there are many well-marked walks around the valley. At **Fox Glacier**, the **Chalet Lookout Walk** starts from the carpark at the end of Glacier View Road and follows the old access track to the glacier that was used until the 1930s. A shelter (the Fox Chalet) stood just below the present lookout, which offers a panoramic view of the lower glacier and its terminal moraine. Since the 1930s, the glacier has receded more than a kilometre (half a mile), leaving the valley floor far below. Allow 75 minutes for this excursion. **Lake Matheson**, a glacial 'kettle' lake, is famous for its reflections of Mounts Cook and Tasman, beloved by photographers. Take Cook Flat Road left off Highway 6 just north of Fox, towards Gillespies Beach. Follow it for 5.5 kilometres (3.4 miles) to a well-marked turnoff to the lake. A very pleasant trail circles the lake through native bush, but you need good hiking shoes for the return section. The best time for photographers to catch a mirror-like reflection of the mountains is very early in the morning. Allow one and a half hours for the circular walk.

The rugged west coast offers excellent fishing in its smallish lakes and swift rivers, where sea-run brown trout predominate. In the **Greymouth** district, the extensive **Grey River** system has the best fishing waters. Nearby **Lake Brunner**, the biggest lake on the west coast, lies in a glaciated hollow among untouched forest about 40 kilometres (25 miles) southeast of Greymouth. Mitchells is a well-known, old-English-style fishing lodge on the lake. Phone (027) 80-163. South of the lake, a small road leads five kilometres (three miles) to the hamlet of Inchbonnie, on the Taramakau River. Rumour has it that a stretch of water in the middle of a dairy farm there is quite wonderful. (Remember to ask permission from the farmer.)

The **Hokitika River** system has recently been attracting a run of sea-run brown trout and salmon in February and March, which has not escaped the notice of fishermen. Perch is also found here, which is good to eat but scorned locally as a poor sporting fish. The upper reaches have rainbow trout.

Harihari, 79 kilometres (49 miles) south of Hokitika, is well known for the fishing in its many glacier-fed streams. Keep to the clear streams, avoiding those with milky glacier-water.

Whataroa, 35 kilometres (22 miles) south of Harihari, is a fishing centre where some very large fish are sometimes caught. A local guide service is available. Phone Whataroa 285. **Lake Wahapo**, ten kilometres (six miles) further south, lies beside the main road. Brown trout offer good sport, and salmon are increasingly common.

Near **Haast**, two seaside lakes with views of snowcapped mountains are well supplied with sea-run brown trout averaging 2.25 kilograms (five pounds) and recently established salmon. Access to the sea makes the lakes a good source of whitebait, too. **Lake Moeraki** lies beside the main road 32 kilometres (20 miles) north of Haast. Its fishing lodge rents boats, rods and nets for whitebait, and it will cook your fish for dinner. **Lake Paringa**, on the sea side of the road 45 kilometres (28 miles) north of Haast, has a lakeside motel that doubles as a fishing lodge and has similar services. For a side trip, the little dead-end road south of Haast crosses several streams that are hardly fished at all. Hearsay has it that they are very good.

Regulations are kept to a minimum to encourage fishermen to come to the west coast. Most lakes and rivers are open all year round, but Lakes Moeraki and Paringa have a closed season for salmon. The 'mixed-bag' limit is seven fish per day, be they trout or salmon. However, Lake Brunner has the restriction of one rainbow trout per day.

The **Westport Golf Club** has an excellent, testing links course that makes for very enjoyable playing. It is south of the Buller River at Phone 8132.

Greymouth Golf Club Kaiata Links is on undulating terrain with a backdrop of fern-filled native forest. The course is pleasant and fun to play. Par 72. Phone 5332.

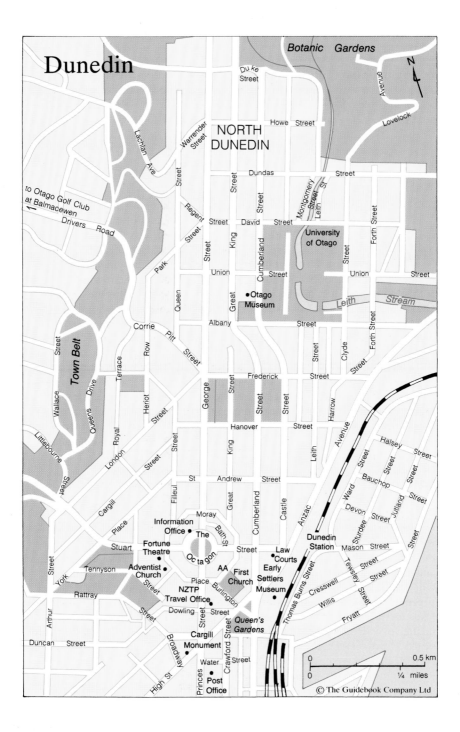

Hokitika Golf Club has a good links course ten kilometres (six miles) to the south. The narrow fairways behind windswept sandhills and beach make it a fine test of accuracy. Par 72. Phone 58–549.

 The only wine found on the rugged, rainy and windy west coast is in restaurants and hotels.

The South

 The South Island broadens out at its southern end into a comfortably rolling agricultural region dotted with tidy townships. In the days when horsepower was hoofed, it was the country's prime oat-growing area—the nose bag of New Zealand. In the age of machines it has turned to sheep and dairying. Sheep in Southland outnumber people 20 to 1. Dunedin, up the east coast, is the main southern urban centre, a solid, rock-ribbed Victorian city. It is the capital of Otago, a broad province that stretches across the island above Southland. The South's second city is Invercargill, in the centre of the south coast. Scottish place names abound throughout the region—Balclutha, Balfour, Clyde, Dumbarton, Earnscleugh, Forsyth.

Scottish settlers came to found a well-planned Presbyterian colony at Dunedin in 1848. Prosperity came with the gold rush of the 1860s, and a new population flooded in, diluting but not drowning its original character. As Dunedin boomed, the canny Scots turned the new wealth into a handsome city built of stone, with as many banks as churches. When the gold was gone, sheep took over. Dunedin set up New Zealand's first freezing works and found new prosperity sending frozen meat to England. Nowadays, Invercargill is the centre of the southern meat-packing industry.

South of Invercargill, across the Foveaux Strait, lies Stewart Island, New Zealand's third major island, which often gets overlooked. The fishing village of Oban occupies a tiny stretch of the island's 1,600-kilometre (1,000-mile) coastline, which otherwise remains virtually uninhabited, a delight for naturalists. A far bigger uninhabited wilderness is Fiordland, which occupies the whole southwestern corner of the South Island. New Zealand's largest and most remote national park is still partly unexplored. This magnificent, wild region of craggy mountains, dense rain forest and spectacular waterfalls is penetrated by far-reaching fiords on one side, and by long-fingered inland lakes on the other, a landscape carved by glaciers. Fiordland is a paradise for nature-lovers and hikers. Its only sizeable town is Te Anau, the starting point of the Milford Track, the famous four-day walk to Milford Sound, one of New Zealand's greatest sights. The spellbinding, 16-kilometre (ten-mile) - long 'sound' is really a fiord, plunging deep and blue between precipitous mountains and waterfalls.

Dunedin

The second-biggest metropolis of the South Island spreads in a horseshoe shape over the hills at the head of Otago Harbour. The site is dramatic, and the ornate stone buildings give the city an air of permanence. Dunedin's Scottish origins are visible in the street names and the statue of poet Robert Burns sitting right at the centre. (The name *Dunedin* is Celtic for Edinburgh.) The city boasts the country's first golf course, its last-remaining kilt-maker and its only whiskey distillery. In March, lads and lasses clad in the tartan dance the highland fling to the skirl of bagpipes in the Octagon Garden, as the city throws itself into its annual Scottish Festival.

Getting There

Air New Zealand flies to Dunedin from all big cities, and Mount Cook Airlines flies from Queenstown. However, the airport is located 29 kilometres (18 miles) south of the city at Momona, a 40-minute ride by Ritchies Coach Lines (phone 779–238) to the Southern Cross Hotel, at 118 High Street, or an expensive taxi ride into town. A pleasant way to travel from Christchurch or Invercargill is by railway. The Southerner, a comfortable train with a buffet car, goes once a day in each direction except Sundays, leaving both ends at about 8.45 am. The trip takes roughly six hours from Christchurch, four hours from Invercargill. Intercity (NZRR) Services, Newmans Coachlines, and H & H Travel Line connect Dunedin with the larger east-coast towns between Christchurch and Invercargill. Others run inland to Alexandra, Queenstown and points between. For those travelling by car, Highway 1, the main east-coast artery, runs right through Dunedin.

Information and Orientation

The city was planned by church members in Scotland before the first settlers arrived. At the centre is the **Octagon**, an eight-sided garden with the statue of Robert Burns and a musical fountain that is the centre of an evening light show from 9 to 10 o'clock. The Octagon also has some important buildings. An outer octagonal road, Moray Place, rings it a block away. A main street bisects the Octagon—called George Street on the north side and Princes Street on the south. Stuart Street forms the east–west axis of a cross. The **New Zealand Visitor Information Centre** is at 48 the Octagon, and the **NZTP Travel Office** is two blocks south on Princes Street. Dunedin is a good city to walk around (see *Focus*, page 210), taking in several sights.

Sights

The **railway station**, on Anzac Avenue at the east end of Stuart Street, is an astonishing bit of architecture completed in 1906. The outside, faced with bluestone, sports a clock tower and copper dome. Inside, this temple to New Zealand Railways has intricate mosaics celebrating railway themes, stained-

glass windows featuring steam locomotives, porcelain cherubs and a ticket office enshrined in scrolls. Don't miss it! The **Early Settlers Museum**, nearby at 220 Cumberland Street, is a treasure house of fascinating objects, from whalebone corsets and antique dental instruments to clocks and veloci-pedes (early pedal-less bicycles). There is a good research and reading room. Open 8.30 am–4.30 pm on weekdays, from 10.30 am on Saturdays and from 1.30 pm on Sundays.

First Church, at Moray Place and Burlington Street, was built of Oamaru stone by the first Presbyterian settlers. Bell Hill, which was flattened for the church, is where early services in Dunedin were held.

Otago Museum, at 419 Great King Street, opposite the university, is widely known for its excellent Pacific art collections and cultural displays. The Maori Hall has outstanding carvings, a reconstructed meeting house and many articles of polished greenstone. Open 9 am–4.30 pm on weekdays, from 10.30 am on Saturdays and from 1.30 pm on Sundays. The **University of Otago**, off Cumberland Street, is New Zealand's oldest campus. Two-toned, ivy-covered stone halls and modern buildings stand amidst lawns and gardens by the Leith Stream. The beautiful **Botanic Gardens**, which boast floral displays, superb rhododendrons and a restaurant, lies to the north, at the end of George Street.

The **Otago Peninsula** extends south of the city into the Pacific Ocean enclosing the harbour. The Royal Albatross Colony and yellow-eyed penguins at its tip are rare sights not to be missed. You need a special reservation, obtainable from the visitor information centre or the NZTP Travel Office. **Lanarch Castle**, halfway along the peninsula (nine kilometres, or 5.6 miles, from the city), is a Victorian folly built in 1871 by a rich New Zealand banker for his wife, the daughter of a French duke. (His life reads like a Victorian melodrama.) The building is copied from a Scottish castle, with a lavishly ornate interior, a Georgian hanging staircase and a dungeon.

North Otago

Oamaru, the chief town of North Otago, is 116 kilometres (72 miles) north of Dunedin. It is most famous for the creamy white limestone quarried nearby. The stone has been used for many impressive buildings, including Auckland's Town Hall and post office, Wellington's Customhouse, Christchurch's Catholic cathedral and Dunedin's First Church, Anglican cathedral and Town Hall. Oamaru's broad, tree-lined streets have many elegant classical limestone buildings dating from the 1870s and 1880s. A good view of the town and coastline can be had from **Lookout Point**, at the eastern end of Tamar Street.

    Moeraki, a small fishing port 38 kilometres (24 miles) south of Oamaru, off Highway 1, is famous for the huge spherical boulders scattered over the nearby beaches and protected in the **Moeraki Boulders Scenic Reserve**. These geological curiosities were formed from minerals and salts on the ocean floor 60 million years ago, their shape resulting from chemical—not wave—action. The boulders appear as the mudstone around them erodes away. Before they received official protection, many more of them littered the area, coming in all sizes, but all except the biggest were carted off as souvenirs.

Invercargill

New Zealand's southernmost city sits on a flat plain near the south coast. Invercargill has the same Scottish roots as Dunedin, and the city's wide, tree-lined streets, laid out in a grid, bear the names of Scottish rivers. The city also has its full share of Scottish weather. Many parks and green areas make it an attractive, open city, and it is surrounded by rolling green sheep farms. Four large freezing works in the area process nearly six million lambs a year, exporting the frozen meat through the port of Bluff, much of it nowadays to the Middle East, where mutton is the meat of choice.

Getting There

Air New Zealand flies to Invercargill from all major cities, and Southern Air runs a service to Stewart Island. There is a railway service to Dunedin and Christchurch (The Southerner, see page 195). Intercity (NZRR) Services has regular connections with Queenstown, Te Anau, Lumsden, Gore and Dunedin, and H & H Travel Line operates daily from Christchurch and Dunedin. For those travelling by car, the flat, well-maintained back roads make this an ideal area to leave the main highways and explore the hinterland. Along the way are a surprising number of deer farms. Introduced to the wild a century ago, deer eventually became a pest, but now they provide income as venison for export.

If you are driving on a Saturday between October and the end of March, keep an eye out for an Agricultural & Pastoral Society (A & P) show, a kind of county fair held in rural communities throughout the country. The smaller the show the better the fun. You are likely to see prize livestock, sewing and knitting displays, sheep dog trials, horse-jumping events and wood-chopping and sheep-shearing competitions. Many farm families take paying guests who want a taste of rural life. It can be a wonderful change from city hotels.

Sights

The hub of downtown Invercargill is the corner of Tay and Dee streets. The Southland Promotion Office/New Zealand Visitor Information Centre is at 82 Dee Street. Phone 86-090. **Southland Centennial Museum and Art Gallery**, on Gala Street by the main entrance to Queen's Park, has good displays on local history, including relics from the country's first-recorded shipwreck, in 1795. It also has live specimens of the rare native tuatara, a lizard-like reptile that is considered a 'living fossil' and believed to live as long as 100 years. Open on weekdays 10 am–4.30 pm, on Saturdays 1–5 pm and on Sundays 2–5 pm. **Queen's Park** is a lovely area in the middle of town with formal gardens, an aviary, a deer park and many playing fields, including an 18-hole golf course. Local Maori have a *marae* (communal compound) close to town serving as a community house and training centre for arts and crafts. **Murihiku Urban Marae** is at Kingswell Heights, off Tramway Road. A recent project is the building and carving of a traditional meeting house on the grounds, under the supervision of a master carver. For visits phone 67–738.

Seafood from Foveaux Strait is the great speciality in this region. Bluff oysters in season (March–August) are especially succulent. On Friday evenings the luxury Ascot Park Hotel, at Racecourse Road and Tay Street, puts on an enormous seafood smorgasbord (with roasts for non-seafood-lovers) that is a weekly social event. Phone 76–195 for prices and bookings.

Bluff, 27 kilometres (17 miles) south of Invercargill, at the end of Highway 1, is Southland's principal port. H & H Travel Line operates a bus service between Invercargill and Bluff. An artificial island in the harbour provides docks and loading facilities for the huge Australian- and Japanese-owned Tiwai Aluminium Smelter on the other side, which uses massive amounts of cheap electricity from the new power plant developed for the purpose at Fiordland's Lake Manapouri after battles—and eventual compromise—with environmentalists. The raw materials come from Australia, and New Zealand counts the electricity as an export item. A large commercial fishing fleet for crayfish and oysters is also based at Bluff. From **Bluff Hill** a lookout gives a panoramic view over the harbour, the Southland plains, Foveaux Strait and Stewart Island. (Turn uphill at the post office and follow the road to the summit.) The view is especially good towards evening, when the fishing boats are heading home.

Stewart Island

Across shallow Foveaux Strait lie Stewart Island and the Muttonbird Islands. Beyond them the open ocean stretches out, home of albatrosses and whales, all the way to Antarctica. Stewart Island is a large, lopsided triangle 60 kilometres (37 miles) long and half as wide. A tiny population of about 450 people clusters around Halfmoon Bay, on the east side, and a number of Maori families live scattered along the north coast. The rest of the island belongs to the birds and animals that inhabit the rocky coves and sandy beaches of the coast and the virgin forests that cover the rugged mountains of the interior. The weather is mild but unpredictable from one hour to the next, forever alternating between sun and rain.

Getting There

Southern Air connects Stewart Island with Invercargill year round and runs as many as four flights a day each way in summer. The flight across the 24-kilometre (15-mile) stretch of water takes about 20 minutes. A 300-passenger ferry plied Foveaux Strait until 1985, but the service was terminated when it failed to pay. Its passing is much mourned. Now, a 50-passenger launch is operated Monday, Wednesday and Friday (daily in the holiday season) by Stewart Island Charter Services in Bluff. The crossing, which can be quite rough, takes about two and a half hours. H & H Travel Line coaches leave from the station at Invercargill and connect with all ferry arrivals and departures. There are hopes for a bigger ferry boat. Both sea and air travel are expensive, and both need bookings in advance. Current timetables are available from the New Zealand Visitor Information Centre in Invercargill.

Sights

Oban is a tiny, friendly village reminiscent of fishing settlements on the coast of Newfoundland or Maine of 30 years ago. Fishing is a far bigger business than tourism, attested to by the piles of cray-pots and fishing nets, and a salmon farm out in Horseshoe Bay. The village has two short streets and a waterfront. High spots are the Department of Conservation's Information Centre, which has good displays, booklets and maps, and the Travel Centre and Tearoom, from which all trips depart. The South Sea Hotel, two

Fjordland National Park

shops, a post office, a library and a small museum complete the town centre. Southern Air has plans to develop the waterfront by putting in a shopping mall and adding a hostel for 72 guests opposite the museum.

Stewart Island has 32 kilometres (20 miles) of paved roads. The **Stewart Island Coach Tour** covers about two-thirds of that total in an hour, leaving the Travel Centre and Tearoom around 11 am. The commentary is marvellous, and the tour is well worth taking. Stewart Island deserves at least a couple of days. Boats can be chartered to delightful Ulva Island and the coves most favoured by seals and penguins. There are magical walks of different lengths through fern-filled forests to sandy beaches. The sunsets and long twilights are legendary—the Maori name for Stewart Island is Rakiura, meaning 'heavenly glow'. If you are lucky, you might even catch a performance by the amateur Stewart Island Players. So many islanders take part in these productions that they have to bring their audiences from the mainland.

The **Muttonbird Islands**, sprinkled off the east and southwest coasts, cannot be visited as they are the exclusive hunting preserve of the Rakiura Maori, who have the right to harvest muttonbirds (migratory sooty shearwaters). The fat chicks, a prized Maori delicacy, are captured by the tens of thousands in April and May and sent to food shops all over the country.

Fiordland

A mere 14,000 years ago, Fiordland was completely covered with ice. Its extraordinary serrated coastline and deep, branching lakes were carved out by glaciers. The ice has left behind a magnificent, untamed land. **Fiordland National Park** is one of the biggest in the world. The huge Te Anau and Manapouri lakes and four smaller, but very deep, lakes create an inland 'coastline' for Fiordland that is almost as daunting as the seaward one.

An immense amount of rain (nearly 6.5 metres, or 253 inches, in Milford Sound, for example) feeds cascading waterfalls and a luxuriant rain forest— the last sub-arctic rain forest in the world still untouched by humans. Towering beech trees shelter a dense undergrowth of shrubs, ferns and moss, the whole clinging to seemingly vertical mountainsides. Lichens and peat moss build up a precarious soil that holds the roots, but when storms dislodge even a few trees, a disastrous 'tree avalanche' can result. Bare scars down every sheer mountain face stand witness. Winter is the driest season, but much of Fiordland's bewitching beauty comes from its wetness.

An incredible insect population lives in this southern region. Most species remain in their forest habitats, but vicious sandflies seek out the few humans around to bite. A Maori legend says that the gods who shaped Fiordland became so entranced by their creation that they stopped working and just sat back to admire it. Hinenui te pou, the goddess of life and death, created *te namu,* the sandfly, to goad them back to work. Be sure to keep plenty of insect repellent on all exposed skin when you are outdoors.

Te Anau, lying just outside the boundary of Fiordland National Park at the south end of Lake Te Anau, is the biggest tourist centre of the region. Manapouri, 19 kilometres (12 miles) south of Te Anau, sits at the mouth of the Waiau River at Lake Manapouri's eastern end. These two towns and the settlement at Milford Sound account for all the urban life in Fiordland.

Getting There

Mount Cook Airlines connects Te Anau with major South Island cities. Fiordland Air and smaller companies fly between Te Anau, Queenstown and Milford Sound. Intercity (NZRR) Services goes to Te Anau from Dunedin, Invercargill and Queenstown. Buses coming from all four directions meet daily at noon in the south-central town of **Lumsden** for a lunch break and exchange of passengers. All depart simultaneously at 1.10 pm. Those travelling by car simply get to Lumsden, on Highway 6 (and famous for good fishing; see *Focus,* page 214), and take Highway 94 west to Te Anau.

Information and Orientation

Te Anau is a small lakeside town completely devoted to tourism. Two dozen hostelries pick up guests from the airport or bus terminal. Most are within easy walking distance of Te Anau's main road and waterfront. Fiordland National Park Headquarters, on the waterfront, provides maps, information and permits for 'freedom' walkers (those not part of an organized group) to walk the Milford Track. Fiordland Travel Centre, opposite the main road on the waterfront, is the biggest agency for tours on land, lake or sea. Phone 7416. Competition is very hot, especially on trips to Milford Sound, and other agencies up and down the main road offer a variety of special deals.

Sights

A two-and-a-half-hour trip to **Te Ana-Au Caves** entails a cruise across Lake Te Anau and an exciting excursion inside limestone grottoes, part of the way by flat-bottomed punt. These 'young' caves have not yet built up stalactites, but their walls are festooned with thousands of twinkling glow-worms. The trips go several times a day, including one after dinner.

    Lake Manapouri is often called New Zealand's most beautiful lake, with the snowcapped Keppler Mountains reflected in its clear, island-studded waters. A tremendous controversy arose in the late 1960s when the national government proposed raising its level by 12 metres (40 feet) and installing a gigantic electric power plant to feed the aluminium smelter at Bluff. A nationwide petition sponsored by environmentalists gathered a quarter of a million names and contributed to the government's electoral defeat in 1972. The incoming Labour government agreed to leave the lake intact and put the power plant 213 metres (700 feet) below ground. The **West Arm Underground Powerhouse** is an awesome sight. Twice-daily tours take visitors to

"The Crime Of Being A Maori"

I

went to Mass at Newman Hall,
Then visited the Varsity Cafeteria
With six Catholic acquaintances.
One wanted to show me the poems he had written,
One talked about the alternate society,
One wanted to convert the world,
One girl in glasses gave me the glad eye,
Another praised the pentecostal movement,
Another hoed into his plate of cheese and camel turds.

I said, "Excuse me a minute, there's a Maori friend of mine,
If he doesn't get a place to crash tonight
The cops will pick him up for the four crimes
They dislike most in Auckland.
Not having a job,
Wearing old clothes,
Having long hair
Above all, for being Maori.

When they shift him to the cells in the meat wagon
The last crime might earn him five punches in the gut.
Could any one of you give him a night's lodging?"

They were extremely sorry.
The bourgeois Christ began to blush on the Cross.
The Holy Spirit squawked and laid an egg.
One had landlord trouble,
One had to swot for exams.
One was already overcrowded,
One didn't know exactly,
One still wanted to show me the poems he had written,
And the last one still silently consumed his plate of camel turds.

I took the Maori lad to Keir Volkerling's place.
He slept on a mattress in the bathroom.
Keir was not a Christian, or a student.
He worked ten hours a day
Digging drains or mixing concrete
To support an average of twenty-five people
Who would otherwise have been in jail
For being out of work,
For having their hair down to their shoulders,
And above all, for the crime of being Maori.

James K. Baxter, Ode to Auckland, 1972

the site by boat from Manapouri village. A bus spirals down for two kilometres (1.2 miles) through a spooky tunnel to a vast granite cavern in the bowels of the earth, where seven giant generators hum. The trip takes about four hours.

Organized tours to **Doubtful Sound** take you by bus over the picturesque **Wilmot Pass** to **Deep Cove**, where the power plant's ten-kilometre (six-mile) -long tailrace tunnel reaches the sea. A launch then takes a cruise on the fiord's still, mirror-like waters between towering cliffs and waterfalls. Doubtful Sound is much bigger than Milford Sound—and equally beautiful. A combined trip to the power plant and Doubtful Sound makes an excellent day's outing. If time is short, flightseeing tours take in the beauties of Doubtful Sound and Milford Sound from the air. Or you can visit the **Milford Track and Milford Sound Audiovisual Theatre**, at 90 Te Anau Terrace, for a stunning 20-minute show of superb scenery employing six projectors and stereo sound.

Milford Sound is the main reason to come to Fiordland. There are various ways to get here and back from Te Anau or Queenstown—by foot along the Milford Track (you need to have made a reservation many months ahead), by small plane, by road or by any combination of these. An airfield at the head of the sound caters to several companies flying the Te Anau-Milford-Queenstown triangle. Half a dozen competing coach tours in Te Anau offer full-day excursions to Milford Sound, including a cruise up the sound. The road to Milford Sound is spectacular, with lookouts and short walks along the way. The drive, by coach or car, takes about three hours with fairly short stops.

Highway 94 follows the shore of Lake Te Anau north for 28 kilometres (17 miles) to a motor lodge at **Te Anau Downs**, where Milford Track walkers take off by launch to start the track at the head of the lake. The road turns inland here and climbs over a ridge into the lovely **Eglinton Valley** and Fiordland National Park. About 12 kilometres (7.5 miles) into the park, a short walkway leads through bird-filled forest to the **Mirror Lakes**, a series of rush-lined pools that sometimes reflect the mountains. From here, a once-famous stretch of road created the optical illusion of a disappearing mountain but trees have now grown up and obscured the effect. **Cascade Creek**, with a hotel and campground, is the next stopping place. The 45-minute loop walk to **Lake Gunn** is superb, if you have time. The road then climbs over the **Divide**, the pass over the mountains, and goes through the most magnificent scenery of all to the **Homer Tunnel**, which is 1.2 kilometres (0.75 miles) long and has been able to take two-way traffic since 1984. The road emerges into the steep **Cleddau Valley**. A few kilometres further, a ten-minute walk leads to a narrow chasm, where a waterfall plunges under a natural bridge. The road ends, after a steep descent, at the THC Milford Resort Hotel.

A cruise up Milford Sound is by far the best way to appreciate its grandeur. The biggest, best-equipped vessel is the *Milford Haven*, operated by Fiordland Travel, which takes passengers 22 kilometres (14 miles) to the open sea at the mouth of the fiord (two hours plus, round trip). The fastest boat is Fiordland Travel's 100-passenger catamaran, the *Fiordland Flyer*, which makes the same cruise in only 70 minutes. Red Boats, operated by THC, take shorter, one- or two-hour cruises to the principal landmarks of the fiord.

The boats glide close to **Bowen** and **Stirling falls**, which tumble 150 metres (500 feet) down sheer cliffs into the dark, still waters of the sound. Triangular **Mitre Peak** soars 1,692 metres (5,551 feet) straight out of the sea to touch the clouds. Seals play along the rocky shore. Crested Fiordland penguins and their cousins, little blue penguins, can sometimes be seen, too. Large bottlenosed dolphins are constant companions of the cruise boats. They ride the invisible pressure wave under the bow, skimming along just below the surface with obvious delight. Bring your camera, binoculars, insect repellent, a warm jacket—and something rainproof, just in case.

Focus

Near **Dunedin**, the protected breeding colony of 16 to 20 pairs of royal albatross at **Taiaroa Head**, on the Otago Peninsula, is an absolute must. The scene from the observatory depends on the placement of the nests, the weather and the month that you come. An average of eight chicks are reared each year. Incubation takes place through December, chicks hatch around the end of January, parents leave the chicks in March and return only every couple of days for feeding. The full-grown chicks depart in September. The colony is closed from 1 September to 25 November, during mating and egg laying. Access to the colony is strictly controlled; tickets are sold for a specific date and time at the NZTP Travel Office on Princes Street (Phone 740–344) or the New Zealand Visitor Information Centre (Phone 774–176).

At **Penguin Place**, also on the Otago Peninsula near Dunedin, rare yellow-eyed penguins come ashore at their nesting place in the late afternoon. A signposted turnoff leaves the road to Taiaroa Head, beyond Harington Point. Pick up the key to a gate at the penguin sign and drive until you reach the end of the road (about four kilometres, or 2.5 miles). There is a small entrance fee.

Stewart Island is generally approached by plane from Invercargill. However, if you cross Foveaux Strait by ferry from Bluff, you may see royal or wandering albatross, mollymawk, sooty shearwater, petrel, prion and any of New Zealand's three species of penguin. On the island there are plentiful birds in the forest, including both Stewart Island brown and little spotted

kiwi, which are sometimes diurnal. Remote Mason Bay, on the west coast, is the most likely place in the country to see kiwis in the wild. A light plane can be chartered to get there. The nearly extinct kakapo (see below under Fiordland National Park) is believed—or at least hoped—to exist on Stewart Island, and the rare Stewart Island robin can still occasionally be found. Pigeons and kaka are found around **Oban**, and an hour's launch trip to bush-covered Ulva Island from Halfmoon Bay can result in a happy day of bird-watching and picnicking.

On the farmland around **Invercargill** you will almost certainly see spur-winged plover. This bird blew in from Australia in the 1940s, started to nest here and has become a common farm bird.

Visitors to **Fiordland National Park** in search of the area's unusual birds use **Te Anau** as a base. The rarest species of all, the secretive, nocturnal kakapo (an owl-like, flightless parrot), is believed to exist near Milford and Doubtful sounds and perhaps on Stewart Island. In 1987 the total known population was 50 individuals, with just five males left in Fiordland. Any signs of kakapo should be reported at once to the Department of Conservation. Twenty-two kakapos were transferred to Little Barrier Island in 1982, and this group represents their best hope of survival.

Te Anau's Wildlife Bird Reserve has succeeded (as has the Mount Bruce Wildlife Centre near Wellington) in breeding the rare takahe, which can be seen here with other native birds. Takahe numbers have declined from 200 pairs in 1948 to about 60 pairs today, in spite of careful protection. The

Acclimatization Societies

If it lives in the wild and flies or swims, it is probably under the jurisdiction of an acclimatization society. There are roughly 22 acclimatization societies in New Zealand, each presiding over an 'acclimatization region', which can range in size from several square kilometres to an entire province. The modern function of these quasi-autonomous non-governmental organizations (QUAN-GOs, for short) bears little relation to the purpose for which they were set up.

During New Zealand's long isolation from the rest of the world—about 20 million years—only one kind of mammal existed here. In a land of birds, that mammal was, naturally, the bat. The first Maori settlers brought dogs and rats from East Polynesia in their canoes. When Captain Cook came, centuries later, he expected to restock his ship's supplies with meat and was surprised to find no large animals at all. He corrected this deficiency on his next voyage by putting pigs ashore to be bred by his Maori friends.

European immigrants who followed brought pigs, goats, horses, cattle and sheep, the arrival of which they documented, and the inevitable mice, rats, cats and dogs, who arrived without documentation. Most of the animals stayed confined in human settlements, but the mice, rats and pigs went wild and multiplied unchecked in the forests. In a word, they *acclimatized.*

As New Zealand filled with settlers, most from England and Scotland, a great desire welled up to turn this virgin land into a new, improved Great Britain. People all over the country spontaneously formed acclimatization societies dedicated to the introduction of every desirable species of plant and animal to see which ones would acclimatize and take root in New Zealand. Many species were brought in for food. Others, like deer, rabbits and trout, provided sport. The Australian possum was desirable for its fur, and pine trees for their timber. Skylarks and thrushes were imported so their song could allay homesickness. The settlers introduced over 130 species of bird, about 40 kinds of fish and over 50 mammals to New Zealand. Of these, about 30 birds, ten fish and 30 mammals became truly established in the wild. The transplants increased their numbers exponentially, and many became pests. The weasels and ferrets brought in to control rampaging rabbits found native birds tastier. Scottish gorse, introduced to form hedges, grew huge and gobbled up pastures.

Finally, the government clamped down on the introduction of new species, and after 1900 the acclimatization societies took over the management of all game birds and freshwater fish. Today they issue hunting and fishing licences. (No licences are needed to hunt mammals, including deer, which are considered pests.) The societies administer hatcheries, run restocking programmes, prevent poaching and provide rangers to enforce national laws.

New Zealand is the only country in the world where wildlife protection and regulation are largely controlled by private societies. The new Department of Conservation is striving to assume this responsibility, but the societies, in their best tradition, have long since become acclimatized to New Zealand's bureaucratic ecology and are likely to prove difficult to dislodge.

culprits seem to be predator stoats and habitat-sharing red deer.

You will probably see falcon around the lake. A tourist trip to Doubtful Sound offers a good chance to see keas at Wilmot Pass and perhaps the Fiordland crested penguin during the boat trip on the sound.

Some of the best bird-watching in New Zealand is in the beech forests of the **Eglinton Valley**, between Te Anau and Milford Sound. On the walk to Lake Gunn from Cascade Creek, you are likely to see yellowheads, kakas, robins, yellow-breasted tits and riflemen—and possibly brown creepers, yellow-crowned parakeets and long-tailed cuckoos. At the Homer Tunnel, keas may steal your food or any bright objects. Rock wrens are found around rock falls and scree. A boat trip to the mouth of **Milford Sound** will include glimpses of the Fiordland crested penguin, if you are lucky.

Dunedin has an excellent **city walk** starting and ending at the Octagon, where the statue of Robert Burns overlooks the heart of the city. Behind him stands St Paul's Anglican Cathedral, with the Civic Centre and library on the right, adjoining the Municipal Chambers (site of the New Zealand Visitor Information Centre). Follow Stuart Street from the fountain to the severe-looking Law Courts on the third corner and the splendid railway station straight ahead. Continue to the right along Lower High Street to the Early Settlers Museum, which is worth a stop. Cross the street to Queen's Gardens, with its war memorial and statue of Queen Victoria. Turn left on High Street, noting the elaborate, gothic Cargill Monument, modelled on Walter Scott's monument in Edinburgh. Two century-old hotels stand at the corner of High and Princes streets. The post office, one block to the left on Princes Street, offers a panoramic view of the city from its seventh floor. Turn right coming out of the post office on Princes Street and walk back towards the Octagon as far as Moray Place. Turn right again and cross Burlington Street to the grounds of the First Church, built by Dunedin's founding fathers. Retrace your steps along Moray Place and cross Princes and View streets. On your left is the city's oldest church, originally the Congregational church, now Seventh Day Adventist. At the corner of Upper Stuart Street is the Fortune Theatre, once a Methodist church. Turn right past the Anglican cathedral and you are back where you started at the Octagon. Allow one to one and a half hours for the walk.

The **Catlins District** is an unspoiled scenic region of coast, river and forest between Dunedin and Invercargill, far from the tourist track. Its centre is **Owaka**, on Highway 92, the coastal route between Invercargill and Balclutha. There are over 20 good walks and hikes here. Especially recommended are Jacks Bay, which has a short trail to a dramatic blowhole (round trip one hour) and the scenic coastal track leading around Surat Bay by False Islet down into Cannibal Bay (two and a half hours one way). The Department of Conservation provides information on all walks and maps at the

Catlins Information Centre in Owaka. Phone 58–341.

Although **Stewart Island** is famous for its long, difficult tramping trails through uninhabited terrain, there are several excellent walks from Oban, taking from an hour or two to half a day. The moss-carpeted, fern-filled rain forest, the rocky coves and beaches, and the scarcity of people make it a delightful place for walkers. The friendly and helpful Department of Conservation in Oban has an excellent booklet entitled 'Stewart Island: Day Track and General Information', which is all you need for a guide.

In **Fiordland National Park** there is a variety of magnificent walks amid the lakes and mountains. Most well-marked, local walks start from the carpark at the outlet of Lake Te Anau, at the town of Te Anau. Follow Te Anau Terrace south along the lakefront to its end, turn right on the road to Manapouri and follow the lake to the control gates. There are lovely **lakeshore walks** to Dock Bay (one and a half hours round trip) and Brod Bay, where there is a well-laid-out **nature walk** (three and a half hours round trip).

There is a fine walk from Lake Te Anau to Lake Manapouri. A gentle track crosses the control gates at the carpark, turns left and follows the winding Waiau River downstream through beech forest to Rainbow Beach, where a swing bridge connects the trail with a side road to the Manapouri–Te Anau Road. This walk takes three to three and a half hours. The trail then goes on for another one and a half hours to a cove on Lake Manapouri's Shallow Bay. There is a hut 15 minutes along the beach to the left. On the return trip, you can arrange to be picked up by car at Rainbow Beach and driven back to Te Anau.

The most famous walk from Te Anau is a full-fledged tramp on the **Milford Track**, often touted as 'the finest walk in the world'. The four-day tramp crosses the 1,154-metre (3,786-foot) Mackinnon Pass and passes Sutherland Falls, the sixth-highest waterfall in the world. You may meet mud and/or snow before emerging at Milford Sound. The tramp can be the crowning achievement for serious walkers who are ready to make the proper preparations. The 54-kilometre (34-mile) Milford is the only track in New Zealand with restricted entry, which means you must walk the track as a member of a Tourist Hotel Corporation guided party, or as an independent walker with a permit from Fiordland National Park. Both methods need bookings and instructions far in advance from the THC (PO Box 185, Te Anau) or through a travel agent. Conducted trips leave Te Anau three times a week from December to early April with guides who provide food and bedding. Backpacks and parkas can be hired from the THC Te Anau Hotel. For independent walkers, the fee for the permit includes hut fees and a launch ride on Milford Sound, but you have to carry your own food and sleeping bag.

*Enshrouded in mist (above); Cook Strait island (right); Bowen waterfall (far right);
Milford Sound, Fjordland National Park (top right)*

Southland boasts dozens of outstanding rivers for trout fishing. Fiordland's two big lakes, Te Anau and Manapouri, normally grouped with the lakes at Queenstown, Wanaka (see *Focus*, page CTR) and others further north in the traditional Southern Lakes District, are described here along with the best fishing rivers of the far south, with which they are conveniently connected by good roads.

Near **Te Anau**, fishing is very good in Lake Manapouri but even better in the rivers north and south of Lake Te Anau. The northern **Eglinton River** is reached from the Te Anau–Milford Sound road (Highway 94), the best spot being grassy Knobs Flat, 62 kilometres (39 miles) from Te Anau. The southern **Waiau River** links Lake Te Anau to Lake Manapouri, winding through ferns and native bush for 19 kilometres (12 miles). Four signposted vehicle tracks lead to the river from the Te Anau–Manapouri road. Other attractive stretches of river can be reached from the Milford Track (see above). The season for both rivers runs from 1 November to 31 May.

Lumsden is right in the middle of excellent fishing country. The road from Lumsden to Te Anau (Highway 94) skirts the upper **Oreti River** just west of Mossburn, about 23 kilometres (14 miles) from Lumsden. Its upper reaches are well-stocked with brown trout. A side road runs south from Mossburn to Wrey's Bush, near Nightcaps, which is on Highway 96. There is exceptional fishing along a 30-kilometre (19-mile) stretch of the **Aparima River**, which runs parallel to the road.

The **Mataura River** is the classic 'best river' of Southland. Some say it is the finest brown trout stream in New Zealand. The Lumsden–Queenstown road (Highway 6) gives access to its fabled upper reaches. (Do not be tempted by Five Rivers, about ten kilometres, or six miles, from Lumsden. Fish are scarce here.) At Parawa, a right turn on Nokomai Gorge Road gives easy access on foot to the river. At Athol, the next village, a small road on the right ends near the river. There is access on foot from the main road north of Athol and from the Black Bridge. At Garston, a side road on the left leads to two excellent places, and the Welcome Rock Lodge caters to fishermen. Fairlight Siding offers the last access to the river from the main road.

Gore is within easy reach of a number of fine rivers, and it has the best, most up-to-date information on the whole region at its sports shop. **Wyndham**, 32 kilometres (20 miles) south of Gore (turn off Highway 1 at Edendale), lies close to the rich lower reaches of the Mataura River. The small Wyndham and Mimihau rivers nearby are also highly recommended. Northeast of Gore, the **Pomahaka River**, a small chalk stream, is said to be unique. In its scenic upper reaches, fish are very large, and in its middle reaches, near Tapanui (38 kilometres, or 24 miles, northeast of Gore on Highway 90), resident and sea-run brown trout are plentiful. Near **Clinton**, 44 kilometres (27 miles) east of Gore on Highway 1, the Waipahi and Waiwera rivers are very good. Consult local fishermen for the best spots.

In the **Dunedin** area, at Ranfurly, on the Taieri River (80 kilometres, or 50 miles, northwest of Palmerston on Highway 85) a new power and irrigation scheme has cleared a willowy swamp and opened up 41 kilometres (25 miles) of river scarcely discovered by fishermen. Rumour says the fishing is fabulous, but you should be prepared for wind.

The season for all the rivers is 1 October to 30 April. Bag limits range from four to 20 a day, so ask on the spot for the local regulations.

Dunedin, with its Scottish heritage, has some tough and splendid golf courses. One of the greatest is the **Otago Golf Club** at **Balmacewen**, located at the north end of the city and founded by Scottish pioneers in 1871. Its pristine, immaculate greens reflect generations of loving care, and club facilities are of the finest sort. However, this is a strenuous, hilly course, and may be too demanding for golfers accustomed to electric golf carts. Par 72. Phone 62–009.

St Clair Golf Club, set among pine groves in the suburb of Tainui, is favoured for international tournaments. The 15th hole is rated one of the 18 best in New Zealand, and the greens are excellent. Visitors are welcome except on Saturdays. Women's day is on Tuesday. Par 72. Phone 877–076.

Chisholm Park Golf Club, a lovely seaside course in the same vicinity as St Clair, tests all facets of a player's game. Par 71. Phone 45–641.

Invercargill has flat golf courses. The **Otatara Golf Club** is one of New Zealand's best, an excellent links-type course. Par 72. Phone 89–002.

Queen's Park, in the centre of Invercargill, has a pleasant, 18-hole public course that is most enjoyable to play. Par 72. Phone 88–371.

Stewart Island has the southernmost golf course in the world. For fun and something to boast about, try the six-hole **Ringa Ringa Heights Golf Course** at Oban. You can rent four clubs and a carrier for NZ$10 at the Travel Centre and Tearoom. The green fee is NZ$5.

There are no vineyards at the southern end of the South Island, but **Dunedin** has a wonderful old brewery to visit. **Speight's Brewery** rolled out its first barrel in 1876, during the gold rush, and has been in business ever since. The small, regional company makes beer in great brewing vessels of burnished copper and open gyles of kauri wood. A cooper's shop for making barrels still exists. The brewery is on Rattray Street at the corner of Dowling Street, three blocks from the Octagon. Guided tours start from its visitor centre at 10.30 am from Monday to Friday, but it is essential to book ahead. Phone 779–480.

Recommended Reading

Most of the books recommended here are published in New Zealand. As New Zealand boasts the highest number of book-buyers per capita in the world, you find good bookshops wherever you go, and the danger is that, by the time you have to fly home, you may find yourself many kilos overweight with books. The solution is to buy some padded envelopes at the post office and send the books by surface mail at the cheap international book rate.

Pope, Diana and Jeremy. *Mobil New Zealand Travel Guide: North Island and South Island* (2 vols) (Auckland: 1987) Available all over New Zealand, this gives an excellent background of history and culture and covers every town in New Zealand, arranged alphabetically. Entertaining and highly readable, this book is a most worthwhile travelling companion.

King, Jane. *New Zealand Handbook* (Chico, California: Moon Publications, 1987) The most complete and reliable general guidebook available. Well organized, easy to use and good on accommodation and restaurants.

Basset, Judith, Sinclair, Keith and Stenson, Marcia. *The Story of New Zealand* (Auckland: Reed Methuen, 1985) A large-format paperback written for young adults, with evocative illustrations and fast-moving, readable text. A delightful way to absorb New Zealand's rough, tough history.

Sinclair, Keith. *A Destiny Apart: New Zealand's Search for National Identity* (Wellington: Allen & Unwin, 1986) A thoughtful analysis of the country's current identity crisis and inner turmoil.

Hulme, Keri. *The Bone People* (New York and London: Penguin Books, 1986) Winner of Britain's prestigious Booker Prize in 1985. A startling, gripping novel about the modern Maori seen through Maori eyes.

Metropolitan Museum of Art. *Te Maori: Maori Art from New Zealand Collections* (New York, Harry Abrams Inc, 1984) The sumptuous catalogue from the great 1984 exhibition 'Te Maori', at the Metropolitan Museum of Art in New York. Priceless, sacred works of Maori sculpture were seen outside New Zealand for the first time. The exhibition, its tour and the interpretive articles in the catalogue helped to spark a Maori renaissance in New Zealand that is still going strong. The articles provide a deep, scholarly understanding of Maori art.

Leland, Louis S, Jr. *A Personal Kiwi-Yankee Slanguage Dictionary* (Dunedin: John McIndoe Ltd, 1980) Does far more than its title suggests, giving much insight into Kiwi attitudes, manners and sub-cultures. This slim pocketbook continues to amuse and inform.

Reed, A W. *A Dictionary of Maori Place Names* (Wellington: A H & A W Reed Ltd, 1961) This pocketbook is sometimes hard to find, but if you see it, pick it up. Maori place names almost always commemorate an event, a slice of life or a piece of mythology, and you can learn a lot from them about life in New Zealand before the arrival of the Europeans.

Bird-watching

Ellis, Brian. *The New Zealand Birdwatchers' Book* (Auckland: Reed Methuen, 1987) Should accompany you the whole way. Easy to read and full of excellent bird lists, expert knowledge, useful tips and precise directions for reaching out-the-way places. We found it indispensable in preparing this guide.

Kelly, Chloe Talbot. *Collins Handguide to the Birds of New Zealand* (Auckland: Collins, 1982) A well-illustrated field guide, light and handy enough to keep in your pocket.

Falla, R A; Sibson, R B and Tubott, E G. *The New Guide to the Birds of New Zealand* (Auckland: Collins, 1981) A big, comprehensive work and an excellent reference.

Harper and Kinsky. *Southern Albatrosses and Petrels Identification Guide* (Wellington: Victoria University Press, revised edition) This locally available manual specializing in pelagic birds is very useful.

Walking

Automobile Association. *The AA Guide to Walkways* (2 vols: North Island and South Island) (Auckland: Lansdowne Press, revised edition, 1987) An excellent compendium selecting a variety of walks— short and long, easy and difficult—with lots of photographs, maps and general information. It cannot cover all the walks, though, because too many exist. Only a few of the recommendations in the AA guide are duplicated here.

Burton, R and Atkinson, M: *A Tramper's Guide to New Zealand's National Parks* (Auckland: Reed Methuen, 1987) Very useful, including all types of walks and giving precise descriptions, grades and times required for each walk. However, the maps at the back are poorly printed and hard to read.

Fly-fishing

Gould, Peter. *The Complete Taupo Fishing Guide* (Auckland and London: Collins, 1983) Exactly what the title promises, including rivers.

Fly Fisher, a magazine published by Rainbow Publishers, PO Box 1746, Auckland, appears on New Zealand newsstands every two months and contains much useful information, especially on the Taupo area. Also, any book by T Norman, a writer for the NZTP in Wellington, is highly recommended.

Wine-tasting

Cooper, Michael. *The Wines and Vineyards of New Zealand* (Auckland and London: Hodder & Stoughton, paperback 1986) The one indispensable book to take with you the whole way. Beautifully illustrated, full of every sort of information, nicely arranged by region and convenient to use. Only one trouble: new wineries are opening with such frequency all over New Zealand that no book can keep abreast of them. You will have to discover those yourself.

Young, Alan. *Australia/New Zealand Wine Year Book* (Malvern: International Wine Academy, annual) Provides an annual update on wines, competitions and sales. Includes maps and is sprinkled with amusing and informative articles. The IWA's address is PO Box 301, Malvern 3144, Australia.

Practical Information

Useful Addresses

Bird-watching

Ornithological Society of New Zealand
PO Box 35337
Brown's Bay
Auckland 10

Royal Forest and Bird
Protection Society
26 Brandon Street
Wellington
Phone (04) 728–154

Department of Conservation
59 Boulcott Street
Wellington
Phone (04) 710–726

Rodney Russ
(New Zealand Nature Journeys)
PO Box 22
Waikari, North Canterbury
(near Christchurch)
Phone (03) 798–729

Walking

New Zealand Walkways Commission
c/o Department of Conservation
59 Boulcott Street
Wellington
Phone (04) 710–726

Fly-fishing

New Zealand Tourist and
Publicity Department
256 Lambton Quay
Wellington
Phone (04) 728–860

The Hunting and Fishing Officer
Tourist and Publicity Department
Private Bag
Rotorua
Phone (073) 85–179

Wine-tasting

Wine Institute of New Zealand
PO Box 39276
Auckland
Phone (09) 33–527

Common Maori Words Found in Place Names

Many place names in New Zealand are made up of Maori words that either describe the place or record something that happened there. The Maori language is spelled with eight simple consonants (h, k, m, n, p, r, t, w), two consonant combinations (wh—pronounced 'f'—and ng) and five vowels (a, e, i, o, u). As in all Polynesian languages (Maori and Hawaiian being among the most widely known), each vowel is pronounced separately, and every word ends with a vowel.

ahi	fire
ahu	mound or heap
aka	South Island form of *whanga* (bay, harbour)
ana	cave
ao	cloud
ara	path or road
ata	shadow
atua	god or demon
awa	river, valley
haere	come or go
hau	wind, famous
hoe	paddle
hou	new
hua	fruit, egg
huka	foam or spray, snow or frost
ika	fish
iti	small
iwi	bone, tribe
kahu	blue
kahui	assemblage, gathering, flock
kai	eat
kainga	unfortified village
kapa	row, line, rank
kau	swim
kino	bad
kohu	mist, fog
kuri	dog
ma	white or clear
ma (short for *manga*)	stream, brook
mangu	black
manu	bird
mata	headland (among other meanings)
mate	dead

maunga	mountain
moana	sea or lake
mot	island or isolated
muri	end
mutu	finished, end
namu	sandfly
nga	the
nui	big, plenty of
o	of, the place of
one	sand, mud or beach
pa	fortified village
pae	ridge or resting place
pai	good
papa	broad, flat, or ground with greenery
po	night
puk	hill
puna	spring of water
puni	encampment
rangi	sky
rau	hundred, many
riki	small or few
rima	five
roa	long
roto	lake
rua	two
ruru	owl
tahi	one, single
tai	coast, sea, or tide
tapu	sacred, forbidden
te	the
tea	white or clear
toa	warrior, brave
toro	explore, discover
umu	oven
uta	inland
wai	water
waka	canoe
wera	hot or burnt
whaka	to make or cause
whanga	bay, harbour
whare	house
whata	raised food-storage platform
whenua	land or country
whero	red

Some Important Events
in New Zealand History

c 950	Polynesian explorer Kupe reaches New Zealand by canoe from Hawaiki. Circles North Island, probably touches South Island and returns to tell his people about the discovery.
c 1150	Explorers Chief Toi and his grandson, Whatonga, arrive by canoe from Hawaiki and find inhabitants. One of them may have stayed in New Zealand while the other returned home to tell his people.
c 1350	Arrival of an organized migration from Hawaiki, including seven or more canoes. Permanent settlement begins.
1503	French seafarer de Gonneville possibly sights New Zealand coast.
1521	Portuguese caravel probably stranded off North Island's west coast.
1576	Spanish sea captain Juan Fernandez may have landed in New Zealand.
1642	Dutch explorer Abel Tasman sails up South Island's west coast and anchors in Golden Bay, but is driven away by a hostile Maori tribe. Tasman thinks he has touched Staten Land off the tip of South America.
1769	English explorer James Cook lands at points on North Island's east coast on first of three voyages. Claims New Zealand for the British Crown.
1790	First European whalers, sealers and kauriwood traders arrive.
1814	First missionaries start converting the Maori to Christianity.
1838	French captain Jean Langlois provisionally buys land on Banks Peninsula in the hope of establishing a French colony in New Zealand.
1840	Treaty of Waitangi between Queen Victoria and Maori chiefs secures New Zealand for the British Empire, with a guarantee of Maori land rights. Wellington is founded as a colony by the New Zealand Company.
1845	First outbreak of fighting as Maori fiercely resist seizure or forced sale of their lands by European colonists.
1848	Dunedin is founded as an organized Scottish Presbyterian colony.
1850	Christchurch is founded as an organized Anglican settlement.
1852	First gold strike is recorded in Coromandel. The first parliament, with two chambers, is established in Auckland.
1855	Earthquake raises Wellington's coastline and harbour floor.

1860	Land Wars break out in the Taranaki and soon spread to other parts of the North Island. Violent conflicts last for two decades.
1861	Gold-rush begins in Otago, in the South Island.
1865	Capital moves from Auckland to Wellington.
1867	First four Maori members of Parliament are elected.
1870	Economic depression sets in as the gold-rush peters out.
1882	First refrigerator ship sails to London in 98 days with cargo of frozen meat. Start of a new economic era for New Zealand.
1893	New Zealand is the first country in the world to give women the vote.
1907	New Zealand, heretofore a colony, becomes a completely self-governing dominion of the British Empire.
1914	New Zealand enters the First World War on the Allied side.
1918	End of the First World War. New Zealand receives control over mandated territory of West Samoa.
1919	New Zealand joins the League of Nations.
1931	Earthquake destroys Napier, raises coast and harbour floor.
1935	Labour Party wins parliamentary majority, introduces the 40-hour work week and starts nationalization.
1939–45	New Zealand fights in Second World War on Allied side.
1947	New Zealand becomes an independent, autonomous member of the British Commonwealth of Nations.
1950	New Zealand contributes troops to UN forces in Korea.
1953	First conquest of Mount Everest by New Zealander Sir Edmund Hillary.
1962	West Samoa gains independence.
1973	Britain joins the European Common Market, ending preferential trade with New Zealand. Start of a new, precarious economic era for New Zealand.
1975	National Party (conservative) wins the general election.
1984	Labour Party is returned to power and initiates neutralist, anti-nuclear foreign policy.

Bird Index

Index of Places